AF802630

BUDGET

BUDGET OF THE UNITED STATES GOVERNMENT

Fiscal Year 1996

THE BUDGET DOCUMENTS

Budget of the United States Government, Fiscal Year 1996 contains the Budget Message of the President and presents the President's budget proposals.

Analytical Perspectives, Budget of the United States Government, Fiscal Year 1996 contains analyses that are designed to highlight specified program areas or provide other significant presentations of budget data that place the budget in perspective.

It includes economic and accounting analyses, such as a balance sheet-type presentation; information on Federal receipts and collections, including user fees and tax expenditures; analyses of Federal spending; detailed information on Federal borrowing and debt; the Budget Enforcement Act preview report; current services estimates; and other technical presentation, such as the national income and product accounts.

It also includes information on management improvements; the budget system and concepts; a listing of the Federal programs by agency and account; and a glossary of budget terms.

Historical Tables, Budget of the United States Government, Fiscal Year 1996 provides data on budget receipts, outlays, surpluses or deficits, Federal debt, and Federal employment covering an extended time period—in many cases beginning in fiscal year 1940 and ending in fiscal year 2000. These are much longer time periods than those covered by similar tables in other budget documents. As much as possible, the data in this volume and all other historical data in the budget documents have been made consistent with the concepts and presentation used in the 1996 Budget, so the data series are comparable over time.

Budget of the United States Government, Fiscal Year 1996—Appendix contains detailed information on the various appropriations and funds that constitute the budget. The Appendix contains more detailed information than any of the other budget documents. It includes for each agency: the proposed text of appropriation language, budget schedules for each account, new legislative proposals, explanations of the work to be performed and the funds needed, and proposed general provisions applicable to the appropriations of entire agencies or group of agencies. Supplemental and rescission proposals for the current year are presented separately. Information is also provided on certain activities whose outlays are not part of the budget totals.

A Citizen's Guide to the Federal Budget, Budget of the United States Government, Fiscal Year 1996, is a new Office of Management and Budget publication that contains a brief summary of the Budget for the general public.

Automated Sources of Budget Information. The information contained in these documents is available in electronic format from the following sources:

- The budget documents are available on compact disc from the Government Printing Office. For more information, see the order form at the back of this document.
- The budget documents can be accessed using a computer modem as well as on the Internet through the U.S. Department of Commerce's STAT-USA information service. There is no charge for use of this service when used to obtain budget information.

  BBS Access: Set your computer communications software parameters to 8-bit words, no parity, and 1 stop-bit, then use your computer to contact STAT-USA's Economic Bulletin Board (EBB) at one of the following modem numbers:

  2400 bps (202) 482–3870
  9600 bps (202) 482–2584
  14400 bps (202) 482–2167

  When connecting to the EBB, use the word GUEST as your login userid. At the EBB's main information menu, select the [P]residential option for a list of budget documents that are available for online viewing or downloading to your computer.

  Internet Access: Budget documents are available through STAT-USA's Internet service using the *file transfer protocol* (ftp), *gopher* and *World Wide Web* (WWW) at the following addresses:

STAT-USA ftp side address ...	ftp.stat-usa.gov/pub/BudgetFY96
STAT-USA gopher side address ...	gopher.stat-usa.gov/BudgetFY96
STAT-USA World Wide Web uniform resource locator	http://www.doc.gov/inquery/BudgetFY96

  For more information on access to STAT-USA information services, call (202) 482–1986.
- Copies of the database used to generate the budget numbers may be purchased from the U.S. Department of Commerce National Technical Information Service, Springfield, VA 22161, telephone (703) 487–4650. Refer to stock number PB95–502340.

GENERAL NOTES

1. All years referred to are fiscal years, unless otherwise noted.
2. Detail in this document may not add to the totals due to rounding.

U.S. GOVERNMENT PRINTING OFFICE
WASHINGTON 1995

For sale by the Superintendent of Documents, U.S. Government Printing Office, Washington, D.C. 20402

ISBN 0-16-045409-3

TABLE OF CONTENTS

	Page
The Budget Message of the President	1
Promoting a Rising Standard of Living For All Americans	
1. Sharing the Benefits of Economic Growth	11
2. Building on Our Economic Record	31
Creating Opportunity and Encouraging Responsibility	
3. Restoring the American Community	55
4. Controlling Violent Crime and Drug Abuse	61
5. Reforming the Nation's Immigration System	71
6. Ensuring a Clean Environment	79
7. Investing in Science and Technology	91
8. Continuing the Commitment to Health Security	101
Projecting American Leadership Around the World	
9. Strengthening the U.S. Role in International Affairs	113
10. Maintaining a Quality Military Force	119
Making Government Work	
11. Reinventing the Federal Government—Phase I	133
12. Reinventing the Federal Government—Phase II	141
13. Other Reforms	159
Summary Tables	
Budget Aggregates	171
1996 Budget Proposals	177
Summaries by Agency/Function	211
Other Summary Tables	219
List of Charts and Tables	225
OMB Contributors to the 1996 Budget	231

THE BUDGET MESSAGE OF THE PRESIDENT

THE FEDERAL GOVERNMENT DOLLAR
FISCAL YEAR 1996 ESTIMATES

WHERE IT COMES FROM...

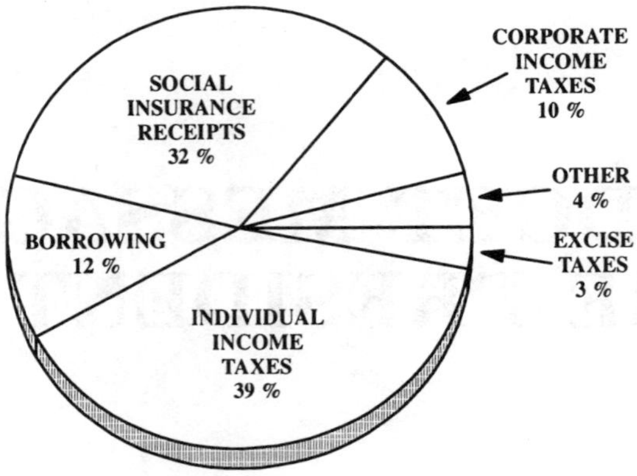

WHERE IT GOES...

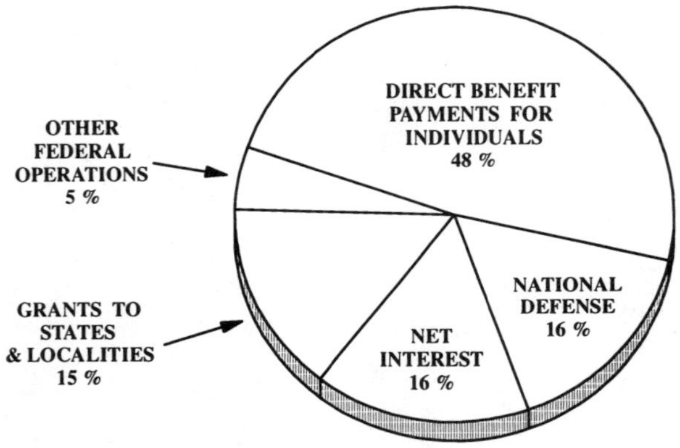

RECEIPTS, OUTLAYS, AND DEFICITS

(In billions of dollars)

	1994	1995	1996	1997	1998	1999	2000
Receipts	1,257.7	1,346.4	1,415.5	1,471.6	1,548.8	1,624.7	1,710.9
Outlays	1,460.9	1,538.9	1,612.1	1,684.7	1,745.2	1,822.2	1,905.3
Deficit (–)	–203.2	–192.5	–196.7	–213.1	–196.4	–197.4	–194.4
On-budget deficit (–)	(–258.8)	(–251.8)	(–262.0)	(–284.5)	(–274.8)	(–283.3)	(–288.6)
Off-budget surplus	(55.7)	(59.3)	(65.3)	(71.4)	(78.4)	(85.9)	(94.2)

THE BUDGET MESSAGE OF THE PRESIDENT

To the Congress of the United States:

The 1996 Budget, which I am transmitting to you with this message, builds on the Administration's strong record of economic progress during the past two years and seeks to create a brighter future for all Americans.

When I took office two years ago, the economy was suffering from slow growth, inadequate investment, and very low levels of job creation. We moved quickly and vigorously to address these problems. Working with Congress in 1993, we enacted the largest deficit reduction package in history. We cut Federal spending by $255 billion over five years, cut taxes for 40 million low- and moderate-income Americans, and made 90 percent of small business eligible for tax relief, while increasing income tax rates only on the wealthiest 1.2 percent of Americans. And while we placed a tight "freeze" on overall discretionary spending at 1993 levels, we shifted spending toward investments in human and physical capital that will help secure our future.

As we fought for our budget and economic policies, we moved aggressively to open world markets for American goods and services. We negotiated the North American Free Trade Agreement with Canada and Mexico, concluded negotiations over the Uruguay Round of the General Agreement on Tariffs and Trade, and worked with Congress to enact implementing legislation for both.

Our economic plan helped bring the deficit down from $290 billion in 1992, to $203 billion in 1994, to a projected $193 billion this year—providing three straight years of deficit reduction for the first time since Harry Truman was President. Measured as a percentage of our economy—that is, Gross Domestic Product (GDP)—our plan will cut the deficit in half.

By reassuring the financial markets that we were serious about getting our fiscal house in order, our plan also lowered interest rates while holding inflation in check. That helped to stimulate private investment and exports, and sparked the creation of 5.6 million new jobs—more than twice the number in the previous four years.

Now that we have brought the deficit down, we have no intention of turning back. My budget keeps us on the course of fiscal discipline by proposing $81 billion in additional deficit reduction through the year 2000. I am proposing to save $23 billion by reinventing three Cabinet departments and two other major agencies, to save $2 billion by ending more than 130 programs altogether, and to provide better service to Americans by consolidating more than 270 other programs. Under my plan, the deficit will continue to fall as a percentage of GDP to 2.1 percent, reaching its lowest level since 1979.

Despite our strong economic record, however, many Americans have not shared in the fruits of recovery. Though these Americans are working harder and harder, their incomes are either stagnant or falling. The problem is particularly acute among those with less education or fewer of the skills needed to compete in an increasingly global economy. To build a more prosperous America, one with rising living standards for all Americans, we must turn our attention to those who have not benefited from the current recovery.

My budget proposes to do that.

Promoting a Rising Standard of Living for All Americans

I am proposing a Middle Class Bill of Rights, which will provide tax relief to middle-income Americans. The Middle Class Bill of Rights includes a $500 per child tax credit for middle-income families with children under 13; expands eligibility for Individual Retirement Accounts and allows families to make penalty-free withdrawals for a range of educational, housing, and medical needs; and offers a tax deduction for the costs of college, university, or vocational education.

Also as part of my Middle Class Bill of Rights, I am proposing to revamp our confusing array of job training programs by consolidating some 70 of them. In my G.I. Bill for America's Workers, I propose to offer dislocated and low-income workers "Skill grants" through which they can make their own choices about the training they need to find new and better jobs.

The G.I. Bill for America's Workers is the final element of my effort to improve the education and skills of Americans, enabling them to compete in the economy of today and tomorrow. In the last two years, we enacted Goals 2000 to encourage States and localities to reform their education systems; revamped the student loan program to make post-secondary education affordable to more Americans; and pushed successfully for the School-to-Work program that enables young Americans to move more easily from high school to training or more education.

And I am proposing to pay for this Middle Class Bill of Rights with specific spending cuts. In fact, I am proposing enough spending cuts to provide more than twice as much in budget savings—$144 billion—as the tax cuts will cost—$63 billion—over five years.

Creating Opportunity and Encouraging Responsibility

By itself, the Federal Government cannot rebuild America's communities. What it can do is give communities some of the tools and resources to address their problems in their own way. My national service program provides incentives for Americans of all ages to volunteer their services in local communities across the country, and earn money for their own education. The budget proposes to invest more in our urban centers as well as in rural areas, and to continue our efforts to build stronger government-to-government relations with American Indian and Alaska Native Tribes. And I will work with Congress to enact comprehensive welfare reform that embodies the principles of work and responsibility for abled-bodied recipients, while protecting their children.

My Administration has worked with State and local law enforcement agencies to help retake the streets from the criminals and drug dealers who, in far too many places, now control them. Congress enacted my crime bill last year, finally answering the cries of Americans after too many years of debate and gridlock. We pushed successfully for the "three strikes and you're out" rule for violent criminals, and we are making significant progress on my promise to put 100,000 more police on the street. Congress also passed the long-overdue Brady Bill, which provides for background checks that will keep guns out of the hands of criminals. In this budget, I am proposing new funds with which States and localities can hire more police, build more space in prisons and boot camps, invest in prevention programs for first-time offenders, and provide drug treatment for many more drug users.

My Administration inherited deep-seated problems with the immigration system, and we have gone a long way toward addressing them. This budget proposes the strongest efforts yet, including funds for over 1,000 new Border Patrol agents, inspectors, and support staff. While working to fulfill the Federal Government's responsibility to secure our borders against illegal immigration, the budget also proposes funds to assist States that are unduly burdened with the health, education, and prison-related costs associated with illegal immigrants.

We must redouble our efforts to protect the environment. My Administration has sought more innovative, effective approaches to do so, and this budget would build upon them. In particular, I am proposing to work more with State and local governments, businesses, and environmental groups on collaborative efforts, while seeking more funds for high-priority programs.

Because investments in science and technology pay off in higher productivity and living standards down the road, I am seeking significant new funding for the Advanced Technology Program at the Commerce Department's National Institute of Standards and Technology, NASA's New Technology Investments, the Defense Department's Technology Reinvestment Project, biomedical research at the National Institutes of Health, and research and development at the National Science Foundation. I am also seeking to strengthen our coordinated efforts through the Administration's National Science and Technology Council and to improve the payment system for federally-sponsored research at colleges and universities.

I remain committed to comprehensive health care reform. The problems that prompted me to send Congress the Health Security Act in November 1993 have not gone away. Health care costs have continued to soar for individuals, businesses, and all levels of government. More Americans are losing their health coverage each year, and many others are staying in jobs only out of fear of losing their own coverage. I am asking Congress to work with me on a bipartisan basis, to take the first steps toward guaranteeing health care coverage to every American while containing costs.

Projecting American Leadership Around the World

We have begun the post-Cold War era and welcome one of its most significant fruits—the continuing efforts of Russia and the newly-independent states to move toward democracy and economic freedom. We propose to continue our support for this fundamental change that clearly serves the Nation's long-term interests.

My proposals for international affairs also promote and defend this Nation's vital interests in Central Europe, the Middle East, and Asia. The budget supports the important role we play in fostering our historic peace process in the Middle East.

With the global economy offering the prospect of new markets for American goods, we are redoubling our efforts to promote an open trading system in Asia, as well as in Latin America and the rest of the globe. I am, for instance, proposing increased funding for our trade promotion agencies, such as the Export-Import Bank, which strengthen our trade position. I am also asking for continued support for the bilateral and multilateral assistance to less-developed nations that can prevent humanitarian crises, as well as support for a strong American response to these crises.

Our military strength works in synergy with our foreign policy. Our forces defend our interests, deterring potential adversaries and reassuring our friends. My Defense Funding Initiative, a $25 billion increase in defense spending over the next six years, marks the third time that I have raised defense spending above my initial funding plan in order to support and maintain the most capable military force in the world. I am determined to ensure a high level of readiness of U.S. military forces, to continue to improve the pay and quality of life for the men and women who serve, and to ensure that our forces are modernized with new systems that will be available near the end of the century.

Making Government Work

None of our efforts can fully succeed unless we make Government work for all Americans. We have made great progress with the National Performance Review (NPR), which I established early in the Administration and which Vice President Gore has so ably run at my direction.

Specifically, departments and agencies across the Government have made substantial progress on each of the NPR's four themes: putting customers first, empowering employees to get results, cutting red tape, and cutting back to basics. The departments and agencies have established customer service standards and streamlined their operations. They also are working with my Office of Management and Budget to focus more on "performance"—what Federal programs actually accomplish. And they are doing all this while we are cutting the Federal workforce by 272,900 positions, bringing it to its smallest size since John Kennedy was President.

We also greatly improved the Federal regulatory system, opening it up more to public scrutiny. We plan to build upon our efforts, to make sure that we are protecting the public while not unduly burdening any one industry or group. We also overhauled the Federal procurement system, cutting mountains of red tape and enabling the Government to buy high-quality goods and services at lower cost.

Despite such progress, however, we are only beginning our efforts. I recently announced a major restructuring of the Departments of Housing and Urban Development, Energy, and Transportation, the General Services Administration, and the Office of Personnel Management. The budget contains details of these restructurings and our related proposals that affect hundreds of other programs.

In the coming months, the Vice President will lead Phase II of our crusade to reinvent Government—an effort to identify other agencies and programs to restructure or terminate, to sort out responsibilities among the Federal, State, and local levels of government, and to choose functions better performed by the private sector.

Conclusion

Our agenda is working. By cutting the budget deficit, investing in our people, and opening world markets, we have begun to lay the foundation for a strong economy for years to come. And by reinventing the Federal Government, cutting red tape and layers of management, we have begun to make Government more responsive to the American people.

This budget seeks to build upon those efforts. It seeks to spread the benefits of our economic recovery to more Americans and give them the tools to build a brighter future for themselves. It also seeks to continue our reinvention efforts—to eliminate or restructure agencies and programs, and to better sort out responsibilities among the Federal, State, and local levels of government.

These proposals will help us to create a stronger economy and more effective Government. I will ask for Congress's help in these efforts.

WILLIAM J. CLINTON

February 6, 1995

PROMOTING A RISING STANDARD OF LIVING FOR ALL AMERICANS

PROMOTING A RISING STANDARD OF LIVING FOR ALL AMERICANS

The Administration's central economic objective is to improve living standards for the greatest possible number of American families. Since 1993, the President has laid a firm foundation—with a series of budget, trade, education, and other policies that have helped generate the remarkable economic recovery of the last two years. With his new Middle Class Bill of Rights and this budget, the President is building upon that foundation to raise take-home pay for Americans today and help them acquire skills and more financial security tomorrow.

Two years ago, ballooning Federal budget deficits were the greatest barrier to rising standards of living. The Government soaked up so much private saving that interest rates soared and businesses could not afford investments to make our economy more productive, and our workers more prosperous. With a balanced package of spending cuts and revenue increases, the President's program brought the deficit down steeply—from \$290 billion in 1992 to a projected \$193 billion in 1995—marking three straight years of deficit reduction for the first time since Harry Truman was President. Through the Vice President's National Performance Review and subsequent legislation, Federal employment has fallen by nearly 100,000 and soon will drop to its lowest level since John Kennedy was President.

On the tax side, the President and Congress increased the earned income tax credit, which cut income taxes for 40 million Americans in 15 million working families. The tax cuts provided relief where it was needed most and, by augmenting low wages, fulfilled the President's pledge to "make work pay." The President also made 90 percent of America's small businesses eligible for tax relief.

Deficit reduction and spending restraint brought interest rates down. Lower interest rates and targeted tax relief jump-started what had been a weak recovery from the 1990 recession. Since this Administration took office in January of 1993, the economy has produced a whopping 5.6 million new jobs, compared to 2.4 million in the prior four years. Yet, inflation remains at the slowest pace in decades.

Rapid job growth and low inflation are prerequisites for rising living standards, widely shared. But, alone, they are not enough.

While freezing total discretionary spending for three budget years, the President shifted billions of dollars to investments in human and physical capital that will help raise productivity and, with it, living standards down the road. He focused on better educating the young, making college more affordable for millions of students, improving workers' skills, and reforming the welfare system to reduce dependency and increase opportunity. He worked with Congress to create the Goals 2000 program, which rewards local schools that set and pursue their own educational milestones, and a direct student loan program, which cut the cost of Federal support for higher education. At the same time, he focused on investments in science and technology and in physical capital.

The economy has improved far more than even the most optimistic forecasters predicted two years ago, and the deficit is much lower than anticipated. And yet, not everyone has joined in the economic recovery. Millions of Americans continue to work harder and harder, only to see their real incomes stagnate or even decline and their jobs remain uncertain. The problems are particularly acute among those with little education or few skills. With this budget, the President builds upon his economic plan with the Middle Class Bill of Rights—both short- and long-term policies to raise the living standards of those hard-working, middle-income Americans. His goal is straightforward: Having created millions of new jobs, he now wants to create jobs that are better and more secure.

The President's Middle Class Bill of Rights has the following four elements:

- For tax relief, the President proposes a middle-income tax cut—a tax credit for families with children under age 13—that will help Americans with the day-to-day costs of raising families.
- To increase the Nation's savings and the financial self-reliance and retirement reserves of American workers, the President proposes expanded eligibility for Individual Retirement Accounts (IRAs). With this provision, most American families will have a tax incentive to make their own investments in their futures. And to help with the major challenges of buying a first home, paying for catastrophic health costs, withstanding the financial pressure of job loss, and financing education (to increase our skills for the competitive economy of tomorrow), the President would create opportunities for penalty-free withdrawals from IRAs.
- To nourish the skills workers need in tomorrow's economy, the President proposes a tax deduction for the costs of post-secondary education. This gives average American families a tax cut if they invest in their children's—or their own—education and skills.
- To equip today's workers, and tomorrow's, with the education and job skills they need to compete effectively in the global economy, the President proposes a G.I. Bill for America's Workers that empowers individuals by awarding them skill grants and provides greater flexibility for State and local governments.

At the same time, the President proposes to build upon his successes in opening foreign markets, to generate more of the high-paying jobs associated with rising U.S. trade. He will negotiate to expand membership in the North American Free Trade Agreement, implement the recent General Agreement on Tariffs and Trade, and seek other bilateral and multi-lateral opportunities to open new markets. He also will restructure U.S. trade promotion programs to target assistance to exporters.

In short, this budget builds on a base of deficit reduction and economic strength by continuing to pursue sound fiscal policies and investments to bolster and further spread our improved living standards. It will make an enviable economic record even better.

1. Sharing the Benefits of Economic Growth

1. SHARING THE BENEFITS OF ECONOMIC GROWTH

A MIDDLE-CLASS TAX CUT

The Problem of Lagging Incomes

On the domestic front, the President's highest priority is to spread the benefits of our economic growth to average Americans whose incomes have remained stagnant or even declined.

The roots of the problems of working Americans date back over 20 years. Rapid technological advances have put a premium on education and job skills. Generally speaking, those with high education and sophisticated skills have benefited in the last two decades; their standards of living have risen. Those without the requisite education and skills, however, have had to work longer hours or more than one job just to maintain their living standards. Even that wasn't enough for the many whose living standards declined.

In recent decades, the middle class has not fully shared in the benefits of a growing economy. From 1980–93, real incomes of the middle one-fifth of households rose by only 0.6 percent, an average of under $200 each (Table 1–1). Incomes of the top fifth, however, grew by 20.8 percent, or about $17,000 each. Even more striking, incomes of the top five percent grew by over 33 percent, or over $41,200.

As a result, the share of total household income enjoyed by the middle class fell. The share going to the middle three-fifths of households fell from 51.8 percent in 1980 to 48.2 percent in 1993. The share of income enjoyed by the top fifth rose from 44.1 percent to 48.2 percent. Thus, by 1993, the top fifth of households was receiving the same share of income as the middle three-fifths.

Moreover, the top five percent enjoyed most of the growth in income of the top one-fifth; its income share rose from 16.6 percent of all household income in 1980 to 20 percent in 1993. Meanwhile, the share of income of the lowest fifth fell from 4.2 percent to 3.6 percent.

Millions of working American families clearly have lagged behind the pace of growing economic prosperity—even in the last two years, when growth in the overall economy has been especially brisk. The President's program is designed to help lift the incomes of the broad middle class of American workers.

A First Step: The 1993 Tax Cut

Two years ago, the President and Congress took a major first step to raise the limited income growth and reduce the tax burdens of lower-middle-income American workers: They made the *earned income tax credit*

Table 1–1. AVERAGE HOUSEHOLD INCOME, BY QUINTILE

(Incomes in constant 1993 dollars)

	Quintile					Top 5 Percent
	Lowest	Second	Third	Fourth	Highest	
1993	7,411	18,647	31,260	48,572	98,589	163,228
1980	7,567	18,834	31,079	45,787	81,638	121,998
Absolute Growth, 1980–93	–156	–187	181	2,785	16,951	41,230
Percent growth 1980–93	–2.1	–1.0	0.6	6.1	20.8	33.8

Source: Bureau of the Census

(EITC) more generous and extended it to more people. Their action greatly reduced the tax burden on these people and, by lifting working families with children above the poverty line, fulfilled the President's commitment to make work pay.

The EITC, which dates back to 1975, was originally designed to offset the burden of the Social Security payroll tax for low-wage workers with children, and to supplement wages as a way to encourage work. Congress extended it for two years in 1976, and increased it while making it permanent two years later. Since then, Congress has periodically increased and refined it. In 1993, the President and Congress chose to make the EITC available for the first time to poor workers *without* children. Today, the EITC is "refundable"—that is, individuals who owe no income taxes still may be eligible for a Federal refund. Consequently, the EITC helps to raise average incomes of working families with incomes in the bottom fifth of Americans.

In 1996, when the recent changes become fully effective, low-income families with two or more children will receive a 40-percent wage subsidy on earnings up to $8,900. That is, each $100 of earnings will entitle workers to a $40 EITC. The maximum credit will be $3,560 for workers who earn between $8,900 and $11,620. The credit is phased out for workers earning between $11,620 and $28,520.

In 1993, the imperative of reducing the deficit precluded the President and Congress from extending middle-income tax relief to more Americans. Now, with the deficit expected to fall again in 1995, the President can continue the tax relief he began in 1993 while maintaining his commitment to fiscal discipline: Under the President's program, every dollar of tax cuts is offset by spending cuts described, in detail, later in this budget.

The President's New Proposal

The President targets his new tax cut squarely at the middle class. More than 60 percent of the benefits will go to families with incomes below $75,000; 87 percent will go to families with incomes below $100,000.[1] (See Table 1–2.)

The President's tax cut has three main elements aimed at strengthening families, promoting education, and encouraging saving:

$500 non-refundable credit for each dependent child under the age of 13: This credit will be fully available to taxpayers with adjusted gross income (AGI) of less than $60,000, then phased out for incomes from $60,000 to $75,000. To insure that the tax cut does not increase the deficit, the credit is phased in only as fast as spending can be cut. That is, the credit will be $300 for 1996, 1997, and 1998, and $500 for 1999 and beyond.

This credit will provide substantial tax relief. For example, a two-parent, two-child family with $50,000 of wage and salary income (in 1995 dollars) and $7,500 of itemized deductions will enjoy a 21 percent cut in taxes—from $4,875 to $3,875—once the credit is fully in place. For hard-pressed working families, this tax saving could serve as a mortgage payment or as a reserve against a significant medical bill or other important expenses.

Deduction for up to $10,000 in post-secondary education and training expenses: This benefit will be available for tuition and fees (for the taxpayer, spouse, or dependents) for any college, university, or vocational program eligible for Federal assistance. Also, taxpayers will be able to take the deduction "above the line"; it will reduce their AGI and not be limited to taxpayers who itemize deductions.

The maximum allowable deduction will be phased in. It will start at $5,000 in 1996 and rise to $10,000 in 1999 and beyond. Taxpayers with AGI (before the deduction) below $100,000 will be eligible for the full deduction; it will be phased out for taxpayers with AGI between $100,000 and $120,000.

[1] By comparison, the Republican "Contract with America" proposals would give 49.9 percent of their benefits to families with incomes over $100,000, and 28.3 percent to those with incomes over $200,000 (the 2.2 percent of families with the highest incomes). Families with incomes under $75,000 would get only 35.3 percent of the benefits. Thus, the small group of families that enjoyed the biggest income gains in recent years would get the biggest tax cuts, while the vast bulk of middle-income families that experienced only modest gains would get a smaller share.

Table 1–2. PERCENTAGE DISTRIBUTION OF THE PRESIDENT'S MIDDLE-CLASS TAX CUT PROPOSAL

(1994 income levels)

Family Economic Income Class [1] (In thousands of dollars)	Number of Families in FEI Income Class (millions)	President's Middle-Class Tax Cut (percent)
0–10	14.9	0.1
10–20	18.4	1.1
20–30	16.0	4.3
30–50	22.4	23.3
50–75	17.4	32.5
75–100	9.9	25.6
100–200	8.8	12.4
200 & over	2.4	0.6
Total [2]	110.7	100.0

Source: Department of Treasury, Office of Tax Analysis, January 9, 1995.

[1] Family Economic Income (FEI) is a comprehensive income concept that is broader than adjusted gross income.

[2] Families with negative incomes are included in the total line but are not shown separately.

(For taxpayers filing as single or head-of-household, it will be phased out over the AGI range of $70,000 to $90,000.) When fully implemented, this deduction could provide tax savings of $1,500 to $2,800 for middle-income families.

Because college costs hit in large lump sums, even upper-middle-income families find them hard to swallow. The prospect of such expenses and a burden of debt upon graduation can deter some families—especially those of lower income—from making this key investment. This deduction will strengthen the economic incentive for doing so, thus promoting long-term increases in productivity and economic growth as well as broadening economic opportunity.

It also will help level the playing field between investments for physical capital and those for human capital. Investments for physical capital, such as plant and equipment, are eligible for deductions for depreciation. Individuals' investments in skills and training, however, generally are not eligible for such deductions.

Greatly expanded Individual Retirement Account (IRA) options: Today, couples with AGI of up to $40,000 can make fully deductible contributions of up to $2,000 to IRAs. The President would double the income limit to $80,000 (phased out at $100,000) for families, and raise it to $50,000 (phased out at $70,000) for individuals.

The President's proposal would extend fully deductible IRAs to the vast majority of taxpayers. Moreover, it would index these income limits, as well as the $2,000 maximum contribution, for inflation; eligibility and income limits would increase over time. In addition, taxpayers eligible for deductible IRAs could select a new "Special IRA," which provides its tax benefits at the time of withdrawal, not contribution. Rather than receive a tax deduction for contributions, individuals could elect to pay no taxes on the money they withdraw from IRAs after at least five years. Finally, individuals with AGI below the eligibility levels could convert an existing IRA to a Special IRA.

Individuals also could withdraw funds early from an IRA without paying the 10-percent penalty—if they use the money for:

- Post-secondary education;
- Purchase of a first home;
- Unemployment spells of 12 weeks or more;

- Care of an incapacitated elderly parent or grandparent; or
- Medical expenses in excess of 7.5 percent of AGI.

From the IRA expansion, too, the tax cut could prove substantial. Taxes for middle-income families could fall $600 to $1,120 if both spouses work and contribute the maximum $4,000 to their IRAs.

Expanded IRAs will promote savings, helping families and the economy as a whole: They will encourage middle-income families to save, enhancing their long-term economic independence; and they will increase the availability of capital to U.S. business, expanding investment and speeding the growth of productivity and incomes.

Currently, the U.S. personal savings rate is low in historic terms and by international comparison, handicapping investment and economic growth. The expanded IRAs will send a signal to Americans that saving is important. The availability of these new opportunities will encourage private financial institutions to spread the word.

SECURING HIGHER INCOMES

> *Education... has a bigger impact on earnings and job security than ever before... Every American needs the skills necessary to prosper in the new economy... So let's invest the fruits of today's recovery into tomorrow's opportunity.*
>
> President Clinton
> Address to the Nation
> December 15, 1994

The President's G.I. Bill for America's Workers, the fourth element of his Middle Class Bill of Rights, will ensure that all Americans—including those who don't benefit from the tax cuts—have the opportunity to get the skills they need. This initiative not only complements other parts of the Middle Class Bill of Rights but also builds on the Administration's success, working with the last Congress, in improving the education system from preschool through college, thus helping to insure that the next generation will enter the workforce better prepared than previous ones. By focusing on adults as well as youth, this education and training initiative would make lifelong learning opportunities for all Americans a reality.

The Lifelong Learning Agenda

The comprehensive set of initiatives for lifelong learning began with successful, bipartisan legislation of the last two years to increase educational opportunity and quality for young people and make college more affordable:

- Head Start Act;
- Goals 2000: Educate America Act;
- School-to-Work Opportunities Act;
- Improving America's Schools Act; and
- Student Loan Reform Act.

Through these laws, the Administration and Congress are making pre-school more effective, helping States set challenging standards for our schools, helping schools incorporate those standards into system-wide elementary and secondary education improvements, enabling high school students to more successfully move from school to work and further education, and making college loans more affordable. These laws help States and localities raise the achievement and skill levels of all students and workers in order to build a sounder economy, and strong democracy, in the future.

The final component of this agenda is the President's new skills initiative. Working with States, communities, and the private sector, it will produce a thorough restructuring of the wide array of Federal education and training programs, make job search assistance more effective, and put more dollars directly in the hands of workers and job seekers who need and want new skills.

For the major components of the Lifelong Learning Agenda, the budget proposes $27.7 billion, an increase of $2.5 billion over the 1995 level—and an increase of $5.2 billion, or 23 percent, over 1993. (See Table 1–3.)

What We Have Achieved

In the U.S., education is mainly a State, local, and private sector responsibility. The

Table 1–3. THE BUDGET INCREASES INVESTMENT IN MAJOR PROGRAMS FOR LIFELONG LEARNING BY $2.5 BILLION OVER 1995, AN INCREASE OF $5.2 BILLION, OR 23 PERCENT OVER THE 1993 LEVEL

(Budget authority, in millions of dollars)

	1993 Actual	1995 Estimate [1]	1996 Proposed	Change: 1995 to 1996	Change: 1993 to 1996
Head Start	2,776	3,535	3,935	+400	+1,159
Goals 2000	....	403	750	+347	+750
Education for the Disadvantaged (Title I)	6,686	7,233	7,441	+208	+755
Professional Development (Title II)	....	320	735	+415	+735
Charter Schools	....	6	20	+14	+20
Education Technology (ED and DOL)	....	40	98	+58	+98
Safe and Drug-Free Schools [2]	582	482	500	+18	–82
School-to-Work (ED and DOL) [included in G.I. Bill for America's Workers entry]					
G.I. Bill for America's Workers	12,426	13,186	14,202	+1,016	+1,776
Total BA, lifelong learning	**22,470**	**25,205**	**27,681**	**+2,476**	**+5,211**
Loans for education and training (in millions of dollars)	17,873	25,757	28,356	+2,599	+10,483

[1] Includes proposed supplementals and rescissions.
[2] Reflects Congress' cut below the appropriation request in 1995.

Federal Government provides less than 10 percent of total public funds spent for these purposes. This tradition of local responsibility and control precludes the possibility of top-down reform. If schools are to improve, States, local school districts, and individual schools—together with parents—must take the lead and play active roles. Quality, equity, and access to education are, however, critical national concerns. Acting as a partner with States, local communities, and the private sector, the Federal Government invests its resources in three primary areas:

- To stimulate reform (e.g., Goals 2000 and School-to-Work);
- To supplement State and local resources for particular, high-priority purposes (e.g., educating the disadvantaged and making schools safer and more drug-free); and
- To make postsecondary education more affordable (e.g., Pell grants, student loans, and the new tax benefits for training).

Head Start—Reforming the Preschool System: Head Start provides comprehensive services, such as education, health care, and nutritious meals, for disadvantaged three-to-five-year-old children and their families. The new infant and toddler initiative that the President and Congress enacted in 1994 as part of the Head Start Act, allocates about four percent of 1996 Head Start funds to reach children under age three and their families.

Evaluations of Head Start children have found short-term gains in IQ scores, better reading and math skills, better emotional adjustment, and improved health. Former Head Start children are likelier to be promoted to the next grade and less likely to be assigned to special education classes. To assure that all Head Start programs consistently deliver the high-quality services needed to produce such results, the Administration and Congress enacted major quality improvements to Head Start in the 1994 reauthorization.

The 1994 Act supports investments to attract and retain workers at Head Start centers, thereby increasing the stability of the program environment and improving the quality of instruction. These investments enable Head Start centers to improve teacher-

Chart 1-1. 32 THOUSAND NEW HEAD START OPPORTUNITIES FOR CHILDREN IN 1996

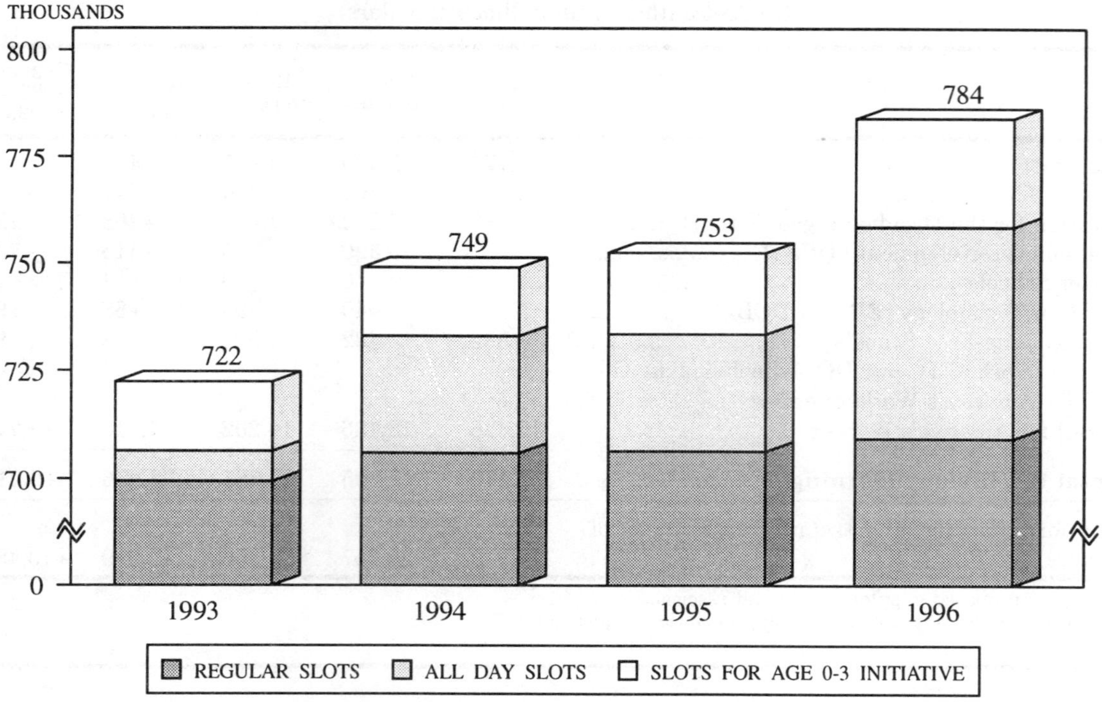

Note: Slots for the age 0-3 initiative in 1993 and 1994 show participation in the Comprehensive Child Development Projects (CCDP) and Head Start Parent Child Centers (PCC).

child ratios, hire education and health specialists, upgrade facilities, and make other changes that local managers deem appropriate to raise the quality of their programs. By May 1995, the Department of Health and Human Services will develop performance measures for evaluating the quality of local programs. The Department is working to ensure accountability and will take prompt action against poorly performing grantees, including termination if necessary.

Having begun the process of improving Head Start's quality, the Administration will focus as well in 1996 on increasing the number of children who benefit from the program. The budget would create 31,500 new opportunities for children, including the provision of full-year, full-day slots, part-time slots, and slots for the new infant and toddler initiative. (See Chart 1–1.) All told, the budget provides for 784,000 slots in 1996, for which it proposes $3.935 billion for Head Start, an increase of $400 million, or 11 percent, over the 1995 level.

Goals 2000: Educate America Act: The 1994 enactment of Goals 2000 marked a new era in education reform, one that engages all schools and students. Goals 2000 codifies the National Education Goals, gives States new reform resources, and sets the expectation that all children will achieve the high standards that States develop. It helps States support local districts and schools in their efforts to align curriculum, instruction, and professional development with challenging new standards. And it helps States make schools more accountable to parents, students and the public.

Goals 2000 draws on research and international comparisons that show that all students can reach far higher academic standards than we have asked of them. It incorporates a strategy far different from prior Federal reform endeavors; it addresses a national problem with a national, not a Federal, strategy. Rather than impose a top-down approach filled with mandates, it focuses on fostering bottom-up, local reform guided by challenging State standards. The goal: To create a long-term, productive partnership among local schools, school districts, States, and the Federal Government to bring all students to higher levels of achievement.

Goals 2000 calls for maximum State flexibility, as reflected in the Education Department's implementation strategy. It imposes no additional constraints and offers States new waiver flexibility through which to bring almost all Federal elementary and secondary education programs into their reform efforts. Each State is tailoring its reform approach to its needs. For example, some States may begin with improved teacher training, others with curriculum redesign, and still others with enhanced parent involvement.

Under Goals 2000, the Federal Government will work with States to carefully evaluate reform. It will help the States learn from each other while it conducts national level research and collects information that States need to support their efforts. Over time, the Federal Government will work with States to create performance indicators for systemic reform, which might include:

- The pace by which States establish objective, high-quality academic content and performance standards, and align professional development and assessment with them;
- The change in the percentage of students who meet or exceed reading and math proficiency levels, as measured by the National Assessment of Educational Progress; and
- The performance of students in high-poverty schools, compared to those in other schools.

The budget proposes $750 million for Goals 2000, an increase of $347 million, or 86 percent, over 1995.

Improving America's Schools Act (reauthorization of the Elementary and Secondary Education Act of 1965): Title I provides funds to raise the educational achievement of children in low-income areas. In 1994, the President proposed and Congress adopted changes to focus Title I resources better on areas with the largest concentrations of low-income children; set the same high standards for those children as for others; and hold schools accountable for making progress toward achieving those standards. States now have much more flexibility to use funds as they deem necessary to achieve better educational results for children. The budget includes $7.441 billion for Title I, an increase of $208 million, or three percent, over the 1995 level.

The new Title II Professional Development program provides funds to States and educational institutions to support the intensive, high-quality training of teachers and administrators. The program will enable educators to achieve higher levels of professional excellence and help students achieve the new academic standards and learn in accordance with new State curriculum designs. The budget includes $735 million for Professional Development, an increase of $415 million, or 130 percent, over 1995.

Of the other elements in the new Act, three are especially significant:

- **Charter Schools**—Funds for States and school districts to support the development of new types of public schools that enhance parental choice and operate substantially free of Federal, State, and local regulations that may impede better student achievement. The budget includes $20 million for Charter schools, an increase of $14 million over 1995's first year funding.
- **Technology for Education**—Activities (including a "Technology Learning Challenge") to create a partnership among States, schools, and the private sector to raise education and training achievement by innovatively using technology. The budget proposes $83 million for the Education Department and $15 million for the Labor Department; the $98 million total represents an increase of $58 million, or 145 percent, over 1995's first year funding.
- **Safe and Drug-free Schools and Communities**—The restructuring of programs

of drug abuse prevention and school violence reduction, giving States and schools more flexibility to use funding to meet their needs. The budget proposes $500 million for these activities, an increase of $18 million over 1995.

School-to-Work Opportunities Act: School-to-Work supports State, local, and private efforts to build an education and training system that helps all youth get the knowledge and skills to move smoothly from school to career-oriented work or to more education or training. States and localities tailor their activities to local needs, such as by developing new curricula that integrate academic and occupational learning; linking high school and one or two years of postsecondary technical education; using mentors to help young people learn the requirements of the workplace; and providing "skill certificates" that employers can trust in choosing a qualified young person.

For example:

- Boston builds on a youth apprenticeship model, integrating paid work experience with new curriculum; and
- Oregon's South Coast Region uses the skill certificate approach, focusing on careers in health care, finance, tourism, manufacturing, shipping, forest products, and commercial fishing.

Recognizing the link between schools and the labor market, the Labor and Education Departments administer School-to-Work jointly through a single office that works with States, localities, and the private sector. The budget proposes $400 million for School-to-Work, an increase of $150 million, or 60 percent, over 1995. (For more discussion, see "Helping Youth," below.)

Reforms of the Student Loan System: The guaranteed loan program structure that evolved over the past 30 years was very costly, hard to administer, and subject to abuse. In response, the President proposed the Student Loan Reform Act, which Congress enacted in 1993.

The Act launched the Federal Direct Student Loan Program to replace the guaranteed lending program, which works through 7,500 lenders and 46 State and non-profit intermediaries ("guaranty agencies"). The new program finances loans efficiently by sending them directly to students and schools through simple electronic transfers. It greatly simplifies borrowing for students, parents, and schools. And for the first time, it gives borrowers substantial repayment flexibility, particularly through the "pay-as-you-can" option—borrowers only repay each year what their income permits. Under this option, nobody needs to fear that borrowing for school might lead to loan defaults or that loan burdens might be too great. The Act extends the Pay-as-you-can option to all borrowers under the old program through "consolidation loans." The Act will save an estimated $6.8 billion from 1995–2000.

Direct lending began successfully in 1994, with 226,000 new loans. To maximize the benefits of direct lending for students, families and schools, and to further lower taxpayer costs, the Administration is proposing to speed up Direct Loan implementation so that all new loans are direct loans by July 1, 1997, saving an additional $5.2 billion from 1996–2000. (See Chart 1–2.)

THE AGENDA AHEAD

During its first two years, the Administration focused on improving education from pre-school through college. These investments are critical to the Nation's future. But we also must provide better opportunities for those adults who are already in the workforce and whose education may prove insufficient to meet the challenges of today's economy, or whose skills may prove equally insufficient to move them into new or better jobs.

The Problem with Job Placement and Job Training Programs

Today's patchwork of Federal job placement and training programs grew up over more than 60 years. Each element was designed with the best of intentions—to respond to a specific concern. In the end, however, the system does not meet the needs of today's economy or fit the President's goal of a streamlined, more effective system.

- The many programs, with their conflicting rules and administrative structures, con-

Chart 1-2. STUDENT LOAN PROGRAM COSTS WOULD BE REDUCED 12 BILLION DOLLARS OVER SIX YEARS, 1995-2000

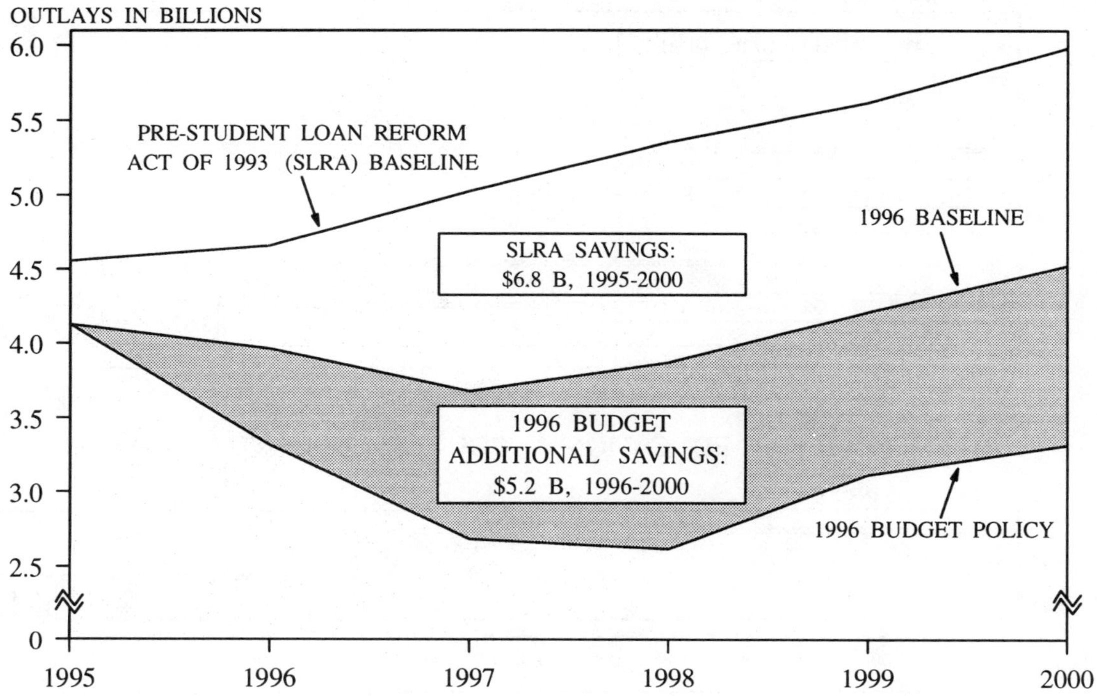

NOTE: Pre-SLRA baseline is adjusted for interest rate, inflation and loan volume differentials, to make them comparable.

fuse the people they are intended to help, add bureaucracy at every level, and waste taxpayer money.

- Not surprisingly, States and localities complain about the problems of coping with so many different Federal rules and reporting requirements.
- In many programs, bureaucrats make choices about jobs and training for individuals, as if individuals cannot choose for themselves; nor is the private sector plugged in enough to help.
- Job seekers and those who seek skill training do not receive high-quality information and assistance. Pell grants and student loans do permit "choice"—recipients use the Federal aid at the institution they choose—but recipients cannot make informed choices because they do not get reliable information on job and career opportunities or on the quality of training providers to choose from.
- The quality of training and related services is uneven, and the programs often do not require accountability for results; institutions continue to get Federal funds regardless of performance.

The Solution: Reinventing Programs by Empowering People, States, and Local Communities

The President intends to help workers, job seekers, local governments, and the private sector meet the demands of the new economy by scrapping the confusing maze of Federal training programs. He would break down traditional hierarchies and bureaucracies, putting most resources directly into workers' hands. Funds also would go directly to States and localities, so they could design the job search and training-related systems that they determine are needed to help youth and adults to qualify for, and get, good jobs.

Chart 1-3. 1.6 MILLION MORE GRANTS AND LOANS FOR PEOPLE TO MAKE THEIR OWN CHOICES OF TRAINING AND EDUCATION

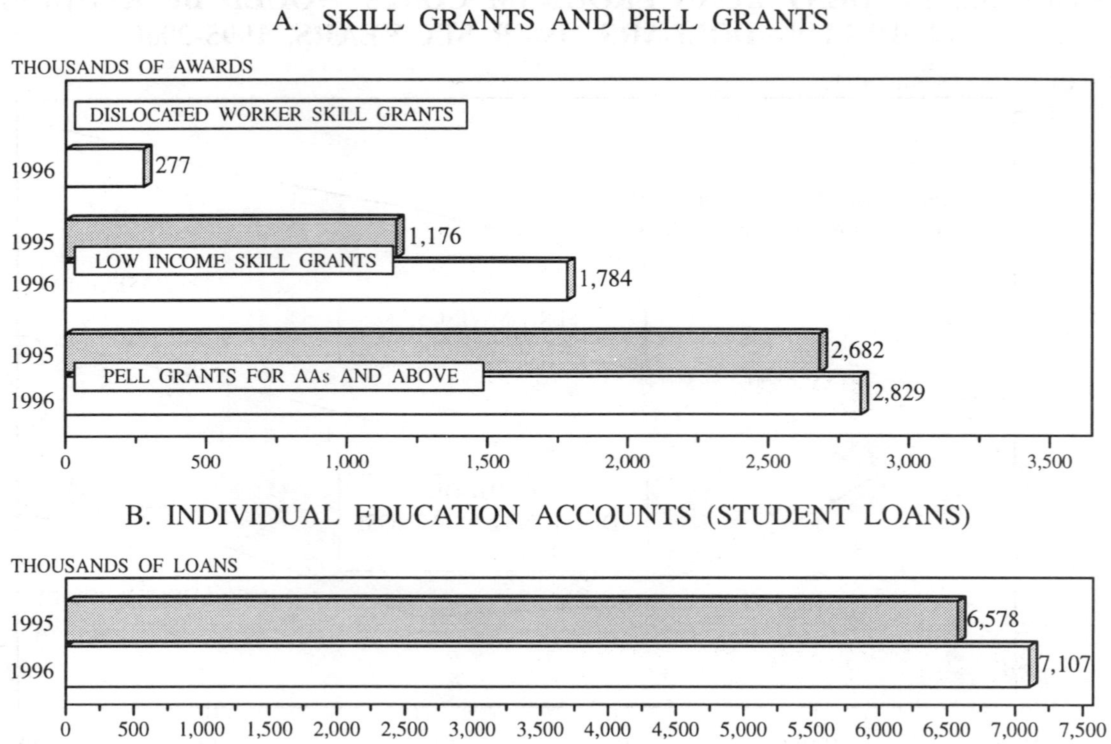

Able to acquire the skills and information they need to compete, workers will have more control over their own futures. Given the opportunity, States and communities will design the job training and related services their citizens need. The Federal Government will ensure that services continue to be provided to the disadvantaged and that the Federal funds in question produce measurable results. Thus, this initiative is based on seven key principles:

1. Empowering individuals;
2. Providing good data to guide choices;
3. Insuring accountability to consumers and taxpayers;
4. Creating leaner government;
5. Providing greater flexibility to State and local communities;
6. Making the private sector a partner; and
7. Creating effective paths from schools to work.

Of the 163 Federal job training programs that the General Accounting Office identified in January 1995, this proposal would incorporate all those that directly support general job search and job training assistance. The budget reflects the inclusion of 70 programs, representing over 60 percent of 1995 funding for the programs GAO identified. (See Table 1–4.) Of the rest, some were terminated or not funded in 1995 and the others are not appropriate for inclusion—for example, some primarily assist business development; others provide physical rehabilitation for the disabled. Thus, they do not fit the description of general job search or training.

While proposing to streamline programs, the President also seeks to increase overall funding by $1 billion, reflecting his belief that—now more than ever—education and training are the ladder into the middle-class and the best insurance that workers have against economic change.

Table 1–4. THE G.I. BILL FOR AMERICA'S WORKERS COMBINES 70 PROGRAMS INTO ONE WORKFORCE DEVELOPMENT SYSTEM, AND INCREASES FUNDING $1 BILLION OVER 1995

(Discretionary budget authority, in millions of dollars)

Sets of Categorical Programs	1995 Enacted	System Components	1996 Proposed
JTPA adult programs	997	Skill and Pell grants to individuals:	
Dislocated worker programs	1,296	Dislocated workers	582
Pell grants	6,247	Low-income persons	3,059
Employment service	912	Pell grants for AA degrees and above	4,480
State postsecondary renew program	20		
Research, evaluation and demonstrations	48	Subtotal, individual grants	8,121
One-Stop Career Centers	120		
JTPA and other youth programs	1,630	State-defined services system:	
School-to-Work (ED and DOL)	250	Adults (including One-Stop)	2,685
Vocational education programs	1,178	Adult and family literacy	490
Adult education and family literacy programs	488	Youth (including School-to-Work)	2,906
Total:		**Total:.**	
Categorical programs	**13,186**	**Better Jobs and Skills System**	**14,202**
Loans for education and training (in millions of dollars)	25,757	Loans for education and training (in millions of dollars)	28,356

The new jobs and skills initiative will allow each State to devise an integrated strategy that unifies all elements of the training and education system. The building blocks are described separately below (though the Federal Government would no longer require States to maintain separate programs).

Helping Adults: The President's proposal would create "Skill grants" for unemployed and low-income workers and job seekers. States would create systems to give individuals the information they need to make informed choices with these grants and ensure that workers are not defrauded by incompetent or unscrupulous providers. The proposal would make 1.6 million more grants and loans available in 1996 than in 1995. (See Chart 1–3.) It also would support State efforts to design new, more flexible, integrated systems that will provide information about jobs and training, counseling, placement assistance, and other services.

- Individuals would get Skill grants or Pell grants of up to $2,620 a year for training;
- The budget proposes $3.6 billion in 1996 for Skill grants for technical education and $4.5 billion for associates and bachelor's degree courses through Pell grants. The student loan programs will provide another $28 billion in loan capital to help finance training and higher education;
- Low-income persons would get Skill grants based on family income and cost of education, in the same way they do now under Pell grants; and
- Dislocated workers who need training would qualify for Skill grants without an income test. Adults who lose their jobs and need skill training to get a new one would receive income support.

The proposal would build upon progress underway through "One-Stop Career Centers" to encourage States and localities to design and implement new systems of placement and training-related services within five years.

- It would provide $2.7 billion, most of it to States to design and operate the new system; and some for Federal activities such as oversight, research, evaluation, and response to multi-State layoffs and natural disasters; and
- It would provide $490 million for adult and family literacy, which the States could use as they want for basic skills instruc-

tion, GED preparation, and English-as-a-second language training.

Helping Youth: Too many young people do not now get the necessary preparation for jobs or for more education by the time they leave high school. Many do not even finish high school, in part because they see no connection between schooling and success in the job market. As discussed above, the School-to-Work Opportunities Act launched a national reform of education and workforce preparation programs for America's youth. Now, to build on and intensify that effort, the President's proposal will help States, communities, and the private sector completely restructure the primary Federal youth training programs.

- Under the proposal, States and localities will continue to receive School-to-Work Opportunities Act funds to link school systems, postsecondary education, and the private sector. These funds phase out by 2001 as systems are implemented;
- The proposal would consolidate most funds under the Perkins Vocational Education Act into one in-school youth grant to States;
- It would consolidate most funds under the JTPA IIC (year-round youth programs), JTPA Summer Youth Jobs programs, and other youth programs into one grant to States to serve dropouts and high-risk youth; and
- It would strongly encourage States and localities to implement an integrated School-to-Work system to serve in-school and out-of-school youth. They could submit a single plan to the Education and Labor Departments to combine Perkins, JTPA, ESEA Title I, and other youth funds. The Federal Government would quickly waive upon request any remaining Federal requirements that impede success.

Maintaining and Enhancing the Private Sector Role: The private sector has an immediate, direct stake in the quality of job training and related systems. It is establishing skill standards that can serve as the basis for holding training providers accountable for results. Under the President's proposal:

- Business and labor will be key partners in designing adult and youth programs and in providing essential data on jobs and skill demands; and
- Government will recognize and give awards to firms that have enjoyed the most success in upgrading the skills of their workforce. The most competitive and productive firms are improving such skills by way of formal training, on-the-job training, and investments in mid-career education, and by empowering workers to take greater responsibility on the job.

Improving the Pell Grant Program: The Pell grant program provides need-based grants to 4 million low- and middle-income undergraduates for vocational training and associates and bachelors degree programs. About half the recipients come from families with under $10,000 in income, and over 90 percent come from families with under $30,000 in income. Awards range from a minimum of $400 up to a maximum limited by annual appropriations.

Studies show that Pell grants help raise the participation rates of low-income students in post-secondary programs. As such, they are another important ladder into the middle class. Currently, about one-third of Pell funds are used for non-degree programs and are not integrated with other Federal and State training activity. Individuals who use these funds get little information about career options or the quality of vocational schools.

In the new skills initiative, Pell grant funds for vocational training would become "Skill grants" (as described above). Recipients would benefit from information about jobs and careers before enrolling in training and would learn the quality of training at each school.

For 1996, the budget would raise the maximum Pell grant to its highest level ever at $2,620, the same as the new Skill grants—a $280, or 12-percent increase, over the 1995 level.

More Accountability at all Levels

The President proposes to make the new education and training system meet the test that businesses face every day: it must deliver value to its customers or risk losing resources. The system will reflect the principles of performance-based management at all levels.

- Individuals will have the resources to buy training, and the detailed reports on the quality and track records of eligible education and training institutions to let them make sound choices. Ineffective institutions will not survive.
- Individuals will be able to use their Federal dollars only at institutions with good track records, in terms of their students' achievement against recognized skill standards and their success in the job market.
- State-designed job search, job information, and training-related services will have to provide data to the public and to the Federal Government on how effectively they are using resources.
- Training providers will have to meet minimum quality standards in order to receive Federal funds.
- Training providers will have to produce customer-friendly "Report Cards," spelling out how well they perform on such factors as job placement of hard-to-employ persons as well as others, and the earnings of graduates in relation to program costs.
- The Labor and Education Departments will assess the system's overall performance at the national level and make its performance the basis for future budget proposals.

WELFARE REFORM

Under true reform, the welfare system would support the President's goal of ensuring that everyone, including welfare recipients, receive the training they need to go to work. It would provide temporary help for Americans who have fallen on hard times, while giving them the tools to return to the economic mainstream.

By that standard, the current system is badly flawed. The vast majority of Americans seem to agree, according to public opinion polls:

- 75 percent believe that welfare is rife with fraud and waste and does little to help poor people;
- 85 percent believe that it should be transformed into a program that creates jobs for the low-income; and
- 89 percent support a two-year welfare limit, after which able-bodied recipients should get a job or do community service.

Today's system does too little to prevent the conditions that lead to welfare dependency, such as teen pregnancy and poor education. It also provides a series of roadblocks for those who want to get off welfare. It does not give many the training they need to be self-sufficient or help them find jobs. Nor does it force most fathers to take responsibility for their families. Low-income parents who want to work often cannot get day care or health care for their children, or find a job with wages high enough to move their families out of poverty.

The President has pledged to "end welfare as we know it." Last year he submitted legislation, the Work and Responsibility Act, to accomplish that goal. This year, he will work with Congress to enact comprehensive welfare reform that embodies the principles of work and responsibility for able-bodied welfare recipients and protects their children.

A Brief History of Our Welfare System

At the turn of the century, our welfare system still reflected the English poor laws. Assistance went to the poor, but often only to those willing to live in poorhouses or to place their children in institutions or with other families as apprentices or indentured servants. Responding to public concerns about the living conditions of large numbers of children, President Theodore Roosevelt convened the first White House Conference on Children in 1909. Conferees agreed that, where possible, children should remain with their families. As a result, many States enacted mothers' pension laws to keep families intact.

The Great Depression spurred further changes to America's decentralized, loose-knit social welfare system. Private and public agencies could not handle the massive needs of so many destitute families. In August 1935, President Franklin Roosevelt signed the Social Security Act, establishing several assistance programs with shared Federal-State responsibility, including Aid to Dependent Children (now Aid to Families with Dependent Children, or AFDC), which is considered the Government's main welfare program.

Welfare Today

First designed primarily to aid widows with young children, AFDC has expanded over the years to serve children whose father or mother is absent, disabled, or unemployed. Rising rates of divorce and out-of-wedlock childbearing, along with an expansion of eligibility and higher participation rates among the eligible, swelled the population of AFDC recipients. In 1936, a half-million individuals received AFDC assistance. Today, 14 million individuals (two-thirds of them children) get such help each year, and the Federal and State governments spend nearly $23 billion a year. (Despite perceptions to the contrary, however, Federal spending on AFDC amounts to less than one percent of the Federal budget.)

Length of Time on AFDC: Today, many believe AFDC fosters long-term dependency. Once a family begins to receive welfare, critics contend, parents may begin to rely on monthly cash payments instead of seeking work. While the charge is true of a small core of people that tend to stay on the rolls for a long time—about 9 percent stay continuously for at least eight years—most AFDC recipients receive assistance only temporarily, as Chart 1–4 shows.

Large numbers of recipients find jobs, and others marry and leave welfare. About 70 percent leave AFDC within two years, according to a recent study. But while they may want to remain independent, many families return to welfare. Some have trouble combin-

Chart 1-4. HOW LONG DOES THE AVERAGE AFDC RECIPIENT STAY CONTINUOUSLY ON WELFARE ?

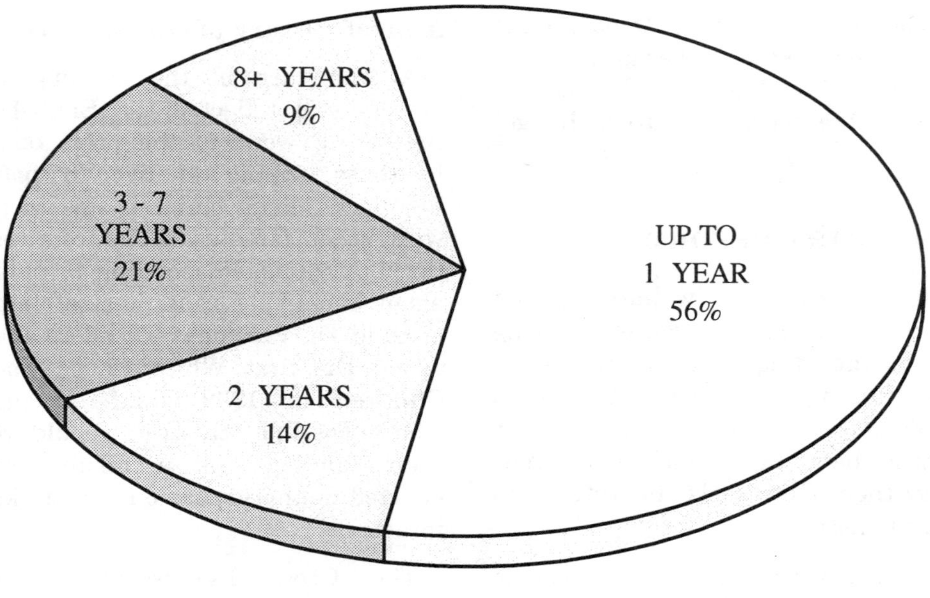

SOURCE: 1994 Greenbook, p. 442.

ing work and family responsibilities; others lack the social and work-related skills to keep a steady job.

Changes in the Family: Critics also contend that the welfare system promotes out-of-wedlock childbearing. To be sure, the percentage of such births nearly tripled between 1970 and 1991; by 1991, 30 percent of all births were by unmarried women. (See Chart 1–5.) But numerous studies have found little or no relationship between these trends and the level of welfare benefits. Instead, out-of-wedlock childbearing seems rooted in broader economic and cultural changes that have affected all segments of society.

Non-Payment of Child Support: Due to changes in the family, by 1992 nearly one of every four children under age 18 in the U.S. lived in a family where the mother had never married or the father was absent because of divorce, separation, or death. A serious related problem is that large numbers of absent parents never assume responsibility for paying child support. In 1989, only 43 percent of low-income women were awarded child support through the court system. (See Chart 1–6).

Nor does a court award always translate into child support itself. Only about half of low-income women who receive a legal order mandating support receive any money. The result is that three-quarters of these families are getting no help from the child's father (57 percent with no award, and 18 percent with no payment, as Chart 1–6 shows).

While the federally-sponsored, State-run child support system has made great strides, collecting about 14 percent more child support in 1992 than 1991 for AFDC-supported families, the system still needs vast improvement. In 1992, only about 12 percent of parents that were absent from AFDC families and being pursued by State agencies actually

Chart 1-5. OUT-OF-WEDLOCK BIRTH RATES IN THE U.S. NEARLY TRIPLED BETWEEN 1970 AND 1991

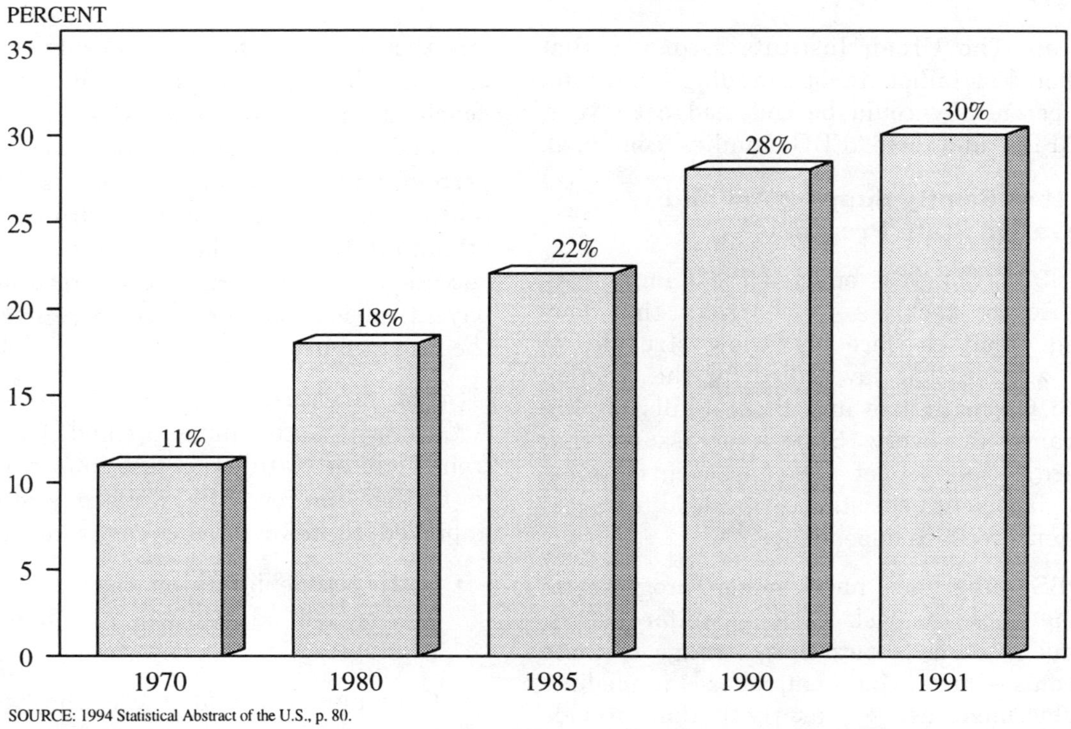

SOURCE: 1994 Statistical Abstract of the U.S., p. 80.

Chart 1-6. MOST POOR WOMEN RECEIVE NO CHILD SUPPORT

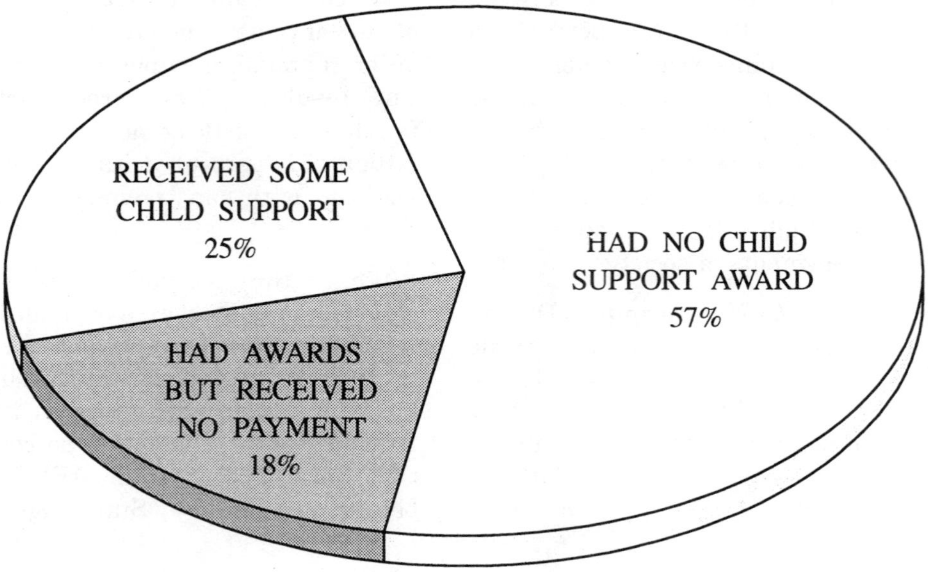

SOURCE: 1994 Greenbook, p. 463.

paid up. The Urban Institute estimates that another $34 billion in outstanding child support potentially could be collected each year, for AFDC and non-AFDC families combined.

The 1988 Family Support Act and Innovative State Programs

In 1988, Congress enacted the Family Support Act to tackle some barriers that low-income families face as they struggle to leave welfare. The law called for the creation of Job Opportunities and Basic Skills (JOBS) programs in every State, to assure that welfare recipients get the education, training, and placement assistance needed to avoid long-term welfare dependence.

JOBS programs have made progress in serving those at risk of long welfare stays. Careful research shows that a range of these programs—those that emphasize immediate job placement as well as those that provide more intensive services—have produced sustained increases in employment and earnings for those on welfare. California's training program has proved successful in moving people from welfare to work. It raised single parents' earnings over three years by 22 percent and cut welfare payments by 6 percent, starting from when enrollees began attending training classes. One particularly successful county, Riverside, returned taxpayers about $3 for each $1 invested in the program over five years.

Since enactment of the Family Support Act, many States have applied for waivers from Federal statutes to test innovative ideas to further improve the welfare system. The approved, State-inspired changes include:

- Setting time limits on cash assistance to able-bodied adults, when employment is available;
- Capping benefits for those who have additional children while on welfare; and

- Requiring children who receive AFDC to attend class regularly.

Because the Administration strongly favors State flexibility, it has approved over 20 waiver proposals—provided they maintain an adequate safety net for children, have a good research design, and do not increase Federal spending.

Work and Responsibility—the Tenets of Comprehensive Reform

The Administration supports the goal of the Family Support Act—to impart self-sufficiency to families—and believes firmly in more State experimentation. It also has proposed certain reforms that lay the foundation for welfare reform. By pushing successfully to expand the Earned Income Tax Credit, the President already has helped to boost the earning power of 15 million low-income families and ensured that many workers will be able to lift their families out of poverty, even in low-wage jobs. With a more robust economy and the skills initiative described above, many more families should be able to escape dependence on welfare. The Administration also remains committed to reform that will guarantee health insurance coverage to every American and contain health care costs for families, businesses and Federal, State, and local governments. This will allow people to retain health coverage as they move from welfare to work.

To build on these proposals and bring about the more fundamental changes needed in welfare, the welfare reform bill that the President submitted last year contained certain key principles:

Impose time limits on AFDC for parents who can work: We should make AFDC a temporary safety net for families in tough circumstances, not a long-term program that fosters dependency. Within two years, most recipients can find jobs in the private sector. Those who have tried and failed, because no jobs are available, still will have to work, in the public sector if necessary. Parents who refuse to participate will receive tough sanctions.

Provide job placement assistance and training: We should convert welfare offices from places that merely write checks to places that move people to work and independence. From the very first day, the new system will focus on helping welfare recipients to find jobs. It will orient job-ready participants to the workplace immediately. And it will refer those who need education, training, or other services to get a job.

Require parental responsibility: We should hold non-custodial parents accountable for maintaining the families they create. Measures such as stiffer penalties for not paying child support, requirements that mothers cooperate more closely with authorities in establishing paternity, and a universal process to establish paternity at birth will help improve the system. Better child support enforcement should deter parents from having children they cannot support, and boost the incomes of single-parent families.

Prevent teen pregnancy: Welfare reform will send a clear message to adolescents: you should not become a parent until you can provide for and nurture your child. Teens must understand that staying in school, postponing pregnancy, and preparing to work are the right things to do. A national campaign will bring together schools, communities, and families to emphasize the importance of delayed sexual activity and responsible parenting. Welfare reform also will change the incentives for teenagers who become parents, by requiring that they live at home or with a responsible adult and attend school.

Ensure that welfare reform does not increase the Federal deficit: A realistic plan to help adult AFDC recipients become independent requires an up-front investment. Although we may reap long-term savings, it costs money initially to give more adults the training and education they need to hold steady jobs, and to pay for child care and other services for those who work. The Administration is committed to covering these costs by cutting spending on other programs.

Ensure States the continued flexibility to experiment with innovative programs that aim to increase self-sufficiency: The cir-

162-000 O - 95 - 2

cumstances facing low-income families may differ greatly across States, each of which offer varied services to help the needy. Since States best understand the unique problems that their welfare beneficiaries face, we should continue to encourage them to develop programs to best address local conditions. We will continue to grant waivers to support State innovation. And we will consult with State and local officials on the best way to insure a successful reform effort at the national level.

The Administration will work with the new Congress to enact fundamental welfare reform, the kind that embodies the principles listed above.

Real reform should mean greater independence, control, and security for all families. It should mean that government helps low-income families to help themselves while protecting their children. It should focus on work and responsibility. And one should not undertake real reform without a full appreciation for the complexities of the issue and the lives of the next generation.

2. Building on Our Economic Record

2. BUILDING ON OUR ECONOMIC RECORD

THE FISCAL RECORD

Although the Federal Government has generated budget deficits for most years since World War II, deficits reached unprecedented peacetime levels in the 1980s. Recent efforts to reduce the deficit—including the 1985 Gramm-Rudman-Hollings law that was supposed to balance the budget—failed, because they evaded the tough choices of which programs to cut and which revenues to raise. When this Administration took office, the deficit had ballooned to nearly $300 billion and was expected to continue rising.

Those ballooning deficits were taking a dear toll on our Nation's economy. They drained the savings of the private sector, raising interest rates above what they otherwise would be. Those higher interest rates deterred business investment in productivity-increasing equipment and factories, and consumer investment in homes and durable goods. Rising budget deficits also inhibited the Federal Government from investing in the skills, knowledge, and infrastructure needed to ensure economic growth, and threatened future generations with a mounting burden of debt. Thus, the deficit legacy of the 1980s imperiled the very foundations of our prosperity.

Through its leadership, this Administration reversed the path of fiscal irresponsibility that had plagued the Federal Government for more than a decade and brought the deficit under control. Its effort paid off. With his economic plan, which Congress enacted in 1993, the President reduced the deficit from $290 billion in 1992 to $203 billion in 1994; we project that it will fall again, to $193 billion, in 1995. For this and other reasons, the economy is well positioned for long-term growth and prosperity.

Moreover, we expect the deficit to remain under control in dollar terms and to fall gradually relative to the size of the economy (measured by Gross Domestic Product, or GDP). We expect our proposals to bring the deficit-to-GDP ratio by 1998 to its lowest level since 1979.

Real deficit reduction is not easy. It forces elected officials to identify specific programs to cut and specific revenues to raise. Every program benefits a constituency which, in turn, voices its unhappiness if its program is slated for cuts. It was only because the President and Congress displayed unusual political courage that they accomplished so much.

How did they do it?

OBRA 1993

The Omnibus Budget Reconciliation Act of 1993 (OBRA) was a $505 billion package of spending cuts and revenue increases—$255 billion of spending cuts and $250 billion of revenues—for the years 1994–98. Spending reductions came from both entitlements and discretionary programs. The revenue increases were targeted almost exclusively at wealthy Americans.

Entitlements: OBRA cut projected spending on entitlements by $71.3 billion over five years, mostly in the fast-growing Medicare program. Savings also came from Medicaid, Federal retirement, farm subsidies, veterans' programs, and the student loan program. In some cases, such as student loans, the plan garnered savings through efficiencies, rather than by requiring cuts in benefits.

Discretionary Spending: OBRA also cut discretionary spending relative to projections. OBRA extended the existing "caps" on discretionary spending, which dated from 1990, through 1998. (This budget proposes to extend them further, through the year 2000.) By not allowing programs to grow with inflation, OBRA's caps reduced projected spending by $108 billion. Through the appropriations process, the President and Congress later agreed on the specific program cuts needed to meet the caps.

Fairer Taxes: OBRA raised revenues from those who were most able to bear that

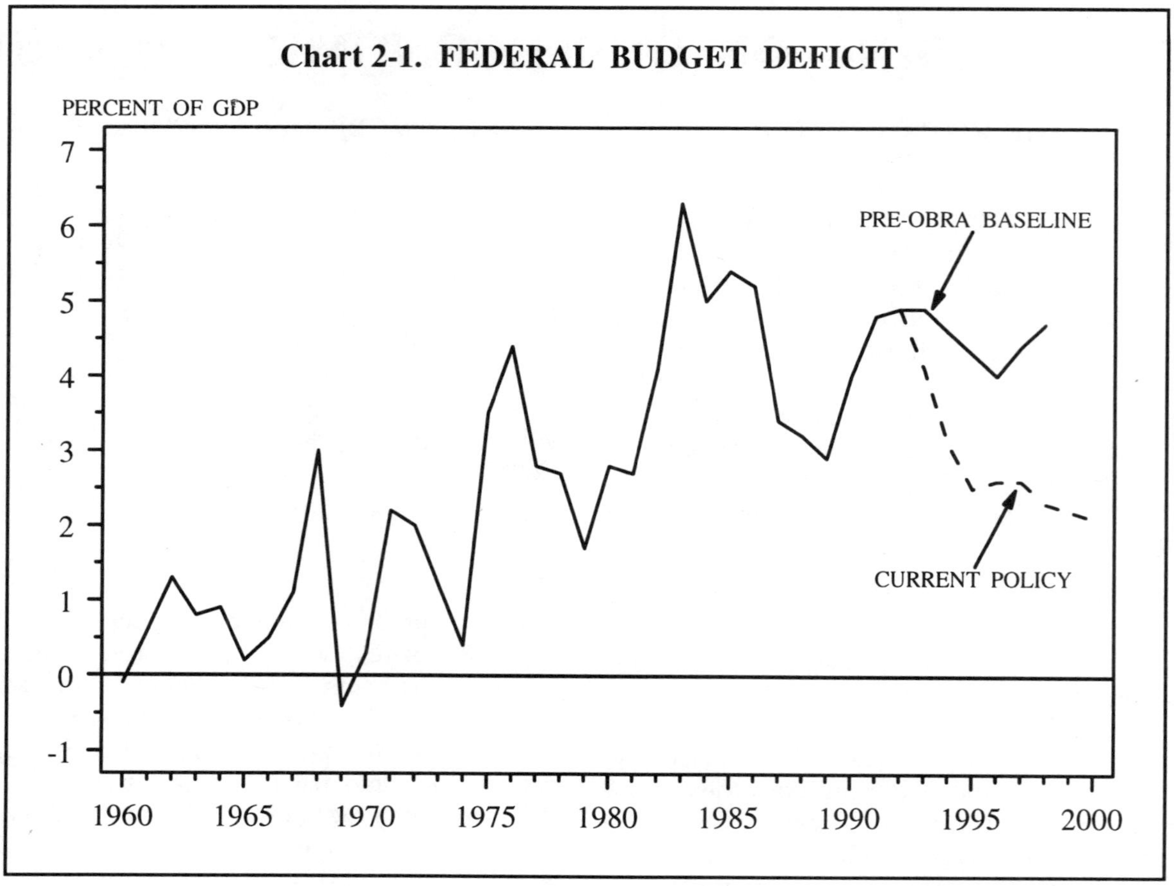

burden. Most taxpayers experienced no increase in their income taxes. To raise $70 billion by 1998, the law created a new marginal tax bracket for families with taxable incomes over $140,000.

OBRA's only broad-based tax increase, raising $24 billion over five years, was a 4.3 cents-per-gallon increase in the Federal gasoline tax. Even with that higher tax, the overall price of gasoline (including the tax) is about the same today as in the early 1980s. In real terms—that is, after adjusting for overall inflation—the total cost of gasoline has fallen significantly.

OBRA also included tax incentives to make the tax system fairer. It expanded the EITC—which, as discussed in Chapter 1, guarantees that any family with children and at least one parent who works full time eventually will rise above the poverty line. Today, the tax system is more progressive than at any time in 18 years.

The Economic Dividend: As we have noted above, OBRA included $505 billion in savings over five years from changes in actual revenue and spending policies. But because the economy responded so well to the plan (as the next section explains), OBRA actually has generated even more savings, bringing the deficit down further (Chart 2–1).

With higher economic growth than expected, the Government received more in business and personal tax payments, boosting Federal revenues. With interest rates lower, the Government has paid out less in interest costs associated with financing the national debt. And with unemployment lower, the Government has spent less on unemployment compensation and other social programs.

All told, the policy changes and the healthier economy have generated not just the $505 billion in savings that was once expected. Instead, the Administration now estimates that OBRA will reduce the accumulated deficits of 1994–98 by some $616 billion.

What Lower Deficits Mean for the Economy

When the President took office, the deficit was rising unsustainably, draining much of the Nation's savings to finance Government activities, keeping interest rates high and imposing a rising burden of debt service on taxpayers—present and future. Before it could move to other problems, the Administration first had to establish a firm plan to bring the deficit under control.

Since OBRA's enactment in the summer of 1993, the economy has performed extremely well. In the year that followed, economic growth averaged 4.4 percent—the best performance in over six years.

Surging Job Creation: Job creation accelerated. Since August 1993, the economy has created over four million payroll jobs—an average of 266,000 jobs a month—bringing the total to 5.6 million since the President took office (Chart 2–2). Over 90 percent have been in the private sector, and 39 percent are classified as either managerial or professional. In short, the economy has generated jobs at a vigorous pace, with a large portion in the highest-paying occupations.

Falling Unemployment: Unemployment, which was over seven percent when the President arrived, keeps falling (Chart 2–3). The unemployment rate fell to 5.4 percent in December, nearing its low point from the end of the last business cycle. (The survey on which the rate is based was redesigned in January 1994, making exact comparisons with prior years difficult).

Confident Consumers: The improving job market has buoyed consumer confidence. After rising by 22 percent in the four months after OBRA was enacted, the Index of Consumer Sentiment fluctuated for most of 1994. Nevertheless, it recently reached a new peak (Chart 2–4).

Consumers have acted on their confidence. Demand for automobiles and other consumer durables has remained strong, and housing starts have climbed to a high level. In the four quarters following OBRA's enactment, real consumer spending rose by 3¼ percent.

Healthy consumer spending is a prerequisite to prolonged economic expansion, and the burst of consumer spending in late 1993 helped accelerate growth and job creation. The rapid rise in consumption, however, has precluded any big increase in personal saving. The personal saving rate has stayed near four percent, similar to the late 1980s.

The Investment Boom: A strong rise in business fixed investment has led the recovery (Chart 2–5). In the last two years, real investment in equipment—led by the new generation of personal computers and related productivity-enhancing devices—jumped by over 18 percent.

Productivity: The key to greater prosperity is greater productivity, and productivity has been rising rapidly. Over the last year, output per hour in the nonfarm business sector is up by over two percent—a rate not seen on a sustained basis in over 20 years.

The recent news is very encouraging, but one cannot yet conclude that higher productivity growth will continue. Productivity rebounded strongly after recessions in the mid-1970s and early 1980s. The real test will be whether the growth rate since 1990 will continue as the business expansion matures. The next few quarters could tell the tale, as the surge in demand abates and the economy approaches its long-run, steady path.

Inflation: While the economy surged, inflation remained subdued. The core rate of inflation, excluding volatile food and energy prices, actually fell in 1994 (Chart 2–6). Low inflation has helped foster consumer and business confidence; previously, high and variable inflation rates made planning difficult. Today's inflation rate, and the promise that inflation will remain under control, help to sustain the current expansion and prolong the boom in investment spending.

Chart 2-2. CHANGES IN PAYROLL EMPLOYMENT
(jobs created December to December)

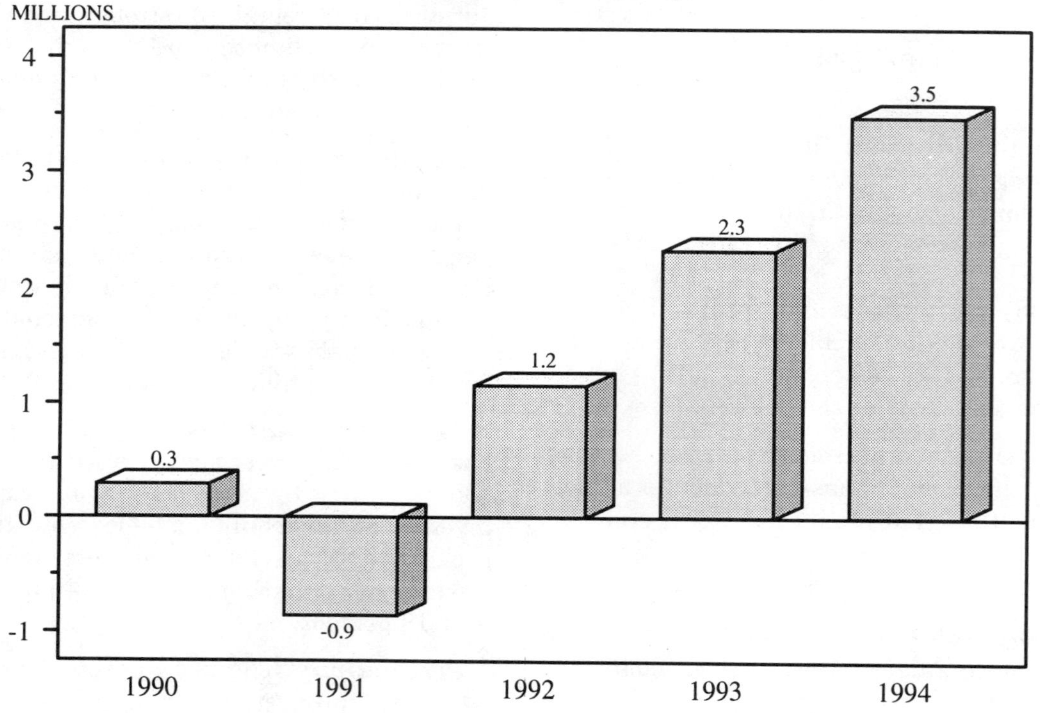

Chart 2-3. CIVILIAN UNEMPLOYMENT RATE

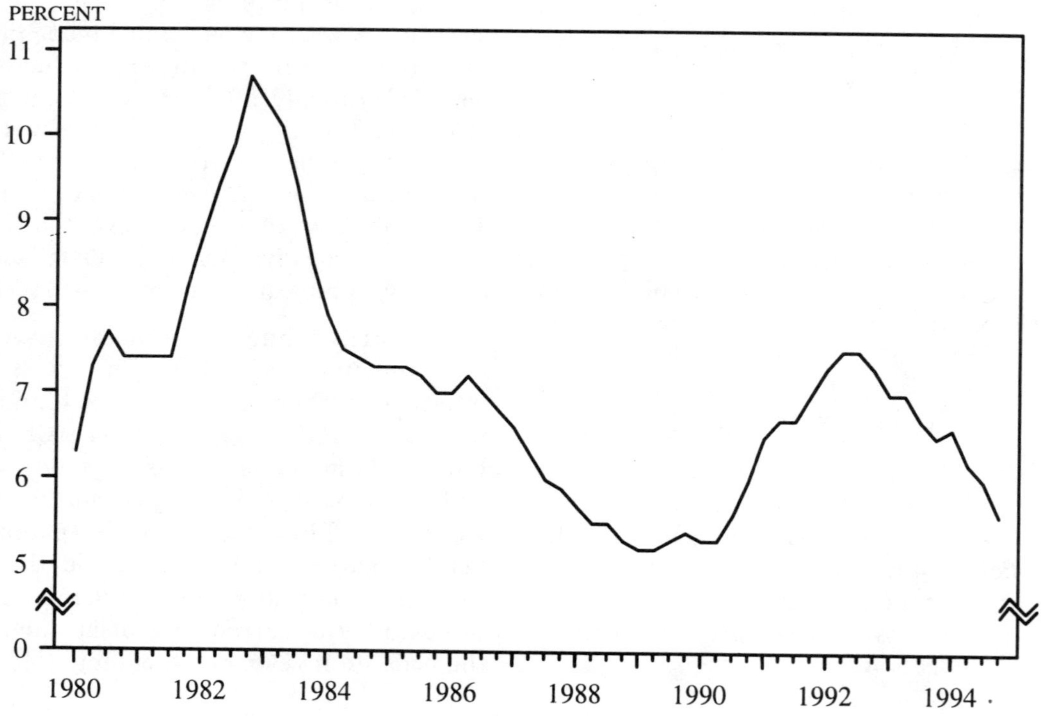

Interest Rates: Interest rates fell sharply in recognition of our serious commitment to deficit reduction. In the past year, interest rates have risen. The Federal Reserve has tightened monetary policy steadily since last winter; the unexpected strength of the expansion increased the demand for credit, and thus its price; and the financial markets reflected fears that the economy could face higher inflation if growth continued unabated. Rapid growth has brought the economy closer to the limits of productive capacity than expected a year ago; but signs of inflation did not emerge. If, as we now expect, the economy attains a steady, sustainable rate of growth in the next year and inflation remains low, the upward pressure on interest rates should ease.

Rapid growth, strong job creation, and low inflation made 1993 and 1994 one of the most successful and prosperous periods on record. Seldom has the U.S. enjoyed such an array of good economic news. Of course, not *all* of the news was good. Family income growth remained slow for the middle class, and the rise in income inequality showed no signs of ending. Even so, many of the nagging problems that had bedeviled the U.S. economy in the previous four years or more faded.

Jobs were plentiful, business was strong, productivity growth was robust, and inflation remained modest. We must maintain these conditions, which are necessary for middle-class prosperity and economic security. Our economic policies proved themselves by reversing the deficit surge and slow productivity growth of the 1980s. We must not return to the failed policies of the past.

What Lower Deficits Mean for You

While benefiting the economy as a whole, the President's deficit reduction plan also has helped average Americans.

Debt held by the public now totals $3-and-a-half trillion—an average of about $50,000 per family. Think of this debt as a $50,000 mortgage, on which the family must pay interest in the form of taxes—forever. Without the President's program, that national mortgage would have grown another $616 billion by 1998—or about $9,000 per American family. Thus, the Administration's efforts have reduced the size of the mortgage that each family owes. A $616 billion reduction in the debt will mean savings in Federal interest costs alone of $42 billion a year (by the year 2000)—or more than $600 per family.

Higher national saving is the ultimate benefit of lower deficits. Greater savings provide capital for investment and boost productivity. While the investment and productivity gains may be small in the short term, they compound and grow over time.

Deficit reduction may bring important intangible benefits that foster a better business climate. The longstanding failure to deal seriously with the deficit encouraged public cynicism about Government and damaged confidence in the economy's future. A budget that seemed out of control suggested that, as a people, we could not govern ourselves. Our renewed willingness to save for the future may, over time, considerably augment the economic benefits of lower deficits.

Finally, deficit reduction is essential to U.S. global leadership, in economic and political terms. A nation cannot provide moral direction and set standards of conduct for its creditors. Trading partners can easily dismiss the concerns of a nation whose trade imbalance is tied to its undisciplined need to borrow money. By contrast, U.S. officials in the last two years have attended international economic forums from a renewed position of strength.

Sustaining Our Commitment to Fiscal Discipline

We must maintain the commitment to fiscal discipline reflected in the President's plan and last year's budget. As a result, this budget directs resources to our Nation's major economic challenges—principally, the short- and long-term measures for the middle class—while providing still further deficit reduction.

Chart 2-4. CONSUMER SENTIMENT

(University of Michigan Index, 1966 = 100)

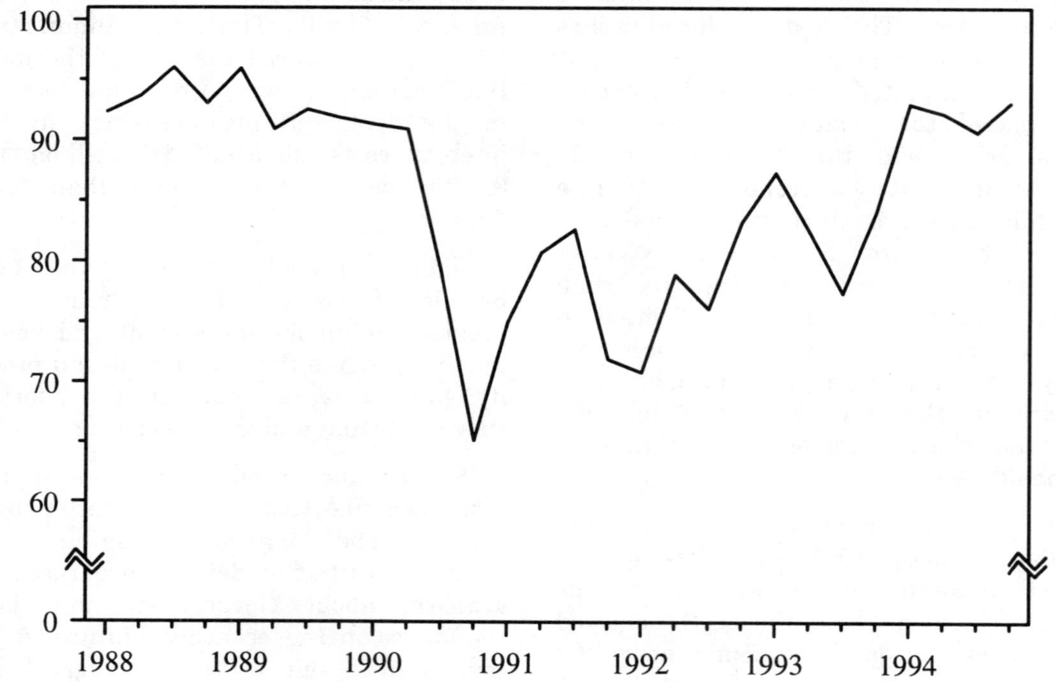

Chart 2-5. REAL BUSINESS FIXED INVESTMENT

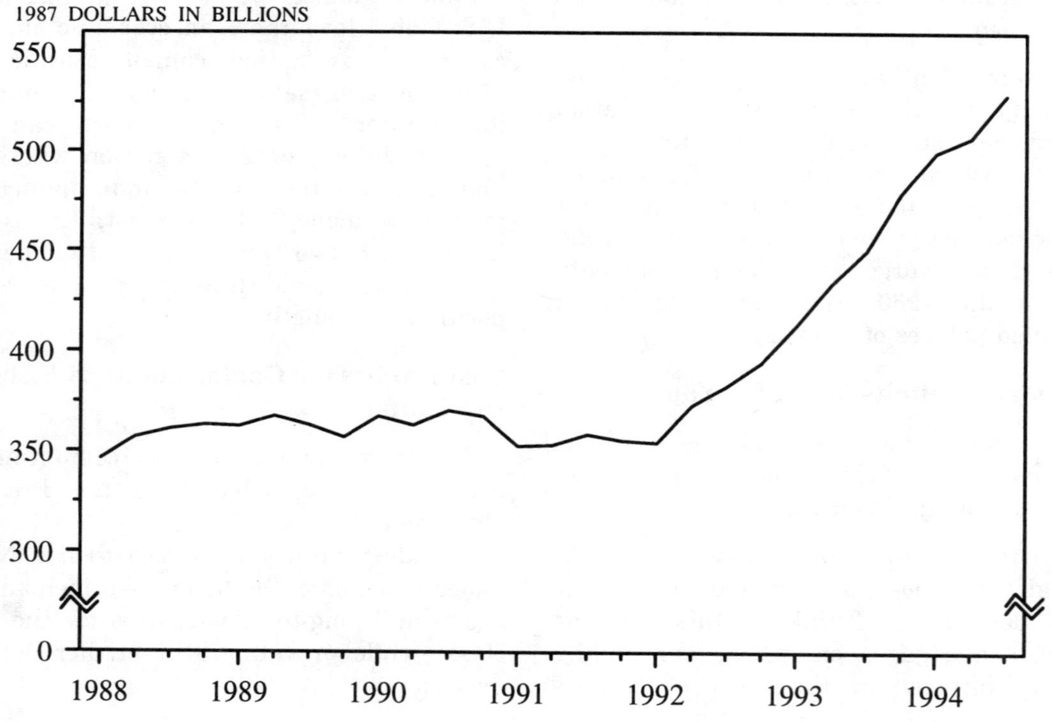

Financing the Tax Cut: The President's middle-class tax cut will reduce Federal receipts by $63.3 billion from 1996 to the year 2000. This budget more than offsets that revenue loss with savings of $26.2 billion from the second phase of reinventing Government, $80.5 billion from other discretionary programs, and $37.4 billion from mandatory programs, other initiatives, and debt service. All told, the budget proposes another $80.6 billion in deficit savings over the next five years (See Table 2–1.)

Savings from Government Restructuring: As outlined in "Making Government Work," this budget envisions savings of $22.8 billion over five years through restructuring five agencies—the Departments of Transportation (DOT), Energy (DOE), and Housing and Urban Development (HUD), the General Services Administration (GSA), and the Office of Personnel Management (OPM). We also expect another $3.4 billion of savings from eliminating some small agencies, streamlining others, and achieving other efficiencies.

From DOE, the budget proposes to save $14.1 billion by realigning programs and resources while privatizing or selling functions. From DOT, it proposes to save $6.4 billion by consolidating programs and transferring air traffic control services to a Government corporation. From HUD, it proposes to save $0.8 billion by consolidating programs and revamping public housing and the Federal Housing Administration. From GSA, it proposes to save $1.4 billion by focusing its mission and transferring some functions to other agencies.

The budget proposes to extend the current caps on discretionary spending for two years beyond their scheduled expiration in 1998, thus cutting this budget category in real—inflation-adjusted—terms. However, we also propose additional savings below the "freeze" level in 1996–2000. We will achieve many

Chart 2-6. INFLATION TRENDS

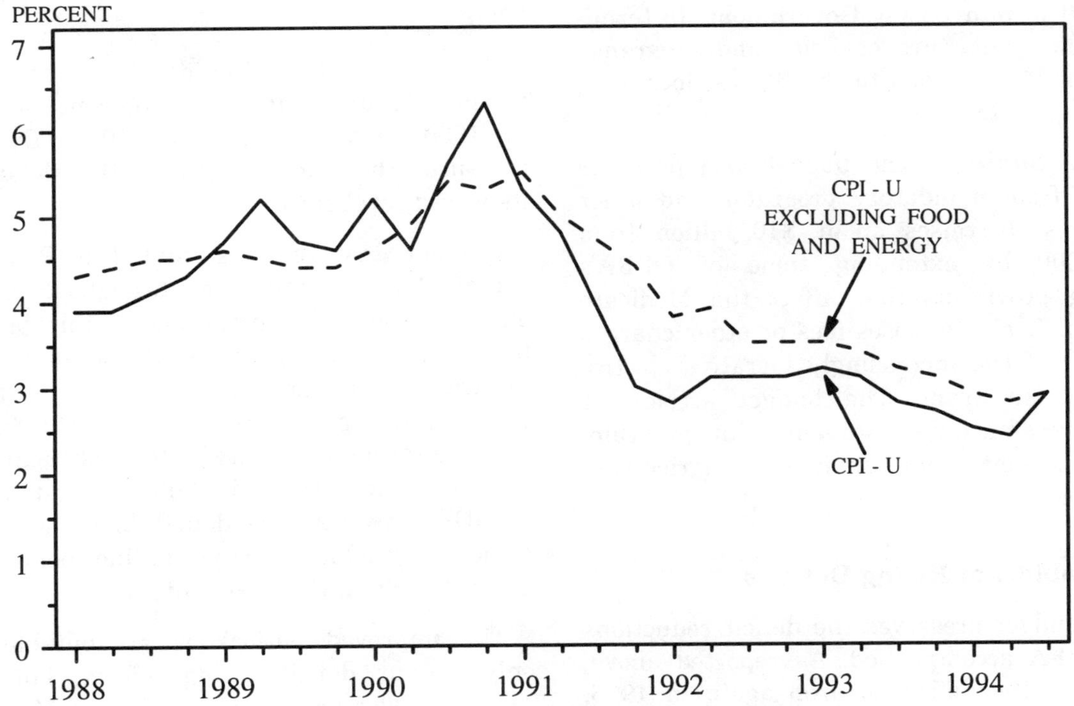

NOTE: CPI - U is the Consumer Price Index for All Urban Consumers. The inflation rate is measured as the change over four quarters.

Table 2–1. FUNDING THE MIDDLE-CLASS TAX CUT AND DEFICIT REDUCTION

(In billions of dollars)

	Estimate 1995	1996	1997	1998	1999	2000	Total 1995–2000
Baseline deficits	192.8	201.1	217.7	209.2	221.3	229.0	
Proposals:							
Middle-class tax cut and additional empowerment zones	0.1	3.9	11.9	12.5	15.2	19.8	63.3
Offsets:							
Reinventing Government, Phase II	0.0	–1.4	–7.3	–8.1	–4.7	–4.8	–26.2
Additional discretionary cap reductions	0.0	–5.1	–4.4	–11.8	–24.1	–35.0	–80.5
Other PAYGO savings	–0.1	–1.6	–4.7	–5.0	–8.9	–11.7	–32.1
Total, offsets	–0.1	–8.1	–16.4	–24.9	–37.8	–51.4	–138.7
Debt service and other non-PAYGO	–0.3	–0.3	–0.1	–0.4	–1.3	–2.9	–5.3
Total, change to baseline deficits	–0.3	–4.5	–4.6	–12.8	–23.9	–34.5	–80.6
Deficits after proposals	192.5	196.7	213.1	196.4	197.4	194.4	
Memorandum:							
Deficit after proposals as a percent of GDP	2.7	2.7	2.7	2.4	2.3	2.1	

of those savings by proposing, as part of Phase II of reinventing Government, to terminate and restructure agencies and programs, and to shift functions to the States, localities, and the private sector.

Other Savings: The budget also proposes savings from mandatory programs and other initiatives. It raises about $10 billion from 1996–2000 by extending some of OBRA's expiring provisions that affect the Medicare program. It also imposes fees or other charges on users of the increasingly lucrative electromagnetic spectrum. The budget accelerates the successful direct student loan program. And it achieves new savings in agriculture programs.

The Problem of Rising Deficits

This budget preserves the deficit reductions that OBRA accomplished. As reported above, we expect the deficit to drop again in 1995, this time to $193 billion. After that, it will fluctuate in a narrow range—rising to $197 billion in 1996 and to $213 billion in 1997, then falling to $194 billion in 2000.

Relative to GDP, the deficit continues to decline. It drops from 2.7 percent of GDP in 1996 to 2.1 percent in 2000. By this measure, the budget returns the deficit to its lowest level since 1979.

Current law requires that the President submit budget estimates through 2000. By enacting the policy proposals in this budget, however, we can preserve the improvement in the deficit for at least the next 10 years. Looking beyond the year 2000, we anticipate rough stability in the dollar amount of the deficit through 2005. As a share of GDP, however, the deficit likely will continue its gradual decline, falling below two percent early in the next century.

The improved outlook is attributable not only to our deficit-cutting efforts, but also to much lower projected spending on Medicare and Medicaid, the Federal Government's two main health programs.

The primary contribution to lower Medicare projections is slower growth in Medicare's Hospital Insurance expenditures. That, in turn, results primarily from slower forecasted hospital cost inflation and slower growth in the complexity of Medicare inpatient cases. Lower Medicaid costs, which continue a trend dating from the President's 1993 budget, are rooted in various factors—actual program experience; improved economic conditions; slower projected growth of the population that receives Supplemental Security Income benefits; slower projected provider cost inflation; and changes in law that have limited the States' use of provider taxes, donations, and disproportionate share payments that had increased the Federal contribution to States.

Though the projected Medicare and Medicaid growth rates are slower, they remain very high. We project that Medicare will grow at an average annual rate of 9.1 percent over the next five years, and that Medicaid will grow at 9.3 percent. These growth rates are nearly three times the projected general inflation rate of 3.2 percent per year (CPI-U), and will double Medicare and Medicaid spending every eight years. As a result, Medicare and Medicaid will rise from 3.4 percent of GDP in the year just ended, to a projected 4.2 percent by 2000 and 4.9 percent by 2005.

These programs' growth is among the main reasons why deficits stay as high as they do in these budget projections. The growth in all Federal health programs, of which Medicare and Medicaid are by far the largest, accounts for almost 40 percent of the total increase in Federal outlays between now and 2000, and is the single most important factor pushing up the deficit.

An increase in Medicare and Medicaid expenditures is unavoidable without universal health insurance coverage, through health reform. We expect the number of people participating in Medicare and Medicaid to increase, bringing insurance protection to some of our most vulnerable citizens. The Medicaid population will grow at a projected average annual rate of 3.8 percent between now and 2000.

But, this expansion in covered populations explains a relatively small part of the increasd Federal spending for Medicare and Medicaid—and could be accommodated without undue pressure on the deficit. More important, from a fiscal standpoint, is that Medicare and Medicaid expenditures per beneficiary keep rising faster than inflation—indeed, faster than inflation plus the general increase in real per capita GDP.

What would the deficit be if health care costs did not rise disproportionately? Chart 2–7 assumes that Medicare and Medicaid expenditures continue rising to accommodate increases in the beneficiary population, but that per capita expenditures rise with the general rate of inflation and the increase in per capita output, not at the higher current rate. Under these assumptions, the deficit would fall to zero.

Beyond the year 2000, the challenge of fiscal discipline will only increase. The aging of the population will continue, even accelerate, as the so-called "baby boom" generation—those born in the first two decades after World War II—begins to retire. This demographic phenomenon contributes to rising expenses for Social Security and for the Federal medical programs which the elderly use heavily. Medicare is largely devoted to those over age 65, and Medicaid is increasingly a program for elderly people needing nursing home care.

PUBLIC INVESTMENT

Throughout his Administration, the President has drawn a clear distinction between the "tax and spend" policies of the past and a new policy of "invest and grow"—between yesterday's Government and that of tomorrow. True investments will translate into stronger productivity and higher living standards for years to come. This budget continues the President's program: to reduce the deficit in order to increase *private* investment, and reallocate the Government's resources to increase true *public* investment.

The Federal Government is, by far, the Nation's single largest investor (Table 2–2). In 1995, it will spend an estimated $235 billion for physical investment, such as struc-

Chart 2-7. THE IMPACT OF MEDICARE AND MEDICAID ON THE FEDERAL BUDGET DEFICIT

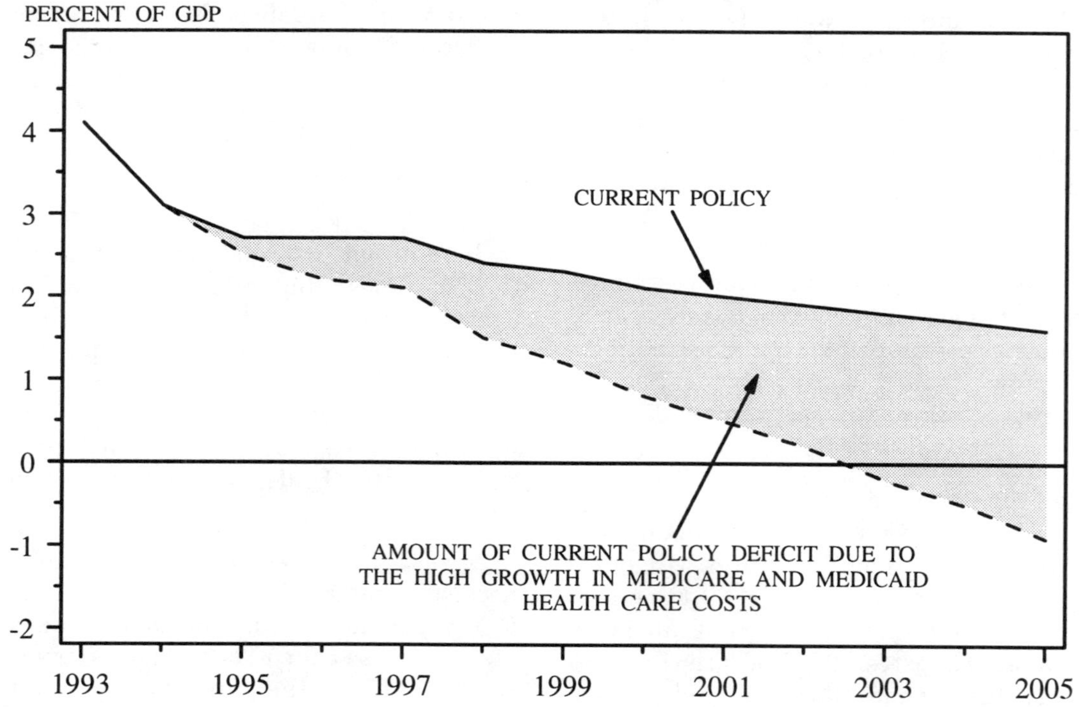

tures, roads, and equipment, and "intangible" investment, such as education and training and research and development (R&D)—about 10 percent of total investment in the U.S. economy.[1]

Government's role in investment is to provide the capital essential for a prosperous economy, cleaner environment, more efficient transportation network, and other worthy goals—but that the market would not provide, or not provide enough of. The private sector could not profitably run many roads and bridges needed to move traffic quickly and safely, and treatment plants needed to provide clean water. States and localities might not clean up emissions that would otherwise flow across jurisdictional boundaries. Publicly supported research yields discoveries that the private sector would not seek because financial returns are too uncertain or too far off. Public support for education and training helps people to invest more than they could on their own.

When businesses and individuals invest, they risk their own money. If the investment pays off, they enjoy a share of the benefits. When Government invests, however, taxpayers incur the costs and the benefits go to the society at large, not to the people making investment decisions. Public investments can have high payoffs but we must choose them wisely, because market forces do not automatically weed out bad choices.

Public investment comes in three major categories, all of which contribute to future productivity.

Federal Investment in Infrastructure: The budget proposes $58.8 billion for 1996 for investment in non-defense physical assets, up $8.6 billion from 1993. Grants to States

[1] For discussions of trends in Federal investment and associated capital stocks, see the *Analytical Perspectives* volume of the budget, Section 2, "Stewardship: Toward a Federal Balance Sheet" and Section 7, "Federal Investment Outlays and Capital Budgeting."

Table 2–2. MAJOR FEDERAL INVESTMENT OUTLAYS

(In billions of dollars)

	1993 Actual	1995 Estimate	1996 Proposed	Change: 1995 to 1996	Change: 1993 to 1996
National Defense [1]	116.6	98.1	91.4	–6.7	–25.2
Total Nondefense	120.1	136.6	137.8	+1.3	+17.8
Physical Investment	50.2	58.6	58.8	+0.2	+8.6
R&D	28.0	30.7	31.7	+1.0	+3.7
Education and Training	41.9	47.2	47.3	+0.1	+5.4
Total	236.7	234.7	229.3	–5.4	+7.5

[1] Including research and development and civilian education and training.

and local governments account for about two-thirds of the total.

While infrastructure spending can be among the most effective ways to boost productivity, we must choose projects carefully. That is why we propose to restructure the Transportation Department, consolidating its infrastructure activities into a single transportation block grant. Local governments will have more flexibility to direct resources to the transportation modes that best address community needs. For the same reason, the Environmental Protection Agency is consolidating 12 grants that total over $600 million, and providing greater State flexibility and simplified administrative procedures. States will direct resources to their most serious pollution problems—air, water, soil, etc.—subject to the fulfillment of national priorities as well. Our goal is more and better infrastructure, at less cost and with less red tape. (For more on these and other proposals to restructure Federal programs, see "Making Government Work.") The President in January 1993 issued Executive Order 12893—requiring increased use of economic analysis and promoting public-private partnerships—to help ensure that our infrastructure investments are as effective as possible.

Federal Investment in Human Capital: The budget proposes $47.3 billion in 1996 for investment in education and training, an increase of $5.4 billion, or 13 percent, over 1993.

Early on, the President enunciated a goal of fostering "lifelong learning" for a changing economy in which only the best-educated, best-trained workers will have the skills to compete effectively enough to boost their productivity and, in the end, their living standards. As Chart 2–8 shows, the earnings of workers with a college degree have risen compared with those with only a high school degree. Men who lack a high school degree have experienced declines in their real incomes since the late 1970s, and their female counterparts have barely had an increase.

To date, this Administration has emphasized improved education from pre-school through post-secondary levels. Working with Congress, the President has launched five major pieces of legislation: to expand and improve the Head Start program; to reward schools that set and pursue their own standards using broad waiver authority; to launch Charter Schools, Safe and Drug-free Schools, and other innovations; to meet the career-training needs of all youth with State, local, and private-sector involvement; and to cut the costs of higher-education loans for our students.

This year, the President will focus on better opportunities for those adults already in the workforce whose initial education has not provided all the skills they need to meet the challenges of today's economy. The President's proposal will consolidate and streamline a patchwork of programs that have built up over 60 years and do not meet today's needs. It will give "Skill grants"

Chart 2-8. ANNUAL AVERAGE EARNINGS OF WORKERS

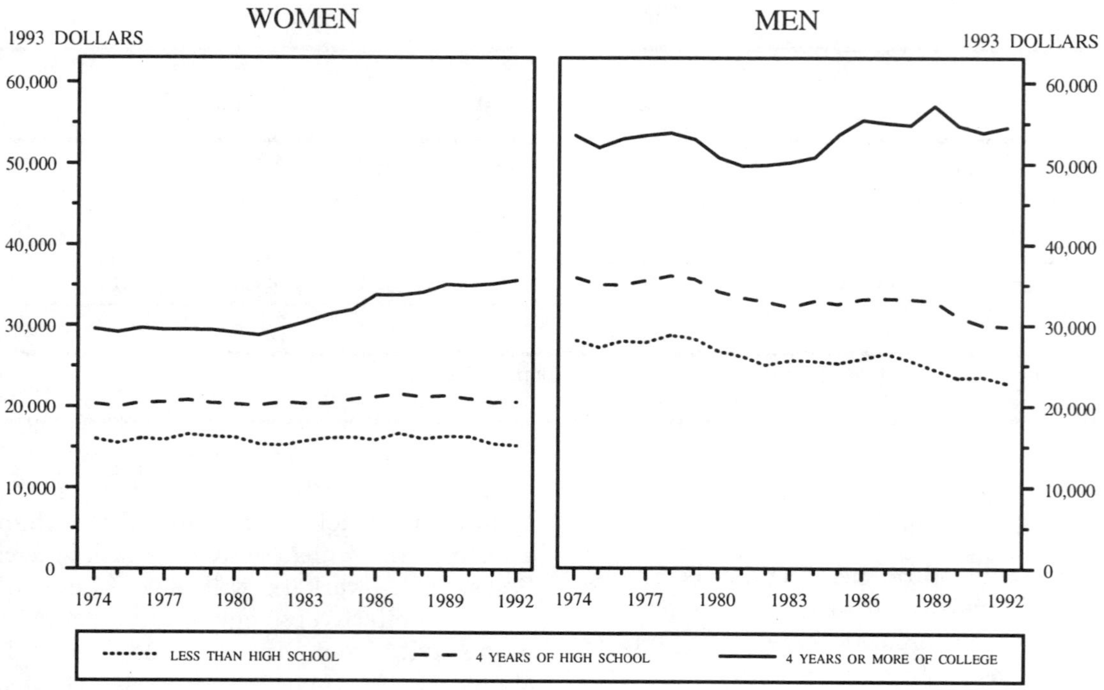

NOTE: Workers 25 years and older, working year round, full time.

SOURCE: Bureau of the Census, Current Population Survey

directly to individuals, like the GI Bill; it will support new, more flexible State systems to provide information about jobs and training; it will ensure access to those who need it, particularly dislocated workers and disadvantaged youth; and it will ensure accountability, with a strong private-sector role, monitoring of results, and quality standards for training providers.

Federal Investment in Science and Technology: The budget proposes $69.4 billion in 1996 for R&D. Nondefense R&D is expected to increase $3.74 billion over 1993. Federal spending accounts for nearly 40 percent of the Nation's R&D spending. Rates of return for R&D are high in the private sector, about 30 percent, and industry R&D may have accounted for about a quarter of overall productivity growth in recent decades. The contribution of federally financed R&D is much harder to estimate, because the Government devotes much of its R&D to products and processes that are not widely bought and sold in the marketplace. Still, the return is probably substantial, through spillovers of developments to the commercial sector (such as lasers and integrated circuits) and earlier basic scientific research whose eventual profitability is hard to discern at first (contributing to advances like fiber optics and disease-resistant hybrid corn).

Commercial firms cannot reap the rewards of basic research; other firms can easily use the knowledge it generates. Thus, despite the high rates of return it produces, the private sector will always do too little basic research to meet society's needs. So, for society at large, the Federal Government plays an important role in promoting and investing in R&D. Through the President's National Science and Technology Council, the Administration seeks to achieve the best possible science on a tight budget. The science and technology program pursues advances in health, business, the environment, information technology, national security, and science itself—with effective management that emphasizes peer review, integration of civilian and military research, cost-shared partnerships with industry, international cooperation, and reform of the payment system for federally sponsored research.

In sum, this budget provides for investment in the truest sense of the word—only in areas that the private sector could not or would not develop. The goal: to make Government an effective support for the private sector, as it creates jobs and prosperity.

EXPANDING TRADE TO CREATE BETTER JOBS

The Administration has worked hard, and with great success, to expand trade and investment, and enhance U.S. competitiveness. Since 1993, we have concluded negotiations on—and the Congress has ratified—two of the largest trade agreements ever completed. The Uruguay Round of the General Agreements on Tariffs and Trade (GATT) reduced trade barriers around the world; and the North American Free Trade Agreement (NAFTA) established a free trade area among the U.S., Mexico and Canada. On the bilateral level, we concluded a number of agreements, including several under the 1993 Framework for a New Economic Partnership with Japan.

We are aggressively examining other avenues to continue expanding opportunities for U.S. exporters. In 1993, the U.S. hosted the meeting of the Asia Pacific Economic Cooperation (APEC) forum. In 1994, APEC made an historic commitment at its Indonesian Summit to eliminate barriers to trade in goods, services, and investment by the year 2020. At the Summit of the Americas meeting last December, Latin American leaders called for a Free Trade Area of the Americas by 2005.

Through its Trade Promotion Coordinating Committee (TPCC), the Administration is working to restructure Federal trade promotion programs to help U.S. exporters take fullest advantage of expanding global markets.

The Importance of Trade

With the globalization of trade in recent decades, the prosperity of the U.S. economy increasingly depends on competing and winning in world markets. In 1993, exports accounted for 10.4 percent of final sales in our economy, compared with only 6.9 percent 20 years earlier. Over 10 million U.S. jobs in 1992 were directly tied to merchandise or service exports, while another five million provided goods or services to export firms. Moreover, export-related jobs pay, on average, 13–17 percent more than the average wages of all U.S. workers. By increasing trade, the U.S. can broaden its economic base, expand the number of high-paying jobs, and provide higher living standards for all Americans.

To expand exports, we must improve the competitiveness of U.S. producers in world markets. However, foreign trade barriers (such as export subsidies, import tariffs and quotas, and product quality standards designed to limit other nations' imports) can make even low-cost, high-quality export goods non-competitive. To give U.S. firms an equal opportunity to compete in foreign markets, the U.S. has played a leading role in negotiations around the world to reduce and eliminate trade barriers on global (GATT), regional (NAFTA), and bilateral (e.g., Japan Framework) bases.

The North American Free Trade Agreement

NAFTA, approved by Congress in late 1993, created a free trade area of over 360 million consumers and over $7 trillion annual output, linking the U.S. to our first and third largest trading partners (Canada and Mexico, respectively). Already, the agreement has stimulated growth and created job opportunities in all three countries.

NAFTA eliminates tariff and most non-tariff barriers for industrial and agricultural products, liberalizes trade in services, and protects U.S. intellectual property rights. Among its highlights:

- The agreement phases out most tariffs and non-tariff barriers in industrial products over 10 years, and most of those in agricultural products over 15 years.
- Investment rules ensure consistent treatment between foreign and domestic firms, eliminate most performance requirements,

and reduce barriers to U.S. investment in certain sectors in Mexico.

- The agreement liberalizes trade in services, including financial services, land transportation, and telecommunications.
- NAFTA's innovative side agreements also require standards of enforcement of national labor and environmental laws, and provide funds for border environmental activities and community adjustment in areas adversely affected by trade liberalization.

NAFTA's effect on the U.S. economy will be positive but relatively small, because Mexico's national income is only four percent of ours, and the U.S. already had a free trade agreement with Canada. Nevertheless, the accord helped to accelerate U.S.-Mexico trade in its first year:

- U.S. exports to Mexico surged by 21.7 percent in the first three quarters of 1994, compared to the same period in 1993—more than twice the growth rate of total U.S. exports. The growth was concentrated in capital goods, automobiles, and high-technology products.
- Imports from Mexico increased by 22.8 percent during this period, particularly in capital goods and automotive parts and vehicles.

This expansion of trade depends on overall economic conditions, so trade flows will fluctuate over time. Still, the evidence so far strongly suggests NAFTA will have beneficial long-run effects for both nations.

The Uruguay Round

The successful conclusion of the seven-year negotiations over the Uruguay Round, and the bipartisan congressional approval, marked a milestone in our efforts to strengthen the economy. GATT will expand U.S. business opportunities abroad and broaden the range of goods and services available to U.S. industry and consumers. For the first time in the 48-year history of GATT, the agreements dealt extensively with reducing non-tariff barriers to trade, incorporated several new product sectors such as agriculture and services under GATT rules, and moved a long way toward establishing a single set of trade rules applicable to all countries.

Tariff Cuts: This agreement will reduce tariffs on U.S. industrial exports by an average of 33 percent overall, and 40 percent in developed countries:

- GATT eliminated tariffs completely in several sectors, including construction equipment, agricultural equipment, medical equipment, steel, pharmaceuticals, and paper products.
- It cut tariffs of major trading partners 50–100 percent for electronic items such as computer parts, semiconductors, and semiconductor manufacturing equipment, and it set tariffs in developed or major developing countries to very low uniform levels (0, 5.5, and 6.5 percent) for the chemical sector.
- It will cap 99 percent of developed country tariffs on industrial products, and 73 percent of developing country tariffs on industrial products, at agreed-upon rates—preventing future increases without compensation.
- The Uruguay Round accords also made significant progress in eliminating quantity restraints (such as quotas) on trade—in some cases replacing quotas with tariff-based equivalents.

New Sectors: By including agriculture and the General Agreement on Trade in Services, the accord greatly broadened the reach of international trade rules.

- The Uruguay Round will cut agricultural tariffs and subsidies, and thereby make it easier for highly efficient U.S. farms and processors to penetrate foreign markets. The agreements cut outlays for export subsidies by 36 percent; reduce the quantity of subsidized exports by 21 percent; convert non-tariff agriculture barriers to their tariff equivalents that will be reduced an average of 36 percent; open previously closed markets (e.g., rice imports in Japan and Korea); and reduce trade-distorting internal subsidies by 20 percent (as the U.S. has already done). Economists estimate that U.S. agricultural exports will rise by

$5 billion to $14 billion in the next five years, and $22 billion to $50 billion over 10 years.

- For the first time, the Uruguay Round extends GATT principles such as most-favored nation and national treatment to service products, where the U.S. is extremely competitive. This opens foreign markets for U.S. exporters in such areas as accounting, advertising, computer services, construction, engineering, and tourism.
- The Uruguay Round agreement clears the way for U.S. creativity and innovation by protecting the intellectual property rights of U.S. entrepreneurs against production piracy in industries such as pharmaceuticals, entertainment, and software.

Widening Participation: By including developing countries as full participants in the new world trading system, the accords ended a serious "free-rider" problem. Developing countries participated in Uruguay Round liberalizations and are now subject to almost all GATT agreements.

Foreign Investment and the Environment: The accords reduced barriers to foreign investment, such as by eliminating requirements that a minimum percentage of production must occur in an importing country—requirements that often restricted foreign operations of U.S. firms. They also broke new ground by endorsing the concept of "sustainable development," granting environmental concerns new stature in international trade and development policy.

Dispute Settlement and the World Trade Organization: The accords also replaced a slow, weak dispute settlement process with a single, effective, enforceable set of rules for prompt settlement. They also provided fairer anti-dumping rules; enhanced tools to fight unfairly subsidized foreign products; equitable guidelines on import-surge safeguards; and stronger, more comprehensive rules on product standards. A new World Trade Organization (WTO) will implement these standards. Contrary to common assertions, the WTO is a major victory for the U.S., which suffered more than any other nation under the prior system. Because WTO decisions do not automatically preempt domestic law in this Nation or any other member nations, the WTO will not compromise U.S. sovereignty.

Multilateral reductions in trade barriers have always generated large, measurable increases in domestic and world growth. The Uruguay Round will be no exception. When fully implemented, these agreements are expected to raise world trade, and generate annual increases in U.S. output of $100 billion to $200 billion. In addition, the net gain in U.S. employment—over and above normal employment growth in the economy in this period—is expected to be just under 500,000 by the tenth year of the agreement.

The Framework for a New Economic Partnership with Japan

In addition to multilateral and regional efforts to expand trade, the U.S. continues to pursue trade liberalization bilaterally. A major focus has been Japan, our second largest trading partner and the nation with which the U.S. has its largest bilateral trade imbalance. Japan has relatively low formal trade barriers outside of agriculture, but also relatively low import penetration in many sectors. For many tradable goods and services, its domestic prices are significantly higher than world market levels. These facts suggest that Japan has significant informal barriers to trade.

In July 1993, President Clinton and then-Japanese Prime Minister Miyazawa announced a Framework for a New Economic Partnership at the Economic Summit in Tokyo. It covers several "baskets" of negotiations, including government procurement, regulatory reforms and competitiveness, major sectors (notably, automobiles and auto parts), economic harmonization, and the implementation of existing agreements.

Despite complications arising from major changes in Japan's government, the U.S. recently negotiated several bilateral trade agreements under the Framework. They include agreements to improve foreign market access in financial services, insurance, flat glass, government procurement of medical technologies and telecommunications equipment, and intellectual property. Other negotiations continue, including in the key areas of Japanese market deregulation and competition policy. The agreements seek to increase foreign access to Japan's markets for all countries, not just the U.S. The U.S. also is seeking progress on automobiles and automobile parts. In October 1994, we initiated a case against Japan under Section 301 of the 1974 Trade Act related to Japan's automobile parts aftermarket.

The Administration's Trade Agenda

Moving forward, the Administration will implement the recent GATT agreements, and seek multilateral agreements on trade barriers in two important sectors in which the U.S. is competitive but which the Uruguay Round negotiators did not address: the financial service and basic telecommunications industries.

Latin America: At the "Summit of the Americas" in December, the Administration launched a new initiative to create a free trade zone to encompass all of the Americas by 2005. When complete, this free trade zone would comprise over 850 million consumers with income of over $13 trillion. As a first step, the Administration will begin negotiations to admit Chile—one of South America's most stable economies—into NAFTA.

Asia: U.S. exports to Asian APEC members grew an average of about 10 percent per year in the past decade. Exports to Asia now account for 29 percent of U.S. exports, a share that's expected to grow. But the Uruguay Round did not eliminate all barriers to trade. Building on their 1993 meeting in Seattle that President Clinton hosted, APEC leaders committed this year to eliminate barriers to trade in goods, services, and investment in the region by 2020. In 1995, APEC ministers will develop a detailed plan for progressive trade liberalization. The Administration will work to see that APEC reforms stay on track. In addition, the Administration will continue to explore market-opening expansions in several key areas of the recent Framework agreements with Japan.

Implementing a "National Export Strategy"

Lower foreign barriers to trade have been a potent tool for expanding U.S. exports. The Administration, however, has taken more steps to help firms compete successfully in these expanding markets. In the 1994 Annual Report of the Trade Promotion Coordinating Committee (TPCC), the Administration established a new strategy to tailor Federal trade promotion support to the needs of exporters in each geographic and sectoral market. As a first step, the Administration is dedicating more resources to six fast-growing sectors where we expect the private demand for export assistance and opportunities for U.S. exporters to be strong.

The TPCC focuses on the 10 "big emerging markets,"[3] which are expected to account for over 40 percent of the growth in potential U.S. export markets over the next two decades. Other fast-growing sectors and markets highlighted in the TPCC annual report include the regions of Latin America and Asia; the traditional U.S. export markets of Canada, Japan, and Western Europe that represent over 50 percent of total U.S. export sales; the economies in transition (e.g., Russia); the service sector, where trade promotion support has been historically weak; and the growing area of trade finance. Through a newly developed unified trade promotion budget and the TPCC, the Administration will continue to give U.S. exporters cost-effective trade promotion support that is unavailable in the private market.

WHAT THE FEDERAL GOVERNMENT DOES

From the broad economic agenda, we now turn to the more detailed discussions of how the Administration proposes to spend the taxpayers' money and to make Government work better. Before we do, however, we should put these details in proper perspective.

As we have all learned too well, the Federal Government cannot solve all of the

[3] Mexico, Brazil, Argentina, China (including Taiwan and Hong Kong), India, Indonesia, South Korea, Poland, Turkey, and South Africa.

Nation's problems. Nor do we propose that it try. In many areas, solutions are more likely to emanate from States or more local units of government, such as counties, municipalities, and school districts. Some solutions, meanwhile, are better left to businesses, churches, community groups, and families.

The Federal Government has a limited, though important, role to play. Clearly, it must provide for the Nation's defense and conduct international affairs. It also must play a large leadership role on problems that cross State lines, such as environmental pollution and air traffic control. In other areas, its role is inherently more limited. It can, for instance, help set the general tone for education reform—but most spending for education comes from States and localities, and only teachers, parents, students, and concerned citizens can really improve their local schools. The Federal Government can help give communities the tools they need to fight crime, but much redevelopment must come from the ground up.

What we can do, and what we are proposing throughout this budget, is to better target Federal resources where they will do the most good, and to give State and local governments more flexibility to allocate Federal resources to address the specific problems before them. As detailed in "Making Government Work," the Administration proposes to capitalize on its earlier successes in reinventing the Federal Government, and it has begun to ask fundamental questions about which agencies and programs work well, which to restructure, and which to eliminate.

In reviewing our proposals, one should keep the whole budget in mind. The proposals discussed in these pages mostly relate to discretionary spending—the $549 billion that Congress votes on each year—which represents

Chart 2-9. 1996 PROPOSED SPENDING BY CATEGORY

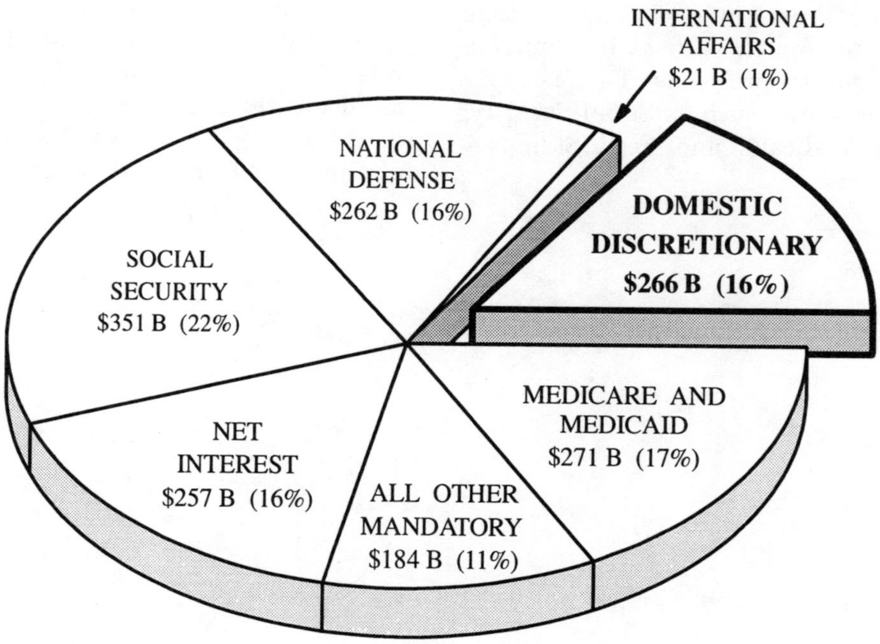

34 percent of the $1.6 trillion in total Federal spending. (See Chart 2–9.)

About half of discretionary spending goes for defense and about $21 billion (or just one percent of the total budget, despite perceptions to the contrary) goes for international affairs. Chapters 9 and 10 explain how the Administration's proposals for defense and international affairs help to project American leadership across the globe.

The other half of discretionary spending includes many of the Federal agencies and programs that people think of when they hear the term "Government"—the FBI, IRS, science and space programs, highway construction, environmental protection, community development, Head Start, and national parks. In many cases, the Administration is not proposing huge sums of money to attack problems. Rather, it seeks to use the Federal Government as a catalyst for State and local decision-making, or to leverage those funds for assistance from State and local governments or the private sector.

Of much greater size, 66 percent of all spending, is mandatory spending—the money that the Federal Government spends automatically unless the President and Congress take specific action to stop it, such as by changing the laws that govern programs. This category includes entitlements—such as Social Security, Medicare and Medicaid, and Food Stamps—through which individuals receive benefits because they meet some criteria of eligibility, such as age or income. It also includes interest on the national debt, the 16 percent of Federal spending that the Government pays to individuals and institutions that buy U.S. securities.

Although the budget proposes no changes in Social Security, which alone accounts for 22 percent of all Federal spending, it does recommend changes to generate savings from several other entitlements; for instance, it proposes a royalty fee for users of the electro-magnetic spectrum. To generate further savings, it recommends extending some expiring provisions that affect Medicare. Moreover, the President continues to support a complete overhaul of the welfare system, to increase opportunity and reduce long-term dependency.

Of greater long-term consequence for the budget as a whole, however, is the President's continued commitment to comprehensive health care reform, as outlined in Chapter 8. The two main Federal health programs, Medicare and Medicaid, continue to grow much faster than the overall rate of inflation. Together, these programs account for 17 percent of Federal spending and, at current growth rates, will double in size in eight years. By helping to control health care costs, reform would slow the rate of growth in Medicare and Medicaid and, in doing so, go a long way toward solving the long-term problem of Federal budget deficits.

CREATING OPPORTUNITY AND ENCOURAGING RESPONSIBILITY

CREATING OPPORTUNITY AND ENCOURAGING RESPONSIBILITY

The President proposes to create opportunity for Americans while encouraging responsibility. He foresees a future in which all Americans feel safer, more secure, and more hopeful about the future.

The President seeks to exert Federal leadership, in partnership with States, localities, and private groups, to reenergize American communities to retake the streets from predatory criminals, to secure the border in order to control illegal immigration, to free the environment of past degradation, to tap the exciting promise of science and technology, and finally, to take steps toward extending health care coverage to all Americans while controlling costs.

The budget would provide the resources to help attain these goals:

- To focus the enthusiasm and energy of Americans of all ages on national problems, the Administration proposes to expand its national service program. It also seeks to fund Empowerment Zones in order to help communities help themselves, to invest more in both urban and rural development through new consolidated performance-based funding for States and localities, to support additional community development banks and financial institutions to help revitalize distressed communities, and to build upon its efforts to work with American Indian and Alaska Native Tribes.
- To capitalize on last year's crime bill and attack crime at its source, the Administration proposes to allocate the resources to hire more police, build more prison space for violent offenders, finance innovative new programs to steer first-time offenders away from a life of crime, and attack drug abuse and drug-related crime by investing heavily in drug treatment programs.
- Building on its significant earlier investments to stop the flow of illegal immigrants, the Administration proposes additional funding to better patrol the border and to assist States with the costs associated with incarcerating criminal illegal aliens, educating the children of illegal aliens, and providing this population with emergency medical care under Medicaid.
- To ensure that environmental protection and economic growth go hand-in-hand, the Administration is pursuing a host of innovative approaches to preserve America's air, water, and natural treasures. It is working more closely with States, communities, industry, and private groups as it seeks to overcome the traditional hostilities that once made such collaboration impossible.
- Through its National Science and Technology Council, the Administration is working to better target its Federal dollars for research and development. By allocating such dollars more wisely, the Administration seeks to better educate the public, fuel job creation and economic growth, and ensure the Nation's continued world leadership in science, mathematics, and engineering.
- After advancing comprehensive health care reform last year further in the legislation process than ever before, the Administration seeks to work with the new Congress to pass legislation that will take the first steps to ensure that Americans no longer have to worry about whether they will have health insurance if they get sick or move from one job to the other, and that costs do not continue bankrupting individuals, businesses, and Federal, State, and local governments.

3. RESTORING THE AMERICAN COMMUNITY

Our fortunes and our posterity also depend upon our ability to answer some questions from within—from the values and voices that speak to our hearts as well as our heads; voices that tell us we have to do more to accept responsibility for ourselves and our families, for our communities, and, yes, for our fellow citizens.

President Clinton
State of the Union Address
January 24, 1995

Communities are the heart of American life. They play host to the schools, churches, synagogues, civic associations, and local events where neighbors come together to share common values and experiences. Communities embody Americans' sense of place, of belonging, of togetherness, and of security, in a time of rapid change.

But American communities, and the idea of community itself, face great pressures. The scourge of violent and drug-related crime threatens communities not only by tearing apart their social fabric, but by keeping residents at home, behind pad-locked doors.

Communities face a multitude of social problems, scarce resources, and a non-profit sector that cannot fulfill all of the requests before it. Though the Federal Government cannot solve the problems of communities, it can at least help provide the tools to generate local solutions. The proposals outlined below attempt to do just that.

Expanding National Service

The President's national service program reflects American values of performing community service, rebuilding communities, rewarding personal responsibility, expanding educational opportunity, and fostering a sense of the common good. Established a year ago, the Corporation for National and Community Service is engaging Americans of all ages and backgrounds to solve problems from inside America's communities.

The Corporation's signature initiative is AmeriCorps. Under it, Americans of all backgrounds engage in full- and part-time service in order to address urgent, local problems. In return for their service, they earn a minimum living allowance and, at the end of their term, an education award to help pay for post-secondary education or repay student loans. Twenty thousand Americans now participate in AmeriCorps. By the end of 1995, AmeriCorps will include 33,000 service positions, 65 percent more than in 1994. Some 200,000 persons have expressed interest in joining up.

The budget proposes about $1.1 billion for the Corporation, an increase of $290 million, or 37 percent, over 1995. The budget would expand programs begun in 1994 and continued in 1995, financing 47,000 positions in 1996 to reach the President's goal of 100,000 AmeriCorps members over a three-year period, 1994–96. The current growth rate reflects the capacity of community organizations to place AmeriCorps members in critical assignments.

The budget also would extend other Corporation programs, including service-learning initiatives for school-age youths, and the National Senior Service Corps for older Americans. In addition, the request would fund the Points of Light Foundation. With these funds, the Corporation will provide opportunities for more than a million Americans to engage in service.

AmeriCorps strengthens America's communities in several ways. National, State, and local organizations operate AmeriCorps programs, designing them individually to meet specific needs. AmeriCorps members do not displace existing volunteers or employees; they participate alongside the men and women already working to solve problems at the community level. They provide a regular source of service that most volunteers, with their time constraints, cannot offer.

The Corporation for National and Community Service operates few AmeriCorps programs itself; its primary work is ensuring quality in AmeriCorps programs that are locally developed and implemented. The Corporation works with States to run competitions that determine what programs will participate in AmeriCorps. Because States best know their own needs, they enjoy considerable autonomy in determining priorities, selecting programs, and offering additional assistance to programs. AmeriCorps is not a mandate for any State or organization, although 48 States and about 1,500 organizations sought AmeriCorps funds last year.

In addition, AmeriCorps seeks to encourage strong partnerships with the private and non-profit sectors. AmeriCorps grantees must raise matching funds from outside the Corporation, and many AmeriCorps programs are underwritten by businesses, including the American Express Company, Fannie Mae, General Electric, IBM, and Timberland.

Following intense competition last year, bipartisan, Gubernatorially-appointed State commissions and the Corporation chose some 450 organizations to participate in AmeriCorps, including Habitat for Humanity, the National Coalition for Homeless Veterans, the National Center for Family Literacy, the National Community AIDS Partnership, the National Multiple Sclerosis Society, the YMCA, and local United Ways across the country.

These organizations now run AmeriCorps programs as varied as the needs that America's communities face:

- In one rural Kentucky county, AmeriCorps members are intensively tutoring half of the second-graders, seeking to raise the average reading level from two grades behind to one grade ahead of standards.
- In Kansas City, AmeriCorps members, working in a coalition of nonprofit organizations with the police department, have helped close 11 crack houses.
- In recent floods in California and forest fires in the Pacific Northwest, AmeriCorps members provided disaster relief and frontline protection to devastated areas.

AmeriCorps members also teach classes, help with community policing, build homes, immunize infants, and assist victims of domestic violence. Some AmeriCorps members act as "volunteer generators" who engage many other citizens in direct service. The Corporation's motto—"getting things done"—expresses AmeriCorps' commitment to achieving direct and demonstrable results.

National service also provides a transforming experience for young people. Individuals who may join in order to earn an educational award leave with a renewed sense of their responsibility to serve throughout their lives. Through AmeriCorps, they also will learn skills that are valuable to their communities and themselves. Communities that plan and implement AmeriCorps programs discover their capacity to meet their own needs, and often draw new institutions and individuals into the common effort. As a result, the effects of a small AmeriCorps program can ripple through an entire community.

With a strong commitment to community-based direction, the Corporation maintains a small Washington staff. Administrative costs included in grants to AmeriCorps programs are statutorily limit to five percent of grant amounts.

Strengthening Community Development Financial Institutions

The budget proposes $144 million, a 15-percent increase in funding over 1995, for the newly-enacted Community Development Financial Institutions Fund. The Riegle Community Development and Regulatory Improvement Act of 1994 created the fund to help existing and new community development lenders expand credit and related financial services in underserved and distressed communities.

Under the program, community lenders can loan to residents and businesses in distressed communities for a wide range of purposes—from mortgage financing for first-time homebuyers, to rehabilitation loans on dilapidated apartments, to commercial loans to start or extend new businesses. Community lenders also will provide basic banking services—checking and savings accounts—to residents.

In exchange, the program makes these lenders eligible for up-front Federal aid. They will, however, have to match such aid, dollar-for-dollar, with capital from other sources. The lenders eligible for Federal aid include community development banks, community development credit unions, revolving loan funds, micro-loan funds, minority-owned banks, and community development corporations.

Advancing Empowerment Zones and Enterprise Communities

On December 23, the Administration designated nine Empowerment Zones (EZ) and 95 Enterprise Communities (EC). At the same time, it designated two supplemental urban EZs to qualify for the same tax incentives, under legislation submitted as part of this budget.

The Empowerment Zones and Enterprise Communities program, enacted as part of the President's 1993 economic plan, empowers communities across the Nation by challenging them to develop and submit a strategic vision for creating jobs and opportunity. Federal contributions include tax benefits, social service grants, and better program coordination.

The competitive application process has encouraged hundreds of communities to plan creatively by requiring them to show a strong relationships between the local government and private sector, and to show how their plans will combine Federal resources with other funds. EZ and EC winners were those that demonstrated the most strength on the following dimensions:

- *Economic Opportunity.*—A plan to create jobs, attract private investment, and expand residents' access to jobs through the region in order to help residents become self-sufficient.
- *Sustainable Community Development.*—A coordinated, comprehensive strategy that includes physical and human development (e.g., safe streets, clean air and water, life-long learning) and a commitment to personal, family, and civic responsibility.
- *Community-based Partnerships.*—A strategic plan for community revitalization based on broad participation of the entire community—residents, community groups, the private and non-profit sectors, educational and religious institutions, and State and local governments.
- *Strategic Vision for Change.*—A vision of what the community will become—e.g., a center for emerging technologies,—and a strategic roadmap that builds on the community's assets and coordinates a response to its needs.

The Administration designated Atlanta, Baltimore, Chicago, Detroit, New York City and Philadelphia/Camden as urban EZs, enabling each to receive $100 million in flexible social service block grant funds. It designated the Kentucky Highlands, Mississippi's Mid-Delta Region, and Texas's Rio Grande Valley as rural EZs, enabling each to receive $40 million.

Urban and rural EZs get tax breaks for businesses in the zones. The two supplemental EZs, Los Angeles and Cleveland, will receive funds from the Department of Housing and Urban Development's (HUD) Economic Development Initiative program. The 65 urban and 30 rural ECs also receive grant funds, and benefit from Federal regulatory waivers from Federal program requirements.

Encouraging Urban and Rural Development

In our restructuring of HUD, we are proposing a new Community Opportunity Funds program to help local and State governments address the most critical economic revitalization and renewal needs of distressed communities.

The new program, for which we propose $4.8 billion in 1996, reinforces and builds on previous Administration initatives—including our new Empowerment Zone and Enterprise Communities program and our welfare reform legislation—that help communities develop strategies to create jobs and promote family economic independence. (For more on this program, see "Making Government Work.")

The Administration's Rural Development Initiative (RDI) has boosted financial assistance to rural communities and businesses for a host of goals—provide affordable housing opportunities, safe drinking water, and adequate wastewater treatment facilities; increase rural employment; and further diversify the rural economy.

For 1994 and 1995, the Administration proposed, and Congress enacted, major increases for RDI programs. This budget seeks to extend that record; it proposes $5.8 billion in grants, loans, and loan guarantees, an increase of $716 million, or 14 percent, over the 1995 enacted level (and 46 percent more than in 1993). Some RDI activities also are key components of Federal assistance to the timber-dependent communities in the Pacific Northwest, of Empowerment Zones and Enterprise Communities, and of the Agriculture Department's (USDA) new "Water 2000" initiative to bring safe drinking water to every home in rural America by the year 2000.

The Administration also proposes to increase the flexibility by which the funding is allocated. It would let USDA State Directors allocate funding between programs, in cooperation with State and local governments and the State Rural Development Councils, whose members include Federal, State, local, and Tribal governments and private sector representatives. The increased flexibility will enable State Directors to target Federal assistance to each State's highest priority programs. It also will save administrative costs by eliminating redundant layers of government.

The nearly $1 billion affected by this new flexible funding will be available to fund grants, loans, and loan guarantees for all of USDA's rural development programs. Included are such programs as water and wastewater disposal grants and loans, community facility direct and guaranteed loans, business and industry direct and guaranteed loans, rural business enterprise grants, and multi-family housing loans for new construction and associated rental assistance.

Boosting Government-to-Government Relations With Native Americans

The budget underscores the Administration's commitment to American Indians and Alaska Natives. In his meeting with Tribal representative last April 29, the President pledged to respect Native Americans' rights to remain who they are and live the way they wish, acknowledged the unique government-to-government relationships between the Federal Government and the Tribes, and reaffirmed the commitment to Tribal self-determination.

That meeting, and the subsequent Listening Conference in Albuquerque, New Mexico have prompted an unprecedented Administration focus on Native American issues. In response to Tribal concerns, this budget represents an effort to place limited resources where they are most needed. Overall, the budget proposes an increase of funding for government-wide Native American programs of seven percent compared to the 1995 enacted level (and 17 percent over 1993).

Two million American Indians and Alaska Natives live in the U.S., half on or near reservations. The income, employment, educational attainment, and health conditions of that half remain below the general population. But, American Indians and Alaska Natives are making progress. In the last 25 years, mortality rates for many diseases afflicting them have fallen sharply, educational attainment has improved, and economic opportunities have increased.

The centerpiece of the Administration's policy toward Tribes is enhanced "self-determination"—allocating needed resources and devolving authority, responsibility, and accountability for Tribal leaders and organizations to provide basic governmental services to Tribal members living on or near reservations. Increased self-determination should improve program delivery, flexibility, and output, making constrained resources go farther and produce better results.

A key component of self-determination is the ongoing program involving "Self-Governance" Tribes. Currently, 29 Tribes have negotiated arrangements with the Interior Department's Bureau of Indian Affairs (BIA), authorizing Tribes to administer BIA funding locally with minimal red tape and second-guessing by Federal employees. The Administration expects Self-Governance Tribes to total 50 in 1996. It also proposes that funds for self-determination contracts—by which Tribes contract with BIA and other agencies to run Federal programs—total over half of BIA's operating budget in 1996.

As shown in Table 3–1, the budgets of BIA and the Department of Health and Human Services' Indian Health Service (IHS) comprise about two-thirds of government-wide funding for Native American programs. Their programs support increased funding for basic services, determined according to Tribal priorities. The budget proposes to allocate about $765 million, or 48 percent of BIA's operating budget, and about $600 million, or 30 percent of IHS' operating budget, in accordance with Tribal priorities. The remainder of the 1996 BIA and IHS budgets support increased funding for Tribal programs and construction in areas such as education, health care, and law enforcement. Overall, the BIA budget will increase by nine percent, and IHS by five percent, from 1995 to 1996.

Reflecting the Administration's commitment to government-to-government relations with Tribes, the Departments of Justice and HUD and the Environmental Protection Agency (EPA) established or are establishing offices to work directly with Tribes on issues of importance to Native Americans. Also, departments and agencies have begun working to better serve Tribal governments and members. Examples include nation-wide seminars, sponsored by the Justice and Interior Departments, to inform Tribes of resources available to them under the Violent Crime Control and Reduction Act of 1994; an inter-agency working group, chaired by EPA, to address rural sanitation issues in Alaska Native villages; an inter-agency Community Enterprise Board subgroup on Indian economic development; new performance-based HUD funds tailored to address the needs of Native American communities; and the White House Office of Intergovernmental Affairs' briefings for Tribal leaders on tax incentives for business investment on Indian reservations, authorized by the 1993 Omnibus Budget Reconciliation Act.

Table 3–1. GOVERNMENT-WIDE NATIVE AMERICAN PROGRAM FUNDING

(Budget authority, in millions of dollars)

	1993 Actual	1995 Estimate	1996 Proposed	Change: 1995 to 1996	Change: 1993 to 1996
BIA	1,647	1,747	1,910	+163	+263
IHS [1]	2,022	2,176	2,274	+98	+252
Subtotal, BIA/IHS	3,669	3,923	4,184	+261	+515
All Other	1,828	2,089	2,246	+157	+418
Total	**5,497**	**6,012**	**6,430**	**+418**	**+933**

[1] Includes Medicaid, Medicare, and private insurance collections.

4. Controlling Violent Crime and Drug Abuse

162-000 O - 95 - 3

4. CONTROLLING VIOLENT CRIME AND DRUG ABUSE

> *We are dedicated to restoring and expanding personal security for people who work hard and play by the rules. We have a comprehensive crime bill that says we need more police, fewer guns, tougher laws, and new alternatives for first offenders. We are asking for a new direction in the control of illegal drugs to make our streets safer.*
>
> President Clinton
> October 1993

The Administration recognizes that crime control is primarily a local responsibility, and that resources to fight it must go where they can do the most good—to support State and local efforts. We can turn the tide against crime and drugs only if the Federal Government works with State and local governments, community groups, parents—indeed, with all segments of society. Our crime fighting strategy contrasts sharply with prior Federal approaches that sought to fight crime largely by expanding the Federal law enforcement bureaucracy.

This budget builds on Administration efforts to make our streets safer by investing substantial sums in our communities for law enforcement and crime prevention, and committing the resources to ensure that dangerous criminals serve their full sentences. It provides funds to hire more State and local police, finances innovative programs to persuade first-time offenders not to view crime as an attractive choice, and continues our attack on hard-core drug abuse and drug-related crime. All told, the budget proposes $22 billion in discretionary and mandatory spending to fight crime in America, an increase of almost 50 percent in the last three years.

CONTROLLING CRIME

The Administration's proposed $21.5 billion in discretionary spending in 1996 to control crime represents an increase of $3.4 billion, or 19 percent, over 1995. (See Table 4–1.) As Chart 4–1 demonstrates, the largest share of this increase would go to assist State and local law enforcement.

Enacting New Crime Control Legislation: The landmark Violent Crime Control and Law Enforcement Act of 1994 sends a clear, strong message about the Nation's law enforcement strategy. It provides a balance between enforcement and prevention programs and tough new sanctions in Federal law, including the "three strikes and you're out" provision for violent criminals, a ban on certain semi-automatic assault weapons, and tougher sentences for gun-related crime.

The law provides:

- New prosecutorial tools to combat growing firearms violations, violent gang activity, predatory sex offenders, and fraud;
- Resources to put well-trained police officers on the street, where communities can and should expect to see results;
- Provisions to help States increase their prison capacities, including incentives to use military style "boot camps," alternatives to incarceration, and better drug treatment programs; and
- Grants to involve community organizations in developing and implementing effective crime prevention programs.

A new trust fund—the Violent Crime Reduction Trust Fund (VCRTF)—will support these new programs. Federal workforce reductions, as required by the Federal Workforce Restructuring Act of 1994, will provide the resources necessary to finance the VCRTF. The six-

Table 4–1. LAW ENFORCEMENT SPENDING BY AGENCY

(Discretionary budget authority, in billions of dollars)

	1993 Actual	1995 Estimate	1996 Proposed	Change: 1995 to 1996	Change: 1993 to 1996
Bureau of Prisons	1.9	2.6	3.0	+0.3	+1.1
Drug Enforcement Administration	0.7	0.8	0.8	+0.1	+0.1
Federal Bureau of Investigation	2.0	2.2	2.4	+0.2	+0.4
Immigration and Naturalization Service	1.0	1.4	1.8	+0.4	+0.8
General Legal Activities	0.4	0.4	0.4	....	....
U.S. Attorneys	0.8	0.9	0.9	....	+0.1
Community Oriented Policing Services	0.2	1.3	1.9	+0.6	+1.7
Office of Justice Programs	0.6	1.1	2.1	+1.0	+1.5
U.S. Customs Service	1.5	1.5	1.5	....	....
Bureau of Alcohol, Tobacco, and Firearms	0.4	0.4	0.4	....	....
U.S. Secret Service	0.5	0.5	0.5	+0.1	....
Judiciary	2.4	2.7	3.1	+0.4	+0.7
All other law enforcement	2.7	2.5	2.8	+0.3	+0.1
Total, Crime Control	**15.2**	**18.1**	**21.5**	**+3.4**	**+6.3**

Table 4–2. VIOLENT CRIME REDUCTION TRUST FUND (VCRTF)

(Discretionary budget authority, in billions of dollars)

	1995	1996	1997	1985	1995	2000	Total 1995–2000
Budget authority ceilings	2.4	4.3	5.0	5.5	6.5	6.5	30.2
Outlay ceilings	0.7	2.3	3.9	4.9	5.6	6.2	23.7
Crime reduction authorization	2.9	4.9	5.4	6.2	6.1	4.8	30.2

year growth pattern for the VCRTF is shown on Table 4–2.

Using Federal Resources To Support Local Law Enforcement: The budget proposes over $4.2 billion to help State and local law enforcement officials, local governments, and community groups fight crime in their own neighborhoods—an increase of $1.7 billion over 1995. (See Table 4–3.) It envisions partnerships among Federal, State, and local governments, and community law enforcement entities, by:

Putting 100,000 More Police On The Street: The budget proposes nearly $1.9 billion to help communities hire more police officers and support community policing. This proposal, a 45-percent increase over 1995, represents significant progress toward the President's commitment to put 100,000 more police on the streets. Already, the Federal Government has awarded over 1,200 grants, adding almost 10,000 more police. This budget request will bring the total to over 40,000 new officers funded by the end of 1996.

Incarcerating Violent Criminals: The budget proposes $500 million in new grants to help States and localities to expand prison space by building new prisons and jails and rehabilitating others, and to construct such alternative facilities as boot camps. At least half of the funds will go to States that have adopted "Truth in Sentencing Laws," ensuring that convicted violent of-

Chart 4-1. 1996 BUDGET REFLECTS THE ADMINISTRATION'S PLAN FOR FEDERAL, STATE, AND LOCAL PARTNERSHIPS TO FIGHT CRIME

(discretionary budget authority)

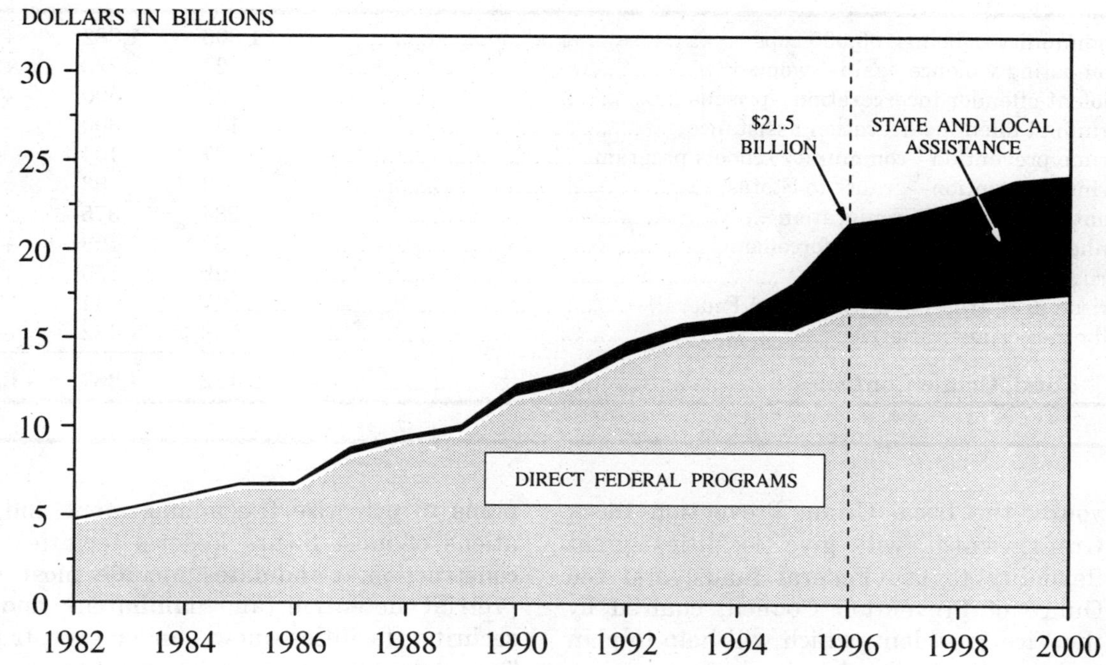

fenders serve at least 85 percent of their sentences behind bars.

Supporting Local Law Enforcement With Federal Resources: The budget proposes $193 million for Federal law enforcement agencies to support State and local law enforcement efforts against violent crime. The funds will help to support court-authorized wiretapping, and to fight firearms crimes and interstate gun trafficking.

Combatting Violence Against Women: The budget proposes $225 million in new State grants to combat gender-based crime. Over half, $130 million, will go for programs to better investigate, prosecute, and convict those who commit violent crimes against women. Another $42 million will go for programs to prevent rape and the sexual exploitation of runaway, homeless, and street youth.

Confronting Domestic Violence: The budget proposes $28 million for State, local, and Tribal governments that implement strong arrest-oriented programs to curb domestic violence. The budget also includes a number of new programs that address rural and community domestic violence through a National Domestic Violence Hotline, programs to aid victims of child sexual and physical abuse, and grants for battered women's shelters.

Funding Effective Crime and Violence Prevention Programs: The budget proposes $93 million for programs to target the causes of violence and crime. The grants address a broad array of conditions that breed crime, and target geographic and demographic populations most vulnerable to criminal activity as a way of life. They include the Model Intensive Prevention Grants, which will target up to 15 chronic, high-crime areas; the Family and Community Endeavor Schools (FACES) Program, which helps local education agencies and community groups set up programs for

Table 4–3. MAJOR VIOLENT CRIME CONTROL INITIATIVES

(Discretionary budget authority from VCRTF, in millions of dollars)

	1995 Estimate	1996 Proposed	Change: 1995 to 1996
Community policing/100,000 cops	1,300	1,882	+582
Combating violence against women	27	229	+202
Violent offender incarceration—prisons	25	500	+476
Criminal alien incarceration assistance	130	300	+170
Crime prevention—community schools programs	37	104	+67
Crime prevention—grants to States	2	93	+91
Controlling illegal immigration	284	375	+91
Enhancing Federal law enforcement	30	193	+163
Drug courts	29	150	+121
Prison drug treatment (State and Federal)	....	41	+41
All other crime initiatives	559	422	–137
Total, Crime Control	**2,422**	**4,287**	**+1,865**

youth; the Local Crime Prevention Block Grant, which will give localities great flexibility to use Federal funds; and the Ounce of Prevention Council, chaired by the Vice President, which will help to plan and coordinate the Administration's crime prevention strategies.

Improving Technology—Digital Telephony: On October 25, the President signed the Communications Assistance for Law Enforcement Act, ensuring the Government's ability to conduct court-authorized wiretaps as the nation converts from analog to digital communications technology. The budget proposes $100 million to reimburse telecommunications carriers for modifying equipment, facilities, and services to continue enabling the Government to conduct wiretaps. The needed funds would come from a 30-percent surcharge on civil monetary penalties and criminal fines (presuming that the needed authorizing legislation is enacted).

Privatizing Federal Prisons: The budget includes $73 million to activate six new Federal prison facilities and expand capacity at five others. The Federal Prison System also will expand its capacity and cut costs through privatization. While the Bureau of Prisons widely uses private facilities to house juvenile offenders and prisoners near the end of their sentences, the Administration plans to privatize the management and operations of most future Federal facilities under construction. Candidates include most future pretrial detention and minimum- and low-security facilities now under construction. The Administration will privatize three of five minimum- and low-security prisons and one detention facility scheduled to open in 1996.

COMBATTING DRUG ABUSE AND DRUG-RELATED CRIME

Drug abuse and drug-related crime costs the U.S. an estimated $67 billion a year and destroys the lives of our most precious resource—our youth. Illicit drug trafficking breeds crime and corruption across the globe, drug use helps to spread AIDS and other deadly diseases, and drug addiction erodes our Nation's productivity. Many of our communities are most acutely affected by drugs and drug-related crime. On many streets, drug dealers control their "turf," making law-abiding citizens prisoners in their own homes.

The Administration's National Drug Control Strategy seeks to eliminate drug use by focusing resources on two goals: (1) reduce demand by expanding effective treatment services and delivering an effective prevention message; and (2) reduce supply through law enforcement, border enforcement, and international cooperation.

The budget proposes $14.6 billion for drug abuse control—$1.3 billion, or 10 percent, more than in 1995. The budget builds on initiatives begun in 1995 by focusing on drug treatment and prevention programs, providing more drug-related crime fighting resources to State and local governments, and maintaining funding for drug interdiction and international efforts. (Table 4–4 shows selected categories of drug control funding.)

Improving Drug Treatment Delivery: The budget proposes $2.8 billion to treat drug abuse, $180 million more than in 1995. The 1996 request, along with administrative savings achieved by consolidating many small grant programs, will make progress toward the Administration's goal of making treatment available to all who want or would benefit from it.

Creating Performance Partnerships: To cut the cost of Government and empower States, localities, and community organizations, the Administration proposes to consolidate a myriad of grant programs. As described in Chapter 12, the budget proposes to consolidate over 100 categorical programs of the Public Health Service into 16 "Performance Partnerships." These partnerships include a $1.3 billion Substance Abuse Performance Partnership for treatment and prevention, providing $60 million more than comparable appropriations in 1995, to allow States to better provide such services. Concurrently, the Department of Health and Human Services' Substance Abuse and Mental Health Services Administration will administer a cluster of grants to train providers, conduct demonstrations, and disseminate the findings nationally.

Funding Treatment Programs That Work: The Administration seeks to address drug abuse where the battle is toughest—in the streets, jails, and urban and rural drug markets. A top priority is treating hard-core users, who consume two-thirds of the $50 billion illicit retail drug trade; commit the largest share of drug-related crime; impose a huge direct and indirect burden on our public health system; overwhelm our criminal justice system; and burden Federal and State prison systems. Economic burdens aside, the human cost of hard-core drug use is a national tragedy.

The Administration is employing a variety of innovative strategies:

- Prison drug treatment helps ensure that prisoners return drug-free to society. The budget proposes over $30 million in new prison treatment funding, adding to current Federal prison treatment programs and supplementing State and local programs.

Table 4–4. DRUG CONTROL SPENDING INCREASES BY $1.3 BILLION

(Discretionary budget authority, in billions of dollars)

	1993 Actual	1995 Estimate	1996 Proposed	Change: 1995 to 1996	Change: 1993 to 1996
Treatment	2.3	2.6	2.8	+0.2	+0.6
Prevention and education	1.6	1.8	2.0	+0.1	+0.4
Criminal justice	5.7	6.3	7.2	+0.9	+1.5
Interdiction	1.5	1.3	1.3	*	–0.2
International	0.5	0.3	0.4	+0.1	–0.1
Intelligence and research	0.6	0.9	0.9	+0.1	+0.3
Total, Drug Abuse Control	**12.2**	**13.3**	**14.6**	**+1.3**	**+2.4**
Supply reduction programs	8.0	8.3	9.3	+1.0	+1.3
Demand reduction programs	4.3	4.9	5.3	+0.4	+1.0

AAA* Less than $50 million.

- Boot camp prison programs offer rigorous discipline, physical conditioning, job training, counseling, and education, and many camps include job placement after a six-month program of drug treatment and follow-up testing. While a six-month boot camp program costs less than the typical five-year average jail sentence imposed on many young drug offenders, society benefits even more by the return of potential taxpayers. The Administration proposes to help finance the construction of new boot camp prisons through its $500 million request for State prison grants.
- Drug courts provide an effective alternative to simply locking up non-violent, first-time drug offenders by offering rehabilitative alternatives to incarceration. Participants must comply with a program of intensive drug treatment, drug testing, case monitoring and management, and follow-on care. Those who do not are processed through State or municipal justice systems and face incarceration. The budget proposes $150 million to expand and improve the drug courts program, a nearly five-fold increase over 1995.

Emphasizing Community-Based Prevention: The budget proposes $2 billion for drug prevention programs, $127 million more than in 1995. This increase comes largely from the many new, innovative, and community-oriented programs authorized by the 1994 crime act:

- Safe and Drug Free Schools and Communities (SDFSC) grants, together with the FACES Program cited above, will fund school-related programs to prevent drug use and drug-related violence in schools. SDFSC programs are augmented by such law-enforcement-supported programs as DARE (Drug Abuse Resistance Education), which seeks to build trust between police and school-age youngsters. Education programs, the heart of our drug prevention effort, combine teacher training and curriculum development with security services to address weapon and drug-related problems at schools.
- The Community Policing initiative includes an estimated $311 million for preventing drug abuse. Community efforts that put "cops-on-the-beat" can help cut the supply of and demand for illicit drugs, increase public awareness, and build cooperation between community groups and law enforcement officials.

Bolstering Drug Law Enforcement: The budget proposes $7.2 billion for domestic drug law enforcement, an increase of $854 million, or 14 percent, over 1995. It concentrates our efforts to maintain Federal law enforcement spending and expand resources for community-based enforcement. The Administration views the Federal role as one of providing leadership and training, fostering inter-Governmental cooperation, and giving incentives to States and localities to become partners with Federal law enforcement in fighting drug trafficking.

The budget, for instance, proposes $110 million for High Intensity Drug Trafficking Areas (HIDTA), $3 million more than in 1995. These funds would pay for a total of seven metropolitan HIDTAs in 1995. The seven receive direct support from Federal law enforcement agencies and grants for local law enforcement agencies to target large drug trafficking organizations operating in these areas of high crime or drug trafficking. The program also earmarks a portion of local grant funding to provide drug treatment services for addicted offenders.

Pursuing Interdiction and International Efforts: The drug trade directly threatens the U.S. and our efforts to promote democracy, economic stability, human rights, and the rule of law. After the National Security Council conducted a comprehensive review of the challenge of international cocaine, the President directed a three-pronged international drug control strategy to emphasize:

- assisting institutions of foreign nations that show the political will to combat trafficking;
- destroying trafficking organizations; and
- interdicting trafficking in both the source and transit countries.

The budget proposes $1.7 billion for international and interdiction programs—$74 million, or 5 percent, more than in 1995. National efforts to interdict drugs entering the U.S.

have begun a gradual shift in the focus of operations from the transit zone to the source country. By focusing on source country control and the availability of better intelligence to direct interdiction forces, the Federal Government can more efficiently suppress and interdict supplies of illicit drugs entering our Nation.

5. Reforming the Nation's Immigration System

5. REFORMING THE NATION'S IMMIGRATION SYSTEM

Our policy is guided by the principle that we will keep unauthorized aliens out of the United States, welcome legal immigrants, and protect refugees from harm. Our solutions rely on working in partnership with States and communities.

President Clinton
October 1994

In working to establish Federal control over the Nation's immigration system, the Administration has pursued two overarching goals. First, it has sought to fulfill the Federal Government's primary responsibility to manage the system and secure the border. Second, it has outlined a vision of shared responsibility with States, boosting funds to those that bear an undue burden from illegal immigration. This budget continues our pursuit of these goals.

The budget proposals are the most aggressive and comprehensive to date. The budget proposes $2.6 billion for the Immigration and Naturalization Service (INS), a 27-percent increase over 1995 (Chart 5–1), and funds for several immigration-related investments in the Departments of the Treasury, Labor, Health and Human Services, and Education (Table 5–1). The proposals will help close the door to illegal immigration while reducing the burdens States bear from the problem.

In particular, the budget proposes major increases for enforcement in three targeted areas—border control and management, interior enforcement, and removal of deportable aliens. A proposed Border Services User Fee, which would generate $200 million in 1996,

Table 5–1. ADDITIONAL SPENDING REQUESTED TO SECURE THE BORDER AND MANAGE IMMIGRATION, AND TO ASSIST STATES WITH THE COSTS OF ILLEGAL IMMIGRATION

(Budget authority, in millions of dollars)

	1993 Actual	1995 Estimate	1996 Proposed	Change: 1995 to 1996	Change: 1993 to 1996
1996 Improved Immigration Programs:					
DOJ/INS	1,493	2,031	2,588	+557	+1,095
Treasury/Customs	270	283	387	+104	+117
DOL/Wage and Hour	95	101	117	+16	+22
Subtotal	1,858	2,415	3,092	+677	+1,234
Assistance to States:					
Incarceration	0	130	300	+170	+300
Health	0	0	150	+150	+150
Education	29	50	100	+50	+71
Subtotal	29	180	550	+370	+521
Total	**1,887**	**2,595**	**3,642**	**+1,047**	**+1,755**

would help INS and Customs facilitate border crossings and improve border management.

To help States with the burdens of illegal immigration, the budget proposes $300 million to help cover costs associated with incarcerating criminal illegal aliens; $150 million to cover some of the emergency medical costs of undocumented immigrants under Medicaid; and $100 million to help school districts with high numbers of immigrant students.

MAINTAINING CONTROL OVER IMMIGRATION

This Administration has taken unprecedented steps and invested the most resources ever to deter illegal immigration. Its actions have produced results. INS saturated the borders of Juarez, Mexico and El Paso, Texas with agents during "Operation Hold the Line"—and the areas witnessed dramatic drops in illegal immigration. INS' more recent deployment of agents and technology in "Operation Gatekeeper" in San Diego is producing similar results.

Our 1996 immigration management and border security proposals build on these achievements. The investment package includes $656 million in new funding, shown in Table 5–2. Most increases are for INS, but the budget also proposes funds for the Treasury and Labor Departments to boost their immigration-related programs.

The top priorities are border control to balance law enforcement and legal crossings; workplace enforcement to reduce the "magnet" of employment; the removal of deportables to ensure that illegal immigrants do not permanently settle in our communities; and the improvement of data and verification systems to assist enforcement. The border fee will finance about 30 percent of these initiatives. Other funding will come from additional direct appropriations, from the new

Chart 5-1. IMMIGRATION AND NATURALIZATION SERVICE BUDGET HISTORY

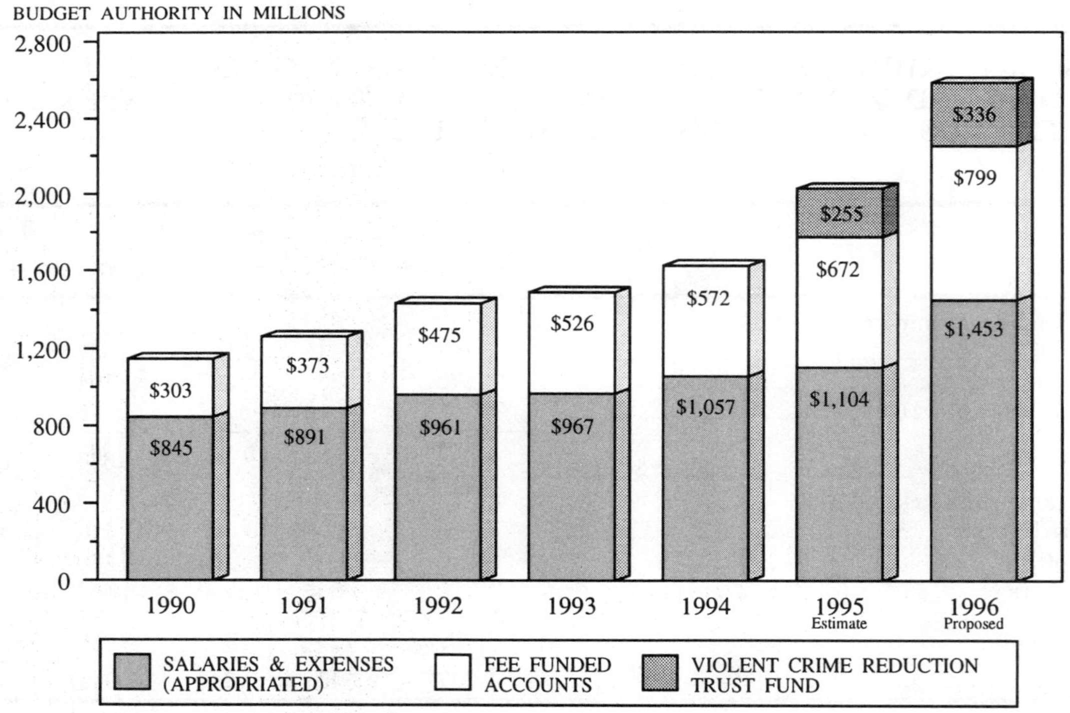

NOTE: Does not include resources for the Immigration Emergency Fund.

Violent Crime Reduction Trust Fund, and from existing INS fees.

Strengthening Border Control and Management

The budget proposes $369 million in new resources for INS and Customs to strengthen border control and management by improving both enforcement and services. For better enforcement, the Administration seeks to deter illegal immigration by raising the risk of apprehension and deportation. For better service, the Administration seeks to place more INS and Customs inspectors at land ports-of-entry, applying new technologies to increase processing efficiency and developing infrastructure to ease port traffic.

Border Services User Fee: A new fee of $3.00 per vehicle and $1.50 per pedestrian crossing the land border ports (with passes available for discounted and unlimited monthly crossing) will partially finance the border control and management initiative. It will help cover the cost of immigration and customs operations at the Nation's 169 land border ports. Experts expect traffic across the U.S.-Mexico and U.S.-Canada land borders to rise dramatically with implementation of the North American Free Trade Agreement (NAFTA). The Administration has already increased border personnel and facilities, but the increases have not kept pace with traffic. Without action, efforts to facilitate cross-border traffic and control illegal immigration will suffer. The Administration's plan provides targeted INS and Customs investments in personnel, technology, and infrastructure. It calls for reinvesting fee revenues to directly facilitate crossings and immigration enforcement.

Several examples demonstrate the promise of a successful fee-for-service proposal. INS and Customs' services at air and sea ports greatly improved after the agencies began collecting processing fees from passengers who use these services. INS reinvests its $6 per-passenger fee to upgrade technology and increase personnel; Customs does so with its $6.50 fee. Services at these ports parallel those provided at land border ports. Travellers at land border ports, however, do not help offset the costs. An INS pilot program, the Dedicated Commuter Lane—in Blaine and Point Roberts, both in Washington—has cut congestion in those areas. For an annual fee, this program allows pre-screened border crossers to pass through ports with an abbreviated inspection.

Several Members of Congress, the Congressional Border Caucus, and the U.S. Commission on Immigration Reform have supported such a border investment program, including fees-for-service, to improve border operations. To implement the fee proposal, the Administration will begin consultations with Congress and the affected States, and bilateral negotiations with Mexico and Canada.

INS Border Personnel Expansion and Systems Modernization: Of the proposed $369 million for border control and management, $140 million is for INS border personnel

Table 5–2. NEW SPENDING INITIATIVES IN THE PRESIDENT'S IMMIGRATION MANAGEMENT AND BORDER SECURITY PLAN

(Budget authority, in millions of dollars)

Strengthening border control and management	+369
Justice/INS	+269
Treasury/Customs	+100
Strengthening interior enforcement	+93
Justice/INS	+82
DOL/Wage and Hour	+11
Removing deportable aliens	+171
Other INS Initiatives	+23
Total	+656

and training. The increase will enable INS to hire over 1,500 new Border Patrol agents, land port inspectors, and support staff across the Nation in 1996. The individuals will serve on INS' mobile deterrence teams, and INS could deploy them quickly at strategic border locations at and between ports of entry to maximize the Administration's "prevention through deterrence" plan. They also could staff more border crossing lanes to reduce traffic delays. With this proposal, this Administration will have increased Border Patrol agents by 1,750, or 44 percent, in the last three years. The multi-year strategy also will add 790 new INS inspectors—a 68-percent increase since 1993.

The INS systems modernization effort, which accounts for $47 million of the $369 million initiative, is among the most critical aspects of the Administration's multi-layered strategy. This effort will:

- Link and analyze information on aliens who have been apprehended or detained;
- Install automated enforcement case tracking systems at five major airports; and
- Upgrade and expand the Interagency Border Inspection System, a joint Customs/INS "look out" system used at ports of entry to identify unauthorized aliens.

The remaining $178 million will go for additional lane construction at ports, Customs Service automation and inspectors, anti-smuggling tactical teams, and a pilot interior repatriation program. These added elements enable the Administration to implement a broad-based strategy to address fully our illegal immigration problems at the border and to assist with legal crossings.

Strengthening Interior Enforcement of Immigration Laws

Employment is a major incentive for illegal immigration. Any comprehensive effort to con-

Chart 5-2. IMMIGRATION AND NATURALIZATION SERVICE SOUTHWEST BORDER STAFFING LEVELS

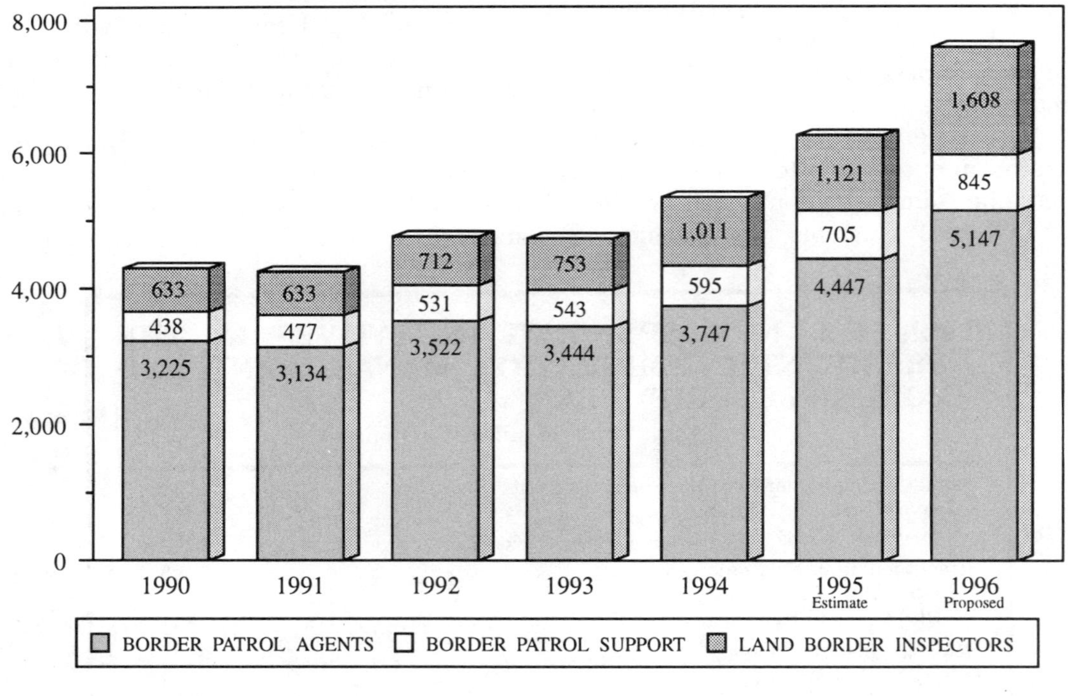

NOTE: The 1996 proposal assumes the area with the greatest need will continue to be the Southwest border. All staffing levels measured by end-of-year employment.

trol illegal immigration also must reduce the "magnet effect" of lucrative U.S. jobs by boosting the costs to both employers and employees if they violate immigration and employment laws. The Administration seeks to revitalize the employer sanctions provision of the 1986 Immigration Reform and Control Act as well as basic employment laws relating to wages and conditions.

The budget provides $65 million to significantly expand the Labor and Justice Departments' efforts to curtail job opportunities for illegal immigrants, and $28 million to test national systems to verify applicants' employment eligibility.

Workplace Immigration and Labor Law Enforcement: The Labor Department's Wage and Hour Division ensures that employers follow basic laws relating to wages and working conditions. It plays a critical role in immigration enforcement because, for the most part, employers who abide by labor standards will not likely subvert the employer sanctions law by hiring illegal immigrants.

This budget proposes to promote higher levels of workplace compliance with employment laws. Among other things, the strategy will dramatically increase the number of Wage and Hour investigations targeted to low-wage industries—such as agriculture and restaurants—in immigrant-affected areas. The targeting likely will increase enforcement activity in those areas by over 50 percent, help cut the economic incentive for illegal employment practices, and, in the end, reduce illegal immigration.

The budget also proposes more funds for the INS employer sanctions program in order to strengthen illegal immigration deterrence efforts in the workplace. Working with other agencies, INS will develop task forces and other special operations that impose sanctions for document fraud violations and criminal conspiracies. Pilot programs in targeted industries that historically have hired illegal aliens are underway in New York and Los Angeles; pilots in other cities will begin in 1996. The budget also proposes resources to link the employer sanctions database in all INS offices, ensuring the timely, accurate sharing of information on all sanctions and document fraud cases.

Verification System Expansion: As quickly as possible, the Administration wants to develop a nationally available employment verification system. The budget proposes $28 million for INS to continue overhauling its records database and infrastructure, in order to improve reliability and usefulness. These resources will support several verification pilots, including an expanded Telephone Verification system pilot project through which 1,000 employers in targeted industries can call INS to verify whether or not an employee is presenting a valid, INS-issued work document. Also, INS will initiate a pilot, working with the Social Security Administration, to determine how to use Social Security numbers to strengthen verification efforts. INS will continue to reduce the number of acceptable work authorization documents while making those documents more tamper proof and counterfeit-resistant.

Removing Deportable Aliens

The magnet of employment will remain strong if INS cannot enforce the immigration laws in our communities and at the border. Lacking adequate detention space, INS already faces a sizable problem in trying to reduce the population of resident illegal aliens. Many of them become a permanent part of the local communities and face little danger of deportation.

The budget, thus, proposes $171 million to implement the Administration's comprehensive National Detention and Removal program—the first serious effort by any Administration to address the problem of resident illegal aliens. The funds will enable INS to double the numbers of deportations, from an estimated 53,000 in 1995 to over 100,000 in 1996. INS will increase its detention capacity to reduce the number of illegal aliens who abscond, locate and remove those who do, and speed the removal process.

HELPING WITH THE COSTS OF ILLEGAL IMMIGRATION

While it continues working to secure the border, the Administration recognizes that the legacy of previous inadequate enforcement unduly burdens some States with the costs of providing health care and education to some undocumented immigrants and incarcerating others.

The Federal Government and the States must continue to share the responsibility for meeting these costs. The Administration believes that a strong partnership among the Federal and State governments, based on the notion of shared responsibility, can help address the problems. We have demonstrated our commitment to work with the States on solutions, and we pledge to continue helping to alleviate the burdens of States with the highest concentrations of illegal immigrants. This budget proposes $450 million in State reimbursements, an increase of $320 million over what Congress appropriated in 1995, and $100 million for Immigrant Education, an increase of $50 million over the 1995 level.

State Criminal Alien Assistance Program (SCAAP): Interviews conducted through the Institutional Hearing Program verified a rise in the number of deportable criminal aliens in State correctional facilities. While the interviews alone cannot measure the precise number of illegal aliens in State facilities, the Administration recognizes its responsibility to work with the States to alleviate their growing burdens. The 1986 immigration law authorized reimbursements to States for the costs of incarcerating illegal criminal aliens. In the first step ever taken to implement that provision, the President proposed a State Criminal Alien Assistance Program in the 1995 budget. SCAAP provides fiscal relief to States burdened by criminal illegal aliens in their correctional facilities. This budget proposes $300 million for SCAAP, the maximum allowed in the Crime Bill and $170 million more than the 1995 appropriation.

Medicaid Discretionary Grant: The Omnibus Budget Reconciliation Act of 1986 required States to pay for emergency medical services, including childbirth, to undocumented immigrants who otherwise meet Medicaid eligibility criteria. The Administration proposes to create a grant program that provides $150 million each year in discretionary funds to help States with a disproportionate burden of funding those emergency services.

Immigrant Education: States with large influxes of immigrants have sought Federal funds to reimburse them for the cost of educating illegal immigrants. Federal education programs do not directly reimburse States for those costs. But programs such as Elementary and Secondary Education Act Title I grants for the disadvantaged give States billions of dollars a year for the special needs of *all* students, including immigrants. This budget proposes $100 million for the Immigrant Education Program, double the 1995 level, to provide grants to school districts that enroll large numbers of recent immigrant students. The budget also seeks to give States more flexibility to distribute the funds to local education agencies with the greatest need, the most effective programs, or both.

Table 5–3. INITIATIVES IN THE PRESIDENT'S PROGRAM FOR ASSISTANCE TO STATES FOR ILLEGAL IMMIGRATION COSTS

(Budget authority, in millions of dollars)

State Criminal Alien Assistance Program	+170
Medicaid Discretionary Grants to States	+150
Immigrant Education Program	+50
Total	**+370**

6. Ensuring a Clean Environment

6. ENSURING A CLEAN ENVIRONMENT

> *Preserving the environment is at the core of everything we have to do in our own country: Building businesses, raising our children to know the difference between right and wrong, and restoring the fabric of our society.*
>
> President Clinton
> April 1994

In his April 1994 Earth Day speech, the President set forth his vision for protecting the environment, enunciating four principles to guide his Administration's efforts:

- A healthy economy and a healthy environment go hand in hand.
- We must reinvent the way we protect the environment, making Government a partner, not an overseer.
- Government should work with local citizens, not over them.
- We should restore U.S. leadership on the international environment.

This budget will ensure that the Federal Government can fulfill its roles of preserving and protecting the environment, including: maintaining and enhancing America's national parks, forests, wildlife refuges, other public lands, and marine sanctuaries; undertaking important basic research to fill gaps in our environmental knowledge; and ensuring compliance with national health and environmental standards.

The Administration is working to fundamentally change the way Government protects our environment and our health—with innovation, flexibility, and fairness. The budget targets increases to selective programs that will have the most impact, while recognizing that the Government also must do more with existing resources.

NEW WAYS OF DOING BUSINESS

To carry out the President's principles, the Administration has developed several new approaches for preserving and enhancing the environment.

Common Sense Reforms: The Environmental Protection Agency (EPA) developed the "Common Sense" Initiative to find ways to make environmental protection cleaner, cheaper, and smarter. It represents a fundamentally different vision of environmental policy.

In this initiative, EPA is bringing together Federal, State, and local government representatives, environmental leaders, union officials, and industry executives to examine the full range of environmental requirements affecting six pilot industries (automobile assembly, computer and electronics, iron and steel metal plating and finishing, petroleum refining, and printing). The six teams will seek opportunities to transform complicated, inconsistent regulations into comprehensive strategies for environmental protection.

Performance Partnerships: EPA is working with States to improve environmental results by providing more flexibility, in exchange for appropriate measures of performance and accountability. By consolidating State grants, EPA would let States and other recipients target resources to their most pressing needs without compromising national priorities and legislative requirements.

Today, the States administer many Federal environmental programs. EPA provides the States with grant funds of over $600 million. The funds, however, are divided into numerous media-specific categories (e.g., air, water), and States cannot transfer funds between programs. EPA proposes to offer States one or more performance partnership grants, rather than up to 12 media-specific grants. States could use the funds for multimedia or single media pollution prevention, control, and abatement—provided the States comply with environmental statutes and, as appropriate, national priorities that EPA establishes for single media programs. EPA also proposes to let States tailor grant funding to their organizational structures and consolidate administrative procedures to cut costs.

Ecosystem Management: Ecosystem Management is designed to restore and maintain the health, sustainability, and biological diversity of ecosystems while supporting sustainable economies and communities. The following are four examples of this approach.

Northwest Forest Plan (Oregon, Washington, and northern California): The President convened the Forest Conference in April 1993 in Portland, Oregon, to address the unresolved issues of protecting and using the forests of the Pacific Northwest. The resulting President's Forest Plan for a Sustainable Economy and a Sustainable Environment is a model for forest management, economic development, and agency coordination. Its implementation represents the Federal Government's first effort to develop and adopt a common management approach to the lands it administers throughout an entire ecological region, based on sound science and the law.

Federal courts have now lifted injunctions, allowing timber sales in owl habitat to move ahead for the first time in three years. The Plan will improve forest management and end the confusion and gridlock of past policies. The forest management approach focuses protection on key watersheds and valuable old growth ecosystems, while eventually allowing timber sales of 1.1 billion board feet per year in the Pacific Northwest.

In an unprecedented effort, Federal, State, and local officials, Tribes, and private landowners are working together to develop and monitor implementation. In 1994, this effort provided $340 million in grants, loans, and other resources to the region through the coordinated efforts of 12 Federal agencies. The Federal Government plans to spend $357 million in 1995 to continue the initiative, and the budget proposes $390 million in 1996. The Forest Plan is protecting Northwest forests and putting people back to work.

South Florida Ecosystem Restoration Initiative: The South Florida Ecosystem contains the Everglades and other nationally and internationally significant natural resources and supports a population of over five million people. The ability of the ecosystem to sustain its human and natural populations depends on its long-term viability and sustainability as a natural system. The budget proposes total funding of $99 million for the initiative in 1996, a 10 percent increase over 1995.

The Administration established the South Florida Ecosystem Task Force to lead and coordinate the efforts of Federal agencies to work closely with the State, local governments, industry, conservation groups, and Tribal governments on restoring the essential hydrologic function of the historical wetlands in and around the Everglades.

Restoration of Prince William Sound (Alaska): The past year has witnessed significant strides to restore the natural and economic resources of Prince William Sound, heavily damaged by the March 1989 Exxon Valdez oil spill. The final Exxon Valdez Oil Spill Restoration Plan, adopted in November, outlines the use of restitution and settlement payments that the Exxon Corporation will make into the next century, totalling $1.1 billion.

Early in 1995, the Trustee Council, comprising Federal and State officials, approved eight resolutions for the Federal and State governments to acquire 500,000 acres of land in the Prince William Sound and Kodiak archipelagos to help implement the Restoration Plan. In 1996, the Administration seeks to acquire environmentally sensitive habitat and implement a comprehensive research and monitoring program in the spill zone. The budget proposes $70 million in joint Federal-State mandatory spending for these activities from the civil settlement.

San Francisco Bay/Delta Estuary (California): For decades, the Federal Government, the State of California, farmers, businesses, and environmental groups have argued about water management of the delta and estuary of the San Joaquin and Sacramento Rivers. The region, known as the "Bay/Delta," provides water for many California farms and cities and serves as a nursery for the region's fish and wildlife resources.

On December 15, the Administration announced a three-year agreement with California on water quality standards. Participating Federal agencies, working with the State, developed standards for the Bay/Delta, and are completing operating procedures for the regional water projects to provide adequate water quality and quantity to meet the needs of farms, cities, and fish and wildlife resources.

Private Sector Partnerships

Climate Change Action Plan: The President's Climate Change Action Plan relies almost entirely on partnerships between Government and the private sector. The Plan includes more than 40 initiatives to fulfill the President's commitment to reduce greenhouse gas emissions to 1990 levels by the year 2000. The budget proposes $336 million, an increase of $104 million, or 45 percent, over 1995, for the Plan.

Instead of relying on command-and-control mandates, the Plan utilizes market incentives and fosters cooperative approaches with industry to reduce greenhouse gases without harming the economy.

In the past year, over 800 electric utilities (the Nation's largest emitting sector), representing 80 percent of the Nation's electricity-generating capacity and 35 percent of carbon dioxide emissions (CO2), have agreed to adopt voluntary measures to cut greenhouse gas emissions. In addition, over 1,600 organizations, largely from the private sector, have joined EPA's Green Lights program—a voluntary public-private partnership to prevent pollution through the widespread use of energy-efficient lighting.

For another example of a private sector partnership, see the discussion on the Partnership for a New Generation of Vehicles (PNGV), the "Clean Car" initiative, in Chapter 7, "Investing in Science and Technology."

Environmental Justice

Federal agencies have moved aggressively to carry out Executive Order 12898—issued on February 11, 1994, and designed to focus Federal attention on the environment and human health conditions in minority and low-income communities, promote non-discrimination in Federal programs that substantially affect human health and the environment, and improve access and public participation in human health and environmental matters.

A 17-member inter-agency working group chaired by EPA has worked since March 1994 to ensure implementation and address specific issues. Federal agencies continue to work to finalize the agency-wide environmental justice strategies that the Order required.

Anticipating and Avoiding Problems

National Biological Service (NBS): Responding to an Administration proposal, Congress appropriated funds to create the Interior Department's National Biological Survey in 1994. A Secretarial Order in early 1995 changed its name to the National Biological Service, to more accurately portray its mission. NBS, which merged the congressionally authorized biological science capabilities of seven Interior bureaus, includes 15 Science Centers and 60 Cooperative Research Units in universities across the country.

NBS will develop objective scientific information and make it accessible to all interested parties, enabling the society at large to enjoy economic growth while minimizing environmental conflicts.

Salmon

Salmon from the Columbia/Snake River Basin (in Washington, Oregon, Idaho, and Montana) are a significant part of the ecosystem, an important indicator of its viability, and vital to the long-term health of the region's economy. Because salmon runs are declining, the National Oceanic and Atmospheric Administration is preparing a Recovery Plan for Snake River salmon. The Plan will take a watershed approach and address all factors responsible for salmon decline,

Table 6–1. TARGETING RESOURCES TO HIGH-PRIORITY ENVIRONMENT AND NATURAL RESOURCES PROGRAMS

(Budget authority, dollar amounts in millions)

	1993 Actual	1995 Estimate [1]	1996 Proposed	Dollar Change: 1995 to 1996	Percent Change: 1995 to 1996
Priority Investments	7,523	9,597	10,614	+1,017	+11%
Total Spending by Program Category:					
EPA's Operating Program	2,766	2,959	3,362	+403	+14%
Stewardship	16,416	17,627	18,540	+913	+5%
Ecosystem Mgmt. & Reg. Partnerships	82	641	735	+94	+15%
Cleanup and Compliance [2]	13,177	14,325	14,642	+317	+2%
International Cooperation	1,806	2,729	2,905	+176	+6%
Total [3]	**31,693**	**35,062**	**36,203**	**+1,141**	**+3%**

[1] Includes proposed supplementals and rescissions.
[2] For comparability, Cleanup and Compliance figures for 1993 and 1995 have been adjusted to reflect the transfer of facilities from Department of Energy Defense Programs to Environmental Management.
[3] Total adjusted to eliminate double counts and mandatory spending.

including Columbia/Snake River dams, habitat losses, over-harvest, and hatchery operations.

The budget proposes ongoing salmon-related construction and operations appropriations of $244 million for 1996, compared to $196 million enacted for 1995.

ENVIRONMENTAL INVESTMENTS

The Administration proposes to increase funding for environmental and natural resources in five major categories, as shown on Table 6–1. This section describes selected investments and programs. (For high-priority environmental investments and major program funding levels, see Table 6–2.)

EPA's Operating Program

The Administration proposes an increase of 14 percent, to $3.4 billion, for EPA's operating program, which includes most of EPA's research, regulatory, partnership grant (States, localities, and Tribes), and enforcement programs.

The proposal includes $510 million, a 12-percent increase, to carry out the 1990 Clean Air Act Amendments. Cleaner air is one of EPA's major environmental success stories, with ambient concentrations of all major air pollutants falling significantly since 1975 (See Chart 6–1). Nevertheless, as of 1993, 59 million Americans still lived in areas that had not attained health-based clean air standards. To implement the Clean Air Act Amendments, EPA is working closely with States and the private sector to bring remaining areas in compliance through such new approaches as the Common Sense Initiative and environmental performance partnership grants.

Water Quality

EPA provides capitalization grants to Clean Water State Revolving Funds (SRFs), which make low-interest loans to municipalities to improve compliance with the Clean Water Act. The budget proposes $1.6 billion for this program, a $365 million increase over 1995.

The Clean Water SRFs have helped to significantly reduce discharges of pollutants to the Nation's waters, despite rising demands on wastewater treatment facilities (See Chart 6–2). Yet, EPA estimates that municipal wastewater treatment needs are $127 billion, which includes constructing secondary and advanced wastewater treatment facilities and collecting and treating combined sewer overflows.

Table 6–2. PRIORITY INVESTMENTS AND OTHER MAJOR ENVIRONMENT AND NATURAL RESOURCE PROGRAMS

(Discretionary budget authority unless otherwise noted; dollar amounts in millions)

	1993 Actual	1995 Estimate[1]	1996 Proposed	Dollar Change: 1995 to 1996	Percent Change: 1995 to 1996
PRIORITY INVESTMENTS					
Stewardship:					
Clean Water State Revolving Funds (SRFs) (EPA)	1,928	1,235	1,600	+365	+30%
Drinking Water SRFs (EPA)	....	700	500	–200	–29%
Water/Wastewater Grants/Loans (USDA)	508	627	782	+155	+25%
Watershed Restoration (EPA)	50	100	100	....	*%
CA Wastewater Recl. & Reuse Pilot Program (DOI)	....	18	23	+5	+28%
Needy Cities (EPA)	100	100	100	....	*%
Enhanced Federal Natural Resource Protection and Environmental Infrastructure:					
National Parks (DOI)	984	1,078	1,158	+80	+7%
National Forests (USDA)	625	632	649	+17	+3%
Fish and Wildlife (DOI)	506	514	535	+21	+4%
Public Lands (DOI)	293	282	319	+37	+13%
National Biological Service (DOI)	....	167	173	+6	+4%
Subtotal (Enhanced Protection/Infrastructure)	2,408	2,673	2,834	+161	+6%
Recover Fisheries and Protected Species (NOAA)	232	269	304	+35	+13%
Wetlands Plan (Corps/DOI/EPA/Others) (excludes USDA/WRP)	500	620	691	+71	+11%
Ecosystem management and biodiversity partnerships:					
Pacific Northwest Forest Plan (USDA/DOI/DOL/EPA/DOC)	....	357	390	+33	+9%
Everglades/South Florida Rest. (DOI/Corps/EPA/USDA/NOAA)	71	90	99	+9	+10%
Subtotal (Ecosystem/Regional Partnerships)	71	447	489	+42	+9%
Climate change and environmental technology:					
Environmental Technology (EPA)	67	139	192	+53	+38%
Clean Car/PNGV (DOE/DOD/DOC/NSF/Others)	NA	269	371	+102	+38%
U.S. Climate Change Action Prog. (DOE/EPA/USDA/Corps)	8	232	336	+104	+45%
U.S. Global Change Research Program (NASA, DOE, NSF, DOC, Others)	1,531	2,305	2,407	+102	+4%
International cooperation:					
NAFTA Env. Support (EPA/USDA/Treasury/State/DOI)	209	280	291	+11	+4%
Global Environmental Education (NOAA/NASA/NSF/EPA)	....	15	15	....	*%
Total, Priority Investments[2]	**7,523**	**9,597**	**10,614**	**+1,017**	**+11%**
OTHER MAJOR PROGRAMS					
EPA's Operating Program	2,766	2,959	3,362	+403	+14%
Stewardship:					
Wetlands Reserve Program (mandatory) (USDA)	....	93	231	+138	+148%
Conservation Reserve Program (mandatory) (USDA)	1,547	1,743	1,926	+183	+10%
Energy Conservation and Efficiency (DOE)	576	792	924	+132	+17%
Solar and Renewable Energy Research and Development (DOE)	257	389	423	+34	+9%
Land and Water Conservation Fund/LWCF (DOI, USDA)	286	235	235	....	+*%
Cleanup and compliance:					
Federal Facility/Site Cleanup:					
DOE (Environmental Management Program)	6,396	6,859	6,592	–267	–4%
DOD Cleanup	1,604	2,298	2,087	–211	–9%
Others (USDA/DOI/DOT/NASA/DOC)	124	143	178	+35	+24%
Subtotal	8,124	9,300	8,857	–443	–5%
Superfund (EPA)(Non-Federal Facility/Site Cleanup)	1,589	1,431	1,563	+132	+9%
Superfund Orphan Shares (mandatory) (EPA)	....	....	200	+200	*%
Environmental Compliance/Pollution Prevention (DOD)	2,094	2,451	2,611	+160	+7%
International:					
Montreal Protocol (EPA/STATE)	25	38	51	+13	+34%
Multilateral and Bilateral International Assistance (Funds Appropriated to the President/AID)	272	320	351	+31	+10%
Global Environmental Facility (Treasury)	....	90	110	+20	+22%
Total, Other Major Programs[2]	**15,979**	**17,988**	**18,463**	**+475**	**+3%**

* Less than $500 thousand or 0.05 percent.

[1] Includes proposed supplementals and rescissions.

[2] Totals adjusted to eliminate double counts and mandatory spending.

Chart 6-1. REDUCTIONS OF U.S. NATIONAL AMBIENT CONCENTRATIONS OF CRITERIA AIR POLLUTANTS

(percent change, 1975-1993)

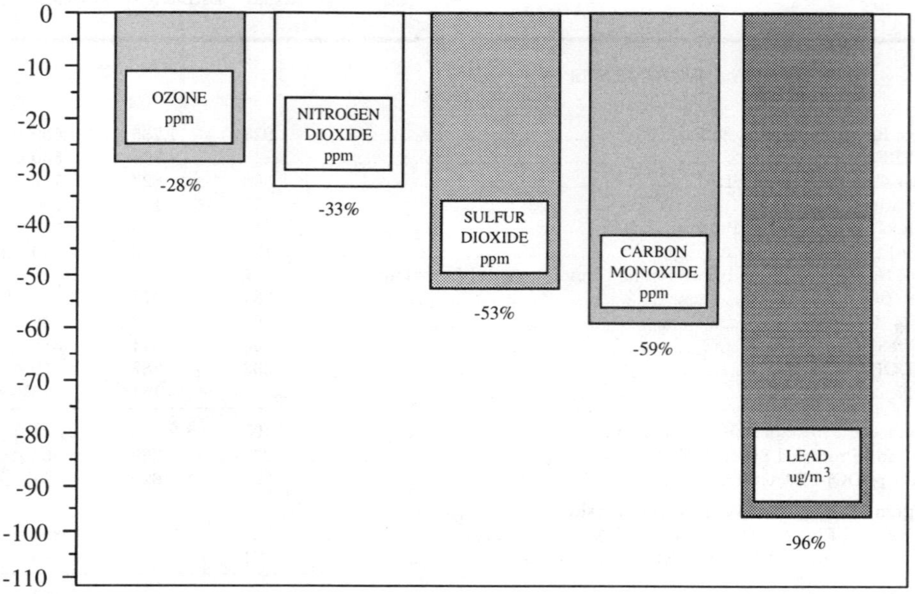

NOTE: ppm is parts per million and ug/m3 is micrograms per cubic meter.

Chart 6-2. U.S. POPULATION SERVED BY SECONDARY TREATMENT OR BETTER

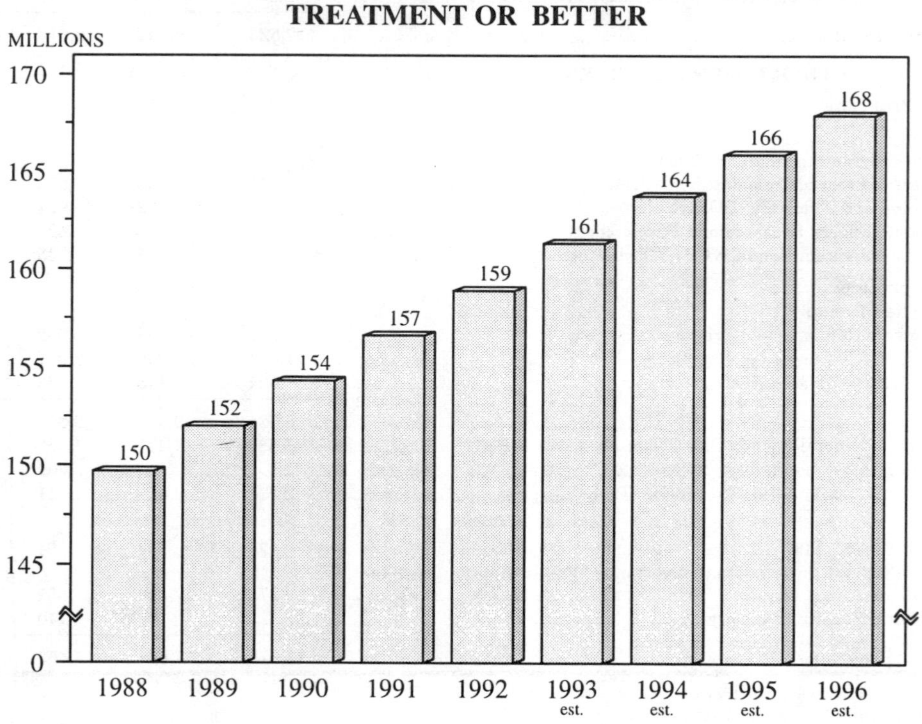

The Administration will apply the revolving loan fund approach to drinking water as well, to meet the treatment requirements of the Safe Drinking Water Act. In 1994 and 1995, Congress provided $1.3 billion for Drinking Water SRFs. For 1996, the Administration proposes another $500 million in budget authority, to become available after Congress authorizes the Drinking Water SRF program.

Also, the Agriculture Department (USDA) is launching a concerted effort to bring safe drinking water to all rural homes through its "Water 2000" project, funded as part of a proposed $782 million in 1996 for water grants and loans.

Superfund

EPA's Superfund program continues to make significant progress to address problems at hazardous waste sites. Through 1994, cleanup activities were underway at 95 percent of the 1,300 sites on the National Priorities List (NPL), with cleanup construction completed at 278 sites. Over the past three years, the program has, on average, cleaned up more sites each year than in its entire first decade (See Chart 6–3).

However, new sites are added to the NPL every year, and EPA estimates that the Federal Government will eventually identify some 3,000 as priorities for cleanup. At the same time, the program attracts criticism for costing too much and accomplishing too little. The Administration proposes to speed cleanups and cut cleanup costs, address the perceived unfairness of the liability scheme, enhance community participation in cleanup decisions, and remove obstacles to economic redevelopment of contaminated sites. The budget includes $1.76 billion for Superfund in 1996, a $332 million increase over 1995.

Chart 6-3. MAJOR PROGRESS IN SUPERFUND CLEANUPS

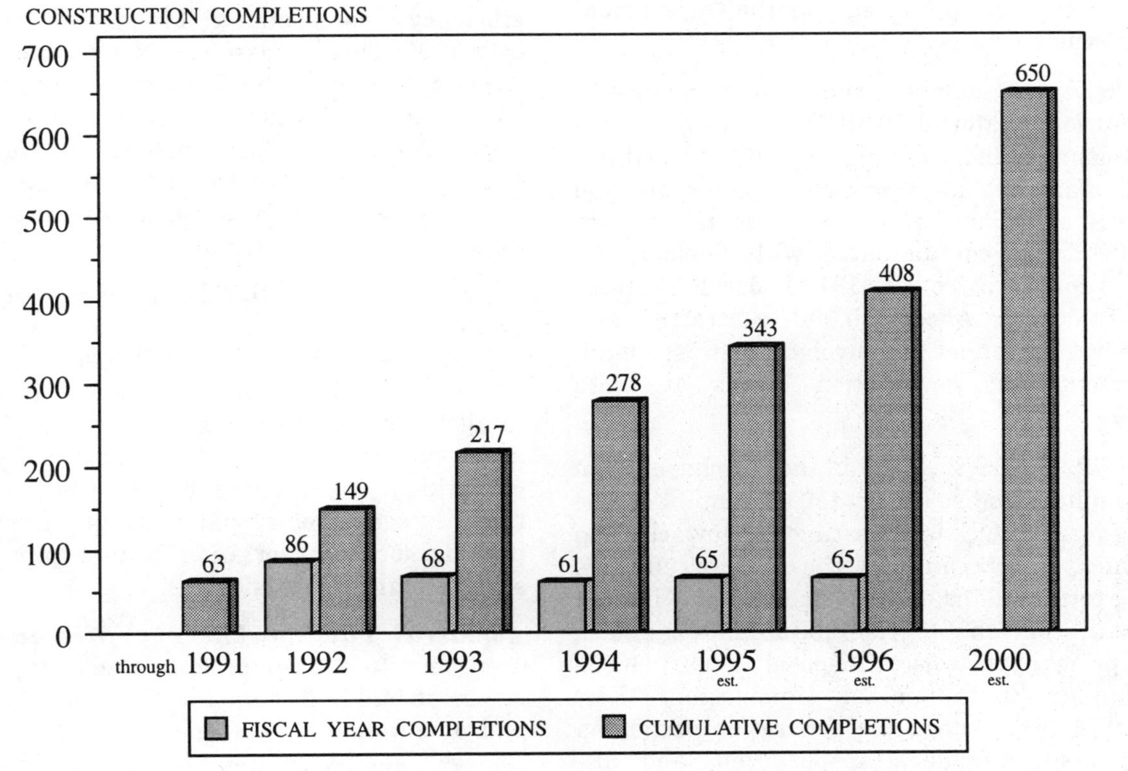

Federal Facilities Cleanup and Compliance

The Federal Government faces an enormous challenge in cleaning up Federal facilities contaminated with radioactive or hazardous waste. The Energy Department (DOE) faces the most complex and costly problems, the result of over four decades of research, production, and testing of nuclear weapons. The Defense Department's (DOD) environmental problems include hazardous wastes similar to those found in the industrial and commercial sectors. In addition, DOD is evaluating the safety and health implications of unexploded ordnance at bombing and test ranges. Thousands of abandoned mines and sites are on public lands managed by the Interior and Agriculture Departments.

The Federal goal for cleanup and compliance is to protect public health and the environment by spending Federal dollars wisely, reducing the risks posed by radioactive and hazardous wastes. Remediation will take many decades to complete. The Federal Facilities Policy Group, an inter-agency task force of officials from Federal agencies with significant cleanup responsibilities, is working to craft a cost-effective clean-up strategy for the Government as a whole.

DOE must safely manage large quantities of nuclear materials while identifying, decommissioning, and cleaning up surplus facilities and managing large stocks of plutonium and other materials. DOE has identified over 14,000 sites contaminated with nuclear and hazardous wastes at 137 Federal facilities in the U.S. About 50,000 contractor and Federal personnel are involved in waste management and remediation efforts at these sites.

In 1996, DOE will shift its emphasis from feasibility studies to actual cleanup. For the long-term, DOE is investing in new cleanup technologies because of the lack of effective long-term stabilization technology, the limited amount of reliable risk data, and the lack of permanent waste disposal sites. DOE's Office of Environmental Management (EM) must safely manage the generation, handling, treatment, storage, transportation, and disposal of DOE nuclear and hazardous waste. The budget proposes about $6.6 billion for this key program.

Meanwhile, DOD continues to make significant progress in cleanup, compliance/pollution prevention, and research and development. The budget provides nearly $5 billion for these programs. To date, DOD has completed the job at over 9,200 sites. Today, 800 military installations have over 10,000 sites where a study or cleanup is underway.

DOD plans to invest about $2.1 billion for environmental cleanup in 1996, including funding from the defense environmental restoration and base closure accounts. The funding will allow the continued identification, investigation, and cleanup of past contamination. For environmental compliance and pollution prevention, DOD plans to invest $2.6 billion in 1996. This funding will allow it to meet current standards in air and water permits, maintain and repair environmental treatment facilities, and begin construction to meet environmental standards.

Energy Efficiency and Renewable Energy

Energy Conservation: At $924 million, DOE's budget for energy conservation and efficiency represents a 17-percent increase over 1995. This increase provides for continued implementation of the Climate Change Action Plan and the Partnership for a New Generation of Vehicles. Also included is funding for "joint implementation" efforts in developing countries, where U.S. technologies can reduce greenhouse gas emissions.

Parking Policy and Environmental Protection: To promote employee use of mass transit, with its associated benefits for the environment, we plan to propose legislation to allow Federal agencies to charge employees a fee no greater than the commercial value of parking. We propose to use the proceeds that exceed the actual cost of providing parking for transportation benefit programs, such as transit subsidies.

Federal Facility Energy Efficiency: We are committed to improving the energy efficiency of buildings that the Government owns and operates. For four agencies—the Defense, Energy, and Veterans Affairs Departments and the General Services Administration—

operation of their facilities is an essential element of their missions. Together, these agencies account for almost 90 percent of all energy consumption in Federal buildings. For 1996, the budget proposes a total of $416 million to help these agencies improve building energy efficiency, seven percent more than 1995.

Solar and Renewable Energy: The DOE solar and renewable energy activities, funded at $423 million, represent a nine-percent increase over 1995. This level maintains the recent growth in photovoltaics and other solar energy research, including photovoltaics manufacturing improvements, and construction of the Solar Two central power prototype in California.

Wetlands Protection

The Administration supports the interim goal of no net loss of the Nation's remaining wetlands, and the long-term goal of increasing the quality and quantity of the wetlands resource base. Wetlands provide important economic and environmental benefits including habitat for fish and wildlife, flood protection, shoreline erosion control, water quality improvements, and opportunities for recreation. The Nation as a whole has lost more than half of the wetlands in the 48 contiguous States.

In August 1993, the Administration announced a comprehensive wetlands plan to protect natural resources without impeding economic growth, and has already taken a number of actions to implement the plan. The budget proposes $922 million in total spending for wetlands restoration, acquisition, protection, research, mapping, monitoring, and education; and for improved non-Federal capabilities for wetlands management.

Wetland Reserve Program: Historically, agriculture has been the leading cause of wetland losses. A quarter of U.S. cropland, over 100 million acres, was obtained by

Chart 6-4. IMPACT OF USDA's WETLAND RESERVE PROGRAM (WRP)

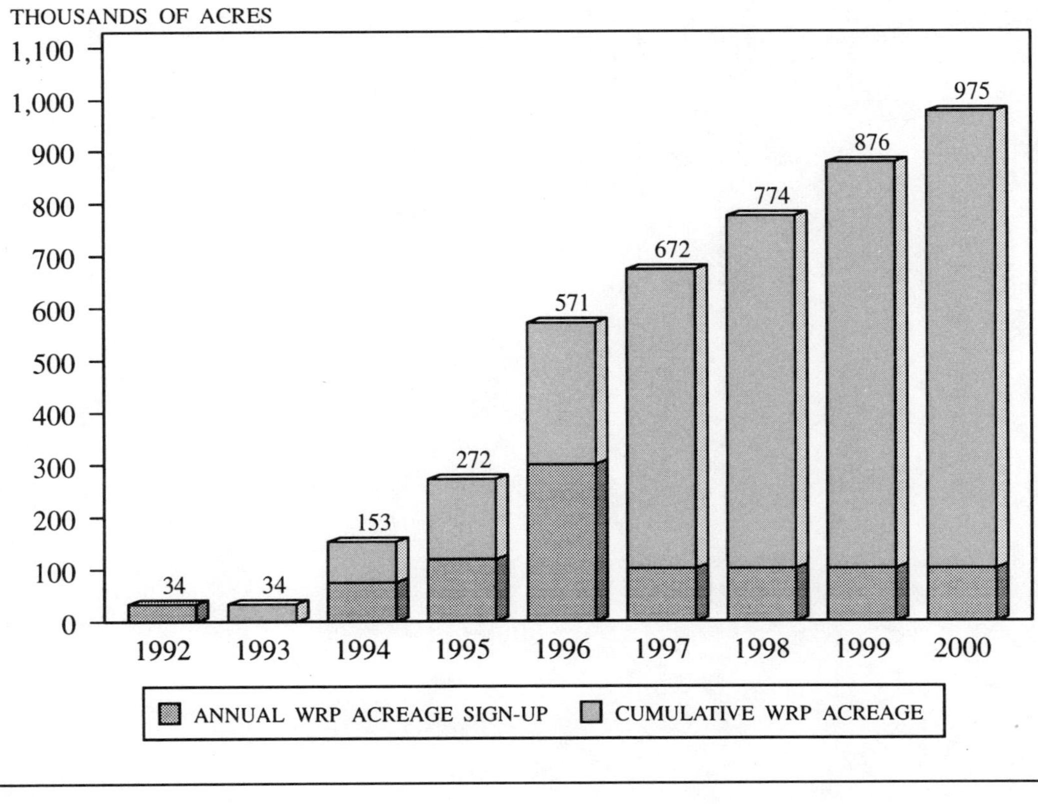

clearing and draining wetlands. The USDA Wetland Reserve Program (WRP) helps offset current and previous wetland losses to cropland.

The proposed level of WRP funding (along with existing restrictions on farmers' use of wetlands) should help the President achieve for 1996 his interim goal of no net loss of the Nation's wetlands acres (See Chart 6–4).

Conservation Reserve Program (CRP)

The Agriculture Department's CRP pays agricultural producers to temporarily take environmentally sensitive (mostly erosion-prone) lands out of production. Producers receive rental payments for 10 years, after which they can again begin producing on these lands.

The first CRP contracts were scheduled to begin expiring in 1995. On December 14, the Administration announced a series of new CRP policies. Among other things, the Administration let contract holders seek early withdrawal from, or modify, CRP contracts on land of lower environmental quality in 1995, with replacement by lands of higher environmental value; let producers extend CRP contracts for up to 10 more years; and let producers apply for permanent conservation easements on CRP lands with high environmental value.

Enhanced Natural Resource Protection

The budget continues the President's commitment to protect the national parks and forests, wildlife refuges, other public lands, and marine sanctuaries. The American people rightly consider these areas special because of their natural beauty and historical significance. These areas also contribute to biological diversity, ecosystem stability, and the preservation of plants and animals that are threatened or endangered.

The budget proposes funding increases with which the national parks will improve visitor services, resource stewardship, and park maintenance. The budget also strengthens the Interior Secretary's initiatives for promoting entrepreneurial management. The Administration will seek legislation to provide the National Park Service with additional authorities to collect user fees and lease facilities.

7. Investing in Science and Technology

7. INVESTING IN SCIENCE AND TECHNOLOGY

For two centuries, the Nation's leaders have agreed that investments in science and technology (S&T) increase productivity and raise living standards. Research and development, commonly known as R&D, is a major component and one of the traditional measures of S&T investment.

Industry R&D may have accounted for about a quarter of overall productivity growth in recent decades, providing rates of return of about 30 percent. Federal R&D has supplemented private R&D in areas where returns are too distant or uncertain for private firms to bear. While the rate of return from federally-financed R&D is much harder to estimate, it is probably substantial, with many economists believing it provides the highest return of any Federal investment. Simply put, S&T is good economic and public policy. This budget proposes $73 billion for all R&D in 1996 (including the category of Facilities), accounting for about 40 percent of our Nation's overall R&D investments.

During the Cold War, many of the Nation's S&T investments went to meet defense and space needs. Today, the Nation faces increasing challenges from global economic competition. We believe that we can significantly improve our competitiveness through a balanced mix of basic research, applied research, and technology development. Though they differ from one another, these three activities are profoundly inter-dependent; we must pursue them all.

To ensure that the Federal Government pursues proper S&T investments, the President created and chairs the National Science and Technology Council (NSTC). In the past year, the NSTC has "reinvented" the way that the Federal government sets priorities among, and coordinates, S&T investments. By pooling the resources of participating agencies, the NSTC has become a "virtual agency," identifying areas where agency research can serve multiple functions. It has worked closely with businesses, universities, State and local governments, and other interested groups. And it has made new funding available to high priority projects by reducing duplication, streamlining management, and eliminating lower priority projects. Through the process, the Administration developed an "investment strategy" to achieve certain S&T goals:

- A healthy, educated public;
- Job creation and economic growth;
- World leadership in science, mathematics, and engineering;
- Improved environmental quality;
- Harnessed information technology; and
- Enhanced national security.

This strategy also includes a set of principles that S&T investments should reflect, such as peer review, cost-shared partnerships, human resource development, international cooperation, and environmental objectives. The Administration views S&T programs that address these goals and principles as higher priorities than others. The President's reports, *Technology for America's Economic Growth: A New Direction to Build Economic Strength* (February 1993) and *Science in the National Interest* (August 1994), describe the strategy and S&T policies in more detail.

In addition, the Administration continues to reshape the Federal R&D budget to maintain balanced investments in basic and applied research, and to ensure that the civilian share of Federal R&D continues to approach 50 percent. Table 7–1 summarizes the Administration's 1996 proposed R&D investments by agency, theme, and share.

162-000 O - 95 - 4

Table 7–1. FUNDING OF RESEARCH AND DEVELOPMENT ACTIVITIES

(Budget authority, dollar amounts in millions)

	1993 Actual	1995 Estimate [1]	1996 Proposed	Dollar Change: 1995 to 1996	Percent Change: 1995 to 1996
By Agency:					
Defense	38,898	36,272	35,161	–1,111	–3.1%
Health and Human Services	10,472	11,676	12,123	+447	+3.8%
National Aeronautics and Space Administration	8,873	9,455	9,517	+62	+0.7%
Energy	6,896	6,637	7,125	+488	+7.4%
National Science Foundation	2,012	2,450	2,540	+90	+3.7%
Agriculture	1,467	1,554	1,499	–55	–3.6%
Commerce	793	1,284	1,404	+120	+9.3%
Transportation	613	687	755	+69	+10.0%
Interior	649	687	697	+9	+1.4%
Environmental Protection Agency	511	589	682	+93	+15.8%
Other	1,308	1,423	1,380	–42	–3.0%
Total	**72,493**	**72,713**	**72,883**	**+170**	**+0.2%**
By R&D Theme:					
Basic	13,362	13,975	14,467	+493	+3.5%
Applied	13,608	14,569	14,686	+117	+0.8%
Development	42,795	42,107	41,768	–339	–0.8%
Facilities	2,727	2,063	1,962	–101	–4.9%
Total	**72,493**	**72,713**	**72,883**	**+170**	**+0.2%**
Civilian:					
Basic	11,951	12,741	13,246	+505	+4.0%
Applied	9,130	10,717	11,022	+305	+2.8%
Development	7,269	8,622	9,031	+409	+4.7%
Facilities	1,979	1,734	1,603	–132	–7.6%
Subtotal	**30,329**	**33,815**	**34,902**	**+1,087**	**+3.2%**
Defense:					
Basic	1,411	1,234	1,221	–13	–1.0%
Applied	4,478	3,852	3,664	–188	–4.9%
Development	35,527	33,485	32,737	–747	–2.2%
Facilities	748	328	359	+31	+9.3%
Subtotal	**42,164**	**38,898**	**37,981**	**–918**	**–2.4%**
By Civilian and Defense Shares:					
Defense Dual-Use	1,702	2,063	1,965	–98	–4.8%
Civilian Share with Dual-Use	44%	49%	51%	NA	NA
Civilian Share without Dual-Use	42%	47%	48%	NA	NA

[1] Includes proposed supplementals and rescissions.
NA=Not applicable.

While the budget proposes to maintain overall R&D funding at roughly the 1995 level, it proposes about $1 billion more for a balanced portfolio of civilian basic research, applied research, and development activities. Under this proposal, the civilian share of R&D should exceed 50 percent by 1996 if the estimates account for so-called "dual-use" defense R&D, and 48 percent if they do not. Table 7–2 highlights some of the Administration's key S&T initiatives.

Table 7–2. FUNDING OF SELECTED SCIENCE AND TECHNOLOGY HIGHLIGHTS

(Budget authority, dollar amounts in millions)

	1993 Actual	1995 Estimate[1]	1996 Proposed	Dollar Change: 1995 to 1996	Percent Change: 1995 to 1996
National Aeronautics and Space Administration:					
Reusable Launch Vehicle Technology Program	....	129	159	+30	+23%
International Space Station	2,262	2,113	2,115	+2	+*%
Aeronautics Initiative	129	347	434	+87	+25%
New Millennium Initiative	67	392	495	+103	+26%
Commerce-National Institute of Standards and Technology:					
Advanced Technology Program	68	431	491	+60	+14%
Manufacturing Extension Partnerships	18	91	147	+56	+62%
In-house R&D	193	259	300	+41	+16%
Defense-Advanced Research Project Agency:					
Technology Reinvestment Project	472	443	500	+57	+13%
Environmental Protection Agency:					
Environmental Technology Initiative	67	139	192	+53	+38%
National Institute of Health:					
Biomedical Reseach	10,326	11,321	11,789	+468	+4%
Department of Energy:					
Basic Research User Facilities	....	....	100	+100	NA
Fusion Energy Research	335	373	360	–12	–3%
Expanded Partnerships and Technology Transfer:[2]					
Federal Technology Transfer Investment	NA	1,611	1,768	+157	+10%
Number of CRADA Partnerships	NA	6,093	6,816	+723	+12%
CRADA Value (Cash and non-cash contributions)	NA	5,104	5,806	+702	+14%
Academic R&D[2]	11,674	11,641	12,504	+863	+7%
Merit Reviewed Research[2]	NA	28,454	29,344	+890	+3%
National Science and Technology Council Initiatives:[2]					
Technology and Learning Challenge	NA	328	335	+8	+2%
Partnership for a New Generation of Vehicles	NA	246	333	+87	+35%
Construction & Building	NA	141	169	+28	+20%
Physical Infrastructure for Transportation	NA	247	321	+74	+30%
Environment & Natural Resources	NA	5,339	5,536	+197	+4%
U.S. Global Change Research Program[3]	1,531	2,118	2,157	+39	+2%
Defense	6	6	6	*	+*%
Health and Human Services	1	31	32	+1	+5%
Energy	305	368	371	+3	+1%
National Aeronautics and Space Administration	917	1,338	1,341	+3	+*%
National Science Foundation	124	169	183	+14	+8%
Agriculture	46	61	67	+6	+9%
Commerce	66	78	97	+19	+24%
Interior	38	31	30	–1	–3%
Environmental Protection Agency	26	32	26	–6	–19%
Smithsonian	3	3	3	*	+*%
Tennessee Valley Authority	....	1	1	–*	–17%
High Performance Computing and Communications	762	1,080	1,142	+63	+6%
Defense	298	384	403	+19	+5%
Health and Human Services	47	68	78	+10	+15%
Energy	100	113	114	+1	+1%
National Aeronautics and Space Administration	82	131	131	–*	–*%
National Science Foundation	233	297	314	+17	+6%
Commerce	2	32	50	+18	+57%
Environmental Protection Agency	....	15	12	–3	–20%
Veterans Administration	....	24	24	+*	+*%
Education	....	16	17	+1	+6%

* Less than $500 thousand or 0.05 percent.

[1] Includes proposed supplementals and rescissions.

[2] These initiatives include double counting of other 1996 S&T initiatives, except for estimates from the Department of Energy.

[3] U.S. Global Change Research Program is a subset of the Environment and Natural Resource initiative.

NA=Not applicable.

Agency Specific Initiatives

NASA Reusable Launch Vehicle Technology Program: The President's National Space Transportation Policy directed NASA to begin fundamental research on a next generation launch vehicle designed to significantly cut the costs of access to space. NASA's budget proposes $159 million to initiate a program in preparation for a White House decision in 1996. Discrete criteria, validated by an external panel, will provide the basis on whether to develop a subscale test vehicle to demonstrate the concept of single stage to orbit. These efforts, in cooperation with the private sector, are the first step to providing inexpensive access to space, and will help reposition U.S. industry atop the global commercial space launch market.

International Space Station: The budget proposes $2.1 billion for the international Space Station, a U.S.-led collaborative effort with the European Space Agency, Canada, Japan, and Russia. The Space Station will be an orbital research facility to study life sciences, materials sciences, engineering research, and advanced technology development. Prior to its assembly in 1997–2002, NASA will conduct at least seven Space Shuttle flights to the Russian Mir space station—three in 1996—to make assembly and operation of the Space Station easier and safer.

NASA Aeronautics Initiative: The aeronautics industry generates about $100 billion a year in revenues, employs roughly 1,000,000 people in high-quality jobs, and generates a larger positive balance of trade than any other U.S. manufacturing industry. NASA develops aeronautical technologies, pursues basic research, and operates national aeronautical facilities for Government and industry. The budget proposes $434 million for the highest priority NASA aeronautics programs—High Speed Research (HSR) and Advanced Subsonic Technology (AST)—an $87 million, or 25-percent, increase over 1995. The budget proposes no additional funding for a national wind tunnel complex. Instead, NASA will use prior-year funds to refine design options and develop financing arrangements with industry to explore a possible 1997 request for funds. As a result, the Administration proposes to reverse an item in a 1995 appropriations bill that rescinds $400 million for the wind tunnels.

NASA New Millennum Initiative (NMI): The NMI is promoting a new class of technology-intensive, smaller, faster, and cheaper space missions. These programs should dramatically reduce costs, increase flight opportunities, and improve mission performance compared to current NASA programs. Each program will have innovative procurement and management approaches and firm performance criteria fixed to a cost cap. These programs will include micro-satellite missions to other planets and the next generation of micro-spacecraft and small rocket technologies. The budget proposes $495 million for the NMI, a $103 million increase over 1995.

Commerce Department's National Institute of Standards and Technology (NIST): Core NIST activities are the Advanced Technology Program (ATP), Manufacturing Extension Partnerships (MEP), and in-house research on measurements, standards, data verification, and test methods. ATP provides cost-shared awards to industry to develop high-risk, enabling technologies to the pre-product development stage. The budget proposes $491 million in 1996 for ATP, $60 million, or 14 percent, more than the 1995 level. This amount will fund 50 new projects and continue 280 existing projects. MEP helps small and medium-sized manufacturers tap into information on the use of modern manufacturing and production technologies. The budget proposes $147 million in 1996 for MEP, a $56 million increase over 1995. It will support 90 MEP centers (75 funded by NIST and 15 funded by the Defense Technology Reinvestment Project, described below). The budget proposes to increase in-house research to $300 million in 1996—$41 million, or 16 percent, more than the 1995 level.

Advanced Research Project Agency/Technology Reinvestment Project (ARPA/TRP): The Technology Reinvestment Project (TRP) implements the Defense Department's strategy of dual-use technologies to cut procurement costs and rapidly insert new technologies into defense systems. ARPA, in the Defense Department, awards TRP funds competitively, on a cost-shared basis, to industry-led projects designed to create new dual-use technologies. TRP projects develop emerging dual-use technologies, such as flat-panel displays and high-density data storage devices, that are critical to national security. At the same time, the projects promote defense technology transfer to commercial applications, to make the technology more widely used and more affordable and accessible to the military. The budget proposes $500 million for TRP in 1996, a $57 million or 13-percent increase over 1995.

EPA Environmental Technology Initiative (ETI): The ETI is a Federal-private partnership to promote R&D and the use of cost-effective environmental technology and pollution prevention approaches. The budget proposed $192 million in 1996, a $53 million or 38-percent increase over 1995.

Biomedical Research (NIH): The budget strengthens the Administration's commitment to biomedical and behavioral research to secure the long-term health of Americans. The proposed $11.8 billion for the National Institutes of Health (NIH) is a $468 million or four-percent increase over 1995 and represents a balanced investment in research directed to areas of high need and promise, and in basic biomedical research that sows the seeds for future progress against disease. The budget proposes targeted increases for HIV/AIDS-related research, breast cancer, and other women's health research; minority health initiatives; high performance computing; prevention research; brain disorders research; environmental cancer research; and gene therapy. NIH's highest priority will remain the funding of research through investigator-initiated research project grants.

Department of Energy (DOE) Basic Research Facilities Initiative: The budget proposes adding $100 million above the 1995 level to significantly enhance the usage of major DOE-operated basic research facilities. These leading-edge facilities serve the university, Government, and industry research community. The budget proposal will facilitate a more efficient use of the facilities, boost the number of users by several thousand over 1995, and improve the quality of service. A fifth of the funds will go directly to users through competitive grants.

DOE Fusion Energy Program: DOE also supports R&D to demonstrate the technical feasibility of fusion energy. The budget includes funds for U.S. participation in the design phase of the International Thermonuclear Experimental Reactor (ITER), analysis of Tokamak Fusion Test Reactor data, and construction of the Tokamak Physics Experiment (TPX). TPX is an experimental device that will improve tokamak machine performance and contribute to the ITER effort. The President's Committee of Advisors on Science and Technology and the Office of Science and Technology Policy are conducting a review of the fusion program. The review will include the ITER and TPX and is scheduled for completion in the summer of 1995. Based on this study, the President will decide upon a fusion energy research strategy. The construction of the TPX will await this decision.

National Science Foundation (NSF): The NSF's charter is to promote scientific progress by awarding competitive grants to institutions for research and education. The budget proposes $2.5 billion for NSF's R&D activities, a $90 million or four-percent increase over 1995 (see Table 7–1). Including NSF's non-R&D education and other activities, the NSF budget would be $3.4 billion. In 1995, the Congress proposed additional funds for a new interagency academic infrastructure modernization program. In the current budget environment, the Administration proposes to rescind the funds.

National Science and Technology Council Initiatives

Expanded Partnership and Technology Transfer: Partnerships with the private sector ensure that federally-sponsored research is relevant for the marketplace. Federal agencies, such as the Defense, Energy, and Agriculture Departments, enter partnerships with industry and the university community, including cooperative research and development agreements (CRADAs). The budget proposes to fund 6,816 CRADAs in 1996, 723 more than in 1995, with a public and private value (in cash and non-cash contributions) of nearly $6 billion. The agencies also propose to invest $1.8 billion in 1996 in technology transfer activities, an increase of $157 million or 10 percent over 1995.

Academic Research: The budget proposes $12.5 billion in 1996 for university-based research, an increase of $863 million or seven percent over the 1995 level. University-based research continues to create knowledge, spur technological innovation, and train the next generation of scientists and engineers. (The Administration's proposed reforms to university overhead are discussed below.)

Merit Reviewed Research and Performance Measurement: One of the Administration's R&D principles is peer evaluation and the competitive selection of Federal research projects (i.e., merit review). The budget proposes $29 billion of merit-reviewed research, an increase of $890 million, or 3 percent, over 1995. Merit reviewed research, now covering nearly 40 percent of the R&D budget, will improve quality and performance.

NSTC Technology and Learning Challenge (TLC): The TLC is a partnership with industrial, educational, and training institutions to use computers, new communication systems, and other advanced technologies to improve the quality, accessibility, and productivity of learning experiences for all Americans. The budget proposes four major focus areas (innovative technologies and demonstration projects, learning tools, evaluation techniques, and cognitive process research). For 1996, nine agencies are proposing $335 million for this effort. An Interagency Technology Office, to be established within the Department of Education, will carry out the initiative.

Partnership for a New Generation of Vehicles (PNGV): The PNGV or "Clean Car" initiative is a partnership with U.S. industry to ensure the global competitiveness of the U.S. automobile industry and its suppliers and improve environmental quality. It is structured around two near-term goals—better manufacturing technologies and better emissions control of conventional engines—and a major long-term goal—developing an attractive, affordable car with three times the fuel efficiency of today's vehicles.

The budget proposes investments in 14 technologies, targeting most Government funding to the third, long-term goal. Eight agencies participate in the initiative: the Departments of Commerce, Defense, Energy, the Interior and Transportation, and EPA, NASA, and NSF. Their combined budget proposal is $333 million in 1996, an increase of $87 million or 35 percent above 1995.

NSTC Construction and Building (C&B): A partnership with U.S. industry, C&B is designed to improve the productivity and safety of building construction practices and the affordability, quality, and environmental characteristics of buildings. C&B has set goals and priorities in three broad areas: technology improvements, such as information and decision technologies; non-technical barriers to improvements, such as regulatory barriers; and the deployment of technology, including training and demonstration projects. Seven agencies are proposing $169 million in 1996, an increase of $28 million (20 percent) over the 1995 level.

NSTC Physical Infrastructure for Transportation: This partnership with industry is designed to improve the quality and lower the cost of building and maintaining highways, bridges, ports, rail lines, airports, and other parts of the Nation's physical transportation infrastructure. The budget provides funds to expand programs associated primarily with accelerating R&D on new materials and with the methods of assessing infrastructure conditions. For 1996, five agencies are proposing $321 million, an increase of $74 million, or 30 percent, over the 1995 level. R&D activities include airport security and pavement technology, and research and technology in highway materials, pavements, and structures.

NSTC Environment and Natural Resources (ENR): The ENR initiative focuses on R&D programs associated with global change, biodiversity and ecosystems, air quality, natural resources and management, water resources, coastal and marine resources, toxic substances, hazardous and solid wastes, and natural disaster reduction. Twelve agencies propose $5.5 billion in 1996, an increase of $197 million or four percent over 1995. The total for ENR includes $2.2 billion for the U.S. Global Change Research Program (USGCRP). As required by law, Table 7–2 lists the agency contributions to the USGCRP—which focuses on issues such as natural climate change, global warming, and ozone depletion.

NSTC High Performance Computing and Communications (HPCC): The HPCC program involves nine agencies and is designed to ensure U.S. leadership in information and communications technologies and help lay the technological foundation for the National Information Infrastructure initiative. It supports research on computer science and engineering, and the development of applications of information technology in commerce, manufacturing, education, public safety, health care, and other fields. The budget proposes $1.1 billion for HPCC in 1996, an increase of $63 million or six percent over 1995. As required by law, Table 7–2 lists the agency contributions to HPCC.

Improving the Payment System for Federally Sponsored Research

The Federal Government spends $12 billion a year on research at the Nation's colleges and universities—$9 billion to support specific research projects and $3 billion to support research facilities and administration. In this budget, the Administration announces several important changes in how the Government pays for research.

These changes will simplify administrative and accounting procedures; promote predictability, stability, equity, and consistency in Federal payments for research; and make the Federal investment in research more understandable to Congress and the public. In the long run, they also will generate cost savings. At this point, however, the Administration proposes to reinvest any initial savings into high priority research.

Most of the proposed changes address the facilities component of research costs. Facilities account for almost all growth in allocated overhead rates over the last decade and explain much of the variation in rates among schools. These changes will be implemented through proposed revisions to OMB Circular A–21, which the *Federal Register* will announce at the time the budget is transmitted. The proposed changes include:

- Establishing limited review of facility construction costs exceeding benchmarks set by Federal and university experts;
- Limiting the current practice of special utility studies, and developing standard benchmarks for utility costs;
- Ensuring that Federal financing policies keep pace with the changing useful-life pattern of scientific equipment, and providing consistent facility cost recovery policies;
- Proposing criteria to appropriately reimburse interest costs;
- Asking the Federal Demonstration Project to develop a model for, and test, direct charging of space costs;
- Increasing the incentives for grantees to maintain lower overhead rates by asking all Federal science funding agencies to review total grant costs in the competitive award process; and
- Eliminating dependent tuition as an allowable benefit, consistent with the Federal Acquisition Regulation.

8. Continuing the Commitment to Health Security

8. CONTINUING THE COMMITMENT TO HEALTH SECURITY

In November 1993, the President sent Congress the Health Security Act, his comprehensive health care reform legislation. It provided one set of solutions to the problems plaguing the health care system: Though the U.S. offers the world's highest quality medical care, many low- and middle-income working Americans cannot afford it. Health care costs continue to rise rapidly, straining private and public budgets at all levels.

The President's bill spurred an unprecedented debate as Americans began to widely discuss the problems facing the health care system. They recognized that many of their neighbors have no health insurance, and that others could lose it just by changing jobs, or if a family member becomes seriously ill.

This debate produced a consensus on several key points. Almost all of the health reform proposals introduced last year included insurance market reforms, such as provisions to prevent insurers from denying coverage to people who have been sick. Many bills recognized the importance of providing health coverage to low- and middle-income Americans, especially children.

Also, the Nation began to examine and test various solutions to the escalating growth in health care costs.

Congressional committees held nearly 200 hearings on such issues as insurance market reforms, coverage, malpractice, and long-term care. After several months of debate, and for the first time in history, a congressional committee approved comprehensive health reform legislation—in fact, four committees did so.[1] And for the first time in history, the Senate brought comprehensive health reform legislation to the floor for debate in August 1994. In the end, however, Congress could not agree on a bill.

[1] Four committees reported five bills: Senate Labor and Human Resources, S. 2296; Senate Finance, S. 2351; House Ways and Means, H.R. 3600; and House Education and Labor, H.R. 3600 and H.R. 1200.

The Costs of Doing Nothing

Americans now share a broad consensus that the U.S. still faces the twin problems of increasing health costs and decreasing coverage. Without action, American families, businesses, and governments will continue to pay the price:

- ***Health costs per person will rise by more than 50 percent by the end of the decade,*** from about $3,300 in 1993 to over $5,000 by the year 2000.
- ***More Americans will lose coverage,*** including many working Americans. The number of uninsured Americans rose by more than one million from 1992 to 1993. Eighty-four percent of the uninsured in 1993 were in working families, and more than 55 percent lived in families headed by full-time workers.
- ***People will continue to stay in current jobs out of fear of losing coverage,*** even when faced with opportunities to move to better jobs. Up to 30 percent of employees say they are afraid to leave their jobs for fear of losing health coverage.
- ***Working Americans bear the full burden of the rising costs of health care.*** Rising employer contributions for their employees' health insurance will continue to come at the expense of growth in real wages. From 1970-1991, real wages and salaries rose a total of 0.4 percent while spending for health benefits increased 243 percent. Unless we do something to control health care costs, American workers take-home pay will suffer.
- ***Businesses will continue to face rising health costs.*** Total health benefit costs per employee rose eight percent in 1993, a slower rate than earlier in the decade, but still nearly three times the rate of gen-

eral inflation. Small firms, in particular, suffer under the current system; insurers charge them up to eight times more than large firms (those with at least 10,000 employees) for administrative costs. Also, in part due to "experience rating" (by which insurers measure the past health records of a company's employees), many small firms pay exorbitant amounts for insurance or cannot get it at all. Small firms often cannot afford to provide any choice of health plans to their employees.

- ***Health care will continue to consume a larger share of government budgets,*** leaving fewer resources for such other priorities as education and job training, transportation and telecommunications infrastructure, and research and development. In fact, over the next five years, almost 40 percent of the growth in total Federal spending will come from health care spending.

Lower Medicare and Medicaid Spending

Fortunately, the two largest Federal health programs, Medicare and Medicaid, are now projected to grow at slower rates than expected when the Administration's Mid-Session Review was released last summer. Under our updated projections, spending in these programs has dropped by $100 billion over the next five years.

Several factors have contributed to the actuaries' lower projections. In Medicare, Hospital Insurance (HI) expenditures have grown more slowly than expected. Slower HI growth results primarily from a decline in forecasted hospital cost inflation and the slower growth in the complexity of Medicare inpatient cases. Other factors, such as effective program management and the success of the Medicare prospective payment system for inpatient hospitals, also may have influenced the lower projections. In Medicaid, the lower cost projections continue a trend dating from the President's 1993 budget, and stem from factors such as actual experience (a decline in the rate of State spending); improved economic conditions; slower projected growth of the population receiving Supplemental Security Income benefits; and successful implementation of regulations to limit States' use of provider donations and taxes that had increased Federal payments.

Together with the earlier spending reductions resulting in part from the President's deficit reduction plan, the 1993 OBRA legislation, these recent changes mean that projected spending on Medicare and Medicaid has dropped by more than $200 billion, and the average annual rate of growth has slowed by several percentage points, for 1994-1998. But despite the progress, spending growth in these programs remains high. (See Chart 8–1.)

The Commitment to Health Care Reform

> *We can pass legislation that includes measures to address the unfairness in the insurance market, make coverage more affordable for working families and children, assure quality and efficiency in the Medicare and Medicaid programs, and reduce the long-term Federal deficit.*
>
> President Clinton, in a letter to congressional leaders
> December 27, 1994

Clearly, the problems have not disappeared. That's why the President remains committed to reforms that will guarantee insurance coverage to every American and contain health care costs for families, businesses, and Federal, State, and local governments. The President has asked the new Congress to work with him on a bipartisan basis to take the first steps toward reaching those goals.

Administration Accomplishments to Date

Part of health care reform is to put the Federal Government's own house in order. In the last two years, the Administration took steps to improve Federal and State health care systems by cracking down on fraud and abuse, implementing administrative simplifications, and giving States more flexibility to administer Medicaid and expand coverage. The Administration also made important investments in public health that will significantly improve the health of Americans.

Highlights of the Administration's efforts to date include:

Chart 8-1. 1996 PROPOSED SPENDING BY CATEGORY: MEDICARE AND MEDICAID

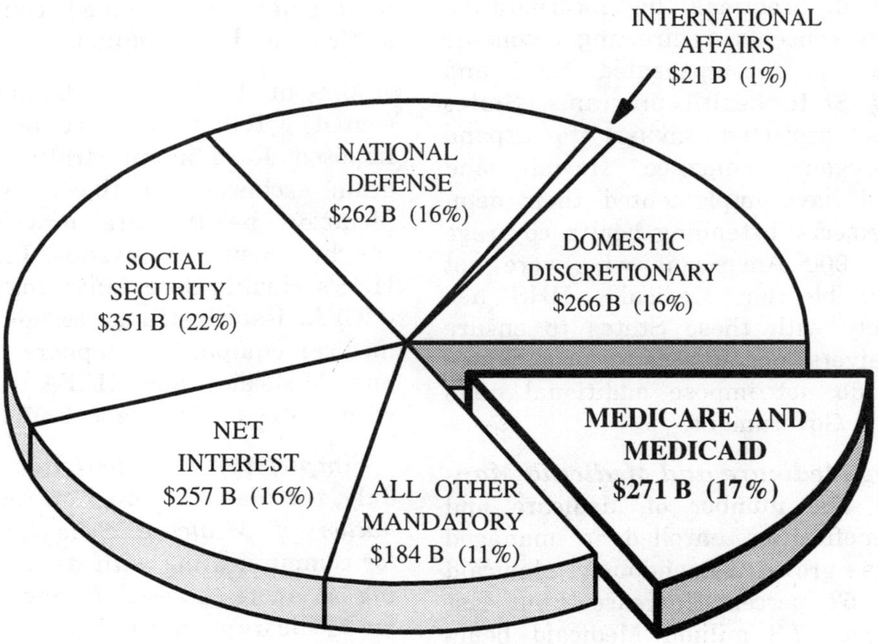

Improving Women's Health: The Administration has placed a high priority on the health of American women, demonstrating this commitment by initiating an unprecedented, comprehensive approach to women's health designed to end the inequities that have plagued research, clinical practice, and public and health care professional education about health and disease in women.

The 1995 Public Health Service budget for women's health included $1.9 billion for research, service delivery, and education programs directly targeting the health of women. The 1996 budget includes significant investments in these areas.

The Administration set an important precedent by establishing the Deputy Assistant Secretary for Women's Health, the first Department-level position in the Department of Health and Human Services (HHS) solely dedicated to improving the health of our Nation's women. Along with the National Institutes of Health (NIH), the new Office on Women's Health has been the focal point for much of the Administration's efforts in women's health:

> Coordinated by the Deputy Assistant Secretary for Women's Health and supported by $10 million from the National Cancer Institute's 1995 budget, the National Breast Cancer Action Plan is a private/public partnership designed to eradicate the threat of breast cancer from the lives of American women. The NIH Women's Health Initiative, the largest research study ever undertaken, continues to explore the major causes of death and disease in older women. In addition, since the President took office, Federal funding for breast cancer research at NIH has increased 65 percent, to $379 million in 1995, and the Department of Defense has funded hundreds of additional research and training grants.

Enhancing State Flexibility to Increase Medicaid Coverage: Under authority of the Social Security Act, the Administration has approved State-wide health reform demonstration programs in Florida, Hawaii, Kentucky, Ohio, Oregon, Rhode Island, and Tennessee. It granted waivers to these States to reform their Medicaid programs by incorporating managed care concepts, redirecting payments to hospitals for uncompensated care, and consolidating State health programs. States will use the projected savings to expand coverage. Oregon, Tennessee, Hawaii, and Rhode Island have implemented their demonstration projects, extending health coverage to about 530,000 Americans who were not otherwise eligible for Medicaid. HHS has worked closely with these States to ensure that the waivers not only save the States money, but do not impose additional costs on the Federal Government.

Expanding Medicare and Medicaid Managed Care: The number of Medicare and Medicaid beneficiaries enrolled in managed care plans has grown tremendously. Medicaid has seen a 62 percent increase from last year, with over 7.8 million Medicaid beneficiaries currently enrolled in managed care plans. Medicare has seen over an 18 percent increase since December of 1993, with 3.1 million Medicare beneficiaries currently enrolled in Medicare managed care. Increasing the role of managed care in Medicare and Medicaid can provide beneficiaries greater continuity of care, improve access to providers, and provide the framework to assure quality. In addition, by increasing the role of managed care, the Medicare and Medicaid programs can benefit from the revolution underway in the private health care market.

Fighting Fraud and Abuse: OBRA 93 contained several provisions to enhance the integrity of Medicaid financing and operations, such as ensuring that liable third parties make reimbursements, that insurers and employers comply with medical child support requirements, and that States operate effective Medicaid fraud control units. These measures were designed to save an estimated $65 million in 1996.

In 1994, HHS's Office of the Inspector General (OIG) recovered over $400 million through settlements. For example, a coordinated effort between OIG and several other Federal and State agencies yielded the largest health care fraud settlement ever to the Federal Government. As a result, a major health care firm that owned over 60 psychiatric hospitals agreed to pay the Federal Government a combined civil and criminal settlement of $379 million.

Also in 1994, the OIG successfully prosecuted 1,169 fraud and abuse cases, and imposed 1,334 administrative sanctions (program exclusions or fines) on Medicare and Medicaid health care providers who were caught abusing the system. Finally that year, HHS's Health Care Financing Administration (HCFA) issued stricter standards for durable medical equipment suppliers under Medicare and Medicaid, and HCFA is now working with States to trace repeat offenders.

Simplifying the Medicare Program: Last July, the Medicare program revised the *Explanation of Medicare Benefits,* its main tool for communicating with its beneficiaries, making it more accessible and understandable for Medicare's elderly and disabled population. Medicare will further refine the document, starting in 1996, when it will become a single, easy-to-read statement of all Medicare claims.

In March 1994, Medicare reduced the paperwork burden on physicians and hospitals. Simply by changing a filing requirement for providers from once a year to one time upon the granting of admitting privileges, Medicare cut red tape while preserving its commitment to quality medical care for all beneficiaries. This regulatory action significantly reduced Medicare's paperwork burden for some 300,000 physicians and 6,000 hospitals.

HCFA, in cooperation with the OIG, is working to be in the forefront of insurance industry practices for guarding against fraud and abuse. As health care delivery systems become increasingly complex, our activities must expand. We are examining innovative methods to fund and carry out these important program integrity responsibilities to detect fraud and abuse and to prevent erroneous payments from the Medicare Trust funds. This program, which will be an integral part of the next round of reinventing government, is expected to yield a significant return on investment.

Preventing Disease through Immunizations: The Administration has made substantial progress towards the goal of immunizing 90 percent of children up to age two by 1996. Immunization rates for some vaccines—such as three doses of DTP[2]—almost reached that level by the end of 1993. Total funding for immunization activities will reach $842 million in 1995, as the Vaccines For Children (VFC) program is implemented. VFC improves access to these lifesaving immunizations for uninsured and Medicaid-eligible children by making publicly-financed vaccines available in private physicians' offices.

What We Propose to Do in the 1996 Budget

In 1996, the Administration will continue to put the Federal house in order by further cracking down on fraud and abuse; making research on, and the treatment of, disease a priority; streamlining the Medicare and public health grants programs; and continuing to provide States greater flexibility in Medicaid. The initiatives include:

Increased Funding for the Ryan White Act—HIV/AIDS Treatment: The budget proposes $723 million for programs authorized under the Ryan White Act, an increase of $90 million, or 14 percent, over 1995. This level will provide funds for categorical grants to cities disproportionately affected by the HIV epidemic; to States to provide medical and support services to infected individuals; and to community-based organizations to provide early HIV/AIDS treatment services and support demonstration projects on pediatric AIDS issues. The 1996 level will provide assistance to an estimated 7–14 new cities that may become eligible for Title I emergency relief grants in 1996.

Since 1993, funding for Ryan White grant programs has increased by 82 percent. The Administration's proposal for 1996 will more than double Ryan White funding since 1993.

Increased Funding for Biomedical and Behavioral Research: The budget continues the Administration's commitment to biomedical and behavioral research, which will pay off in the long-term health and well-being of Americans. The $11.8 billion proposed for NIH—a $466 million, or 4.1-percent, increase over 1995—represents a balanced investment in research directed to areas of high need and promise, and in basic biomedical research which sets the foundation for future progress against disease. The budget includes targeted increases for HIV/AIDS-related research, research into breast cancer and other health concerns of women, minority health initiatives, high performance computing, prevention research, brain disorders research, environmental cancer research, and gene therapy. NIH's highest priority will continue to be financing investigator-initiated research project grants.

Consolidating Programs to Enhance Performance and Streamline the Grants Process—Partnership Grants: The budget proposes to consolidate over 100 categorical Public Health Service (PHS) programs, accounting for spending of $3 billion in 1995, into 14 new grant categories and two existing block grants. The budget also would eliminate many restrictions on how States may use existing PHS grant funds. The new and expanded Partnership Grants represent a performance-based model for Federal agencies, States, and communities to jointly address and ameliorate public health problems. They differ in important ways from past block grant efforts: They represent an increase in total funding over 1995, not a cut, and they encourage performance and results-oriented decisionmaking by using bonus grants. They will also generate administrative savings to HHS.

Streamlining the Medicare Program: HCFA processes millions of beneficiary claims and answers inquiries from beneficiaries and providers. The budget includes $20.2 million for the Medicare Transaction System (MTS), which will bring together all Medicare automated claims processing functions, letting HCFA streamline contractor operations and letting beneficiaries interact more easily with the Medicare program. Currently, more than 10 claims processing systems operate at over 70 contractors. Once MTS is fully implemented, providers will submit virtually all Medicare claims electronically and Medicare will pay them by electronic fund transfers.

[2] Diphtheria-tetanus-pertussis vaccine.

MTS also will generate a more uniform application of coverage and payment policies.

The budget includes $10 million to fund the HCFA "On-Line" proposal, a customer service project for Medicare beneficiaries. Part of the $10 million will finance a thorough needs assessment, which in turn will help identify beneficiaries' and providers' most frequently-asked questions and seek efficient ways to respond.

Providing Federal Assistance to States for Undocumented Immigrants: As discussed in Chapter 5, the Administration proposes to establish a formula-based, discretionary grant program to help States finance the Medicaid costs of undocumented immigrants. The program will help mitigate the costs to States of illegal immigration by providing $150 million a year in discretionary grants. State Medicaid agencies will use the funds to help offset the State and local costs of providing emergency medical services to undocumented immigrants. States with large illegal immigrant populations will be eligible for assistance.

Extending Current Medicare Policies: This budget proposes to extend four current law Medicare provisions: (1) Medicare Secondary Payer protections which allow the Medicare program, like private insurers, to collect payments from primary insurance sources; (2) a provision that maintains the Part B premium at 25 percent of program costs; (3) a provision that assures that the Medicare program does not reimburse excessive costs in skilled nursing facilities; and (4) a similar provision with regard to home health agency services. These provisions, which help reduce Medicare spending, are in effect now but are scheduled to expire unless they are extended. The President does not intend to propose any new Medicare savings proposals outside the context of health care reform.

Special Supplemental Feeding Program for Women, Infants, and Children (WIC): The budget proposes $3.8 billion for WIC, which will raise the annual average WIC participation levels to 7.4 million individuals, up from 5.9 million in 1993.

Building on Success in Immunizing More Children: The Administration proposes $844 million for immunizations in 1996, which will support the purchases of more vaccine to distribute through public health clinics than in 1995 and continued improvements in systems to immunize children. This level reflects the Administration's proposed cut in the vaccine excise tax, which will cut the cost of vaccine for public and private purchasers and save the Federal Government an estimated $75 million in 1996.

PROJECTING AMERICAN LEADERSHIP AROUND THE WORLD

PROJECTING AMERICAN LEADERSHIP AROUND THE WORLD

> *I took this office on a pledge that had no partisan tinge, to keep our Nation secure by remaining engaged in the rest of the world. And ... because of our work together, ... keeping our military strong and prepared, supporting democracy abroad, we have reaffirmed America's leadership, America's engagement. And as a result, the American people are more secure than they were before.*
>
> President Clinton
> State of the Union Address
> January 25, 1994

American foreign and defense policy continues to face complex and swiftly changing international realities. In place of the tense, yet largely predictable, relations structured by the U.S.-Soviet competition, the Nation faces a broad array of conflicts and events that have no obvious central structure. While our foreign and defense policy tools may evolve in this diverse and changing world, our goals and interests remain constant:

- Peace, stability, and strong allies and friends in vital regions;
- A growing U.S. and global economy; and
- Prevention of and humanitarian response to crises that breed future conflict.

The need for strong U.S. leadership on all of these issues is great. The proposed budgets for international affairs ($21.2 billion) and national defense ($258.3 billion) support our leadership position. These two elements are synergistic: we design and prepare our forces and programs to support our national interests and foreign policy goals. Together, these programs create the foundation for American leadership around the world.

9. Strengthening the U.S. Role in International Affairs

9. STRENGTHENING THE U.S. ROLE IN INTERNATIONAL AFFAIRS

International affairs programs and institutions must operate within severe fiscal constraints. While these funds are critical to promoting our vital national interests, they constitute only one percent of the total budget in 1996, requiring a careful focus on their most effective use in supporting the most important goals and objectives. (See Table 9–1 and Chart 9–1.)

1. **First**, and most fundamentally, our international programs must promote and defend our vital interests in regions that have long been central to our national security: Europe, the Middle East, and Asia. Our interests are best served with strong friends and allies, and with the emergence and strengthening of democratic regimes, free markets, and peace and security in these regions. Our budget contains programs that support these vital national interests:

- It continues our strong commitment to strengthen democracy and the emergence of free market economies in the new independent states (NIS) of the former Soviet Union. We have replaced confrontation with the Soviet Union with cooperation with Russia, Ukraine, and the other new nations around Russia. In our own long-term interest, we must continue to support and encourage the development of democracy and a free market in Russia and continue to reduce the nuclear threat from this region by cooperating in mutually verifiable nuclear arms reductions and strengthening non-proliferation regimes. Our budget supports the same efforts in the emerging nations around Russia, especially Ukraine, whose survival and freedom are important to peace and stability in the region. Our budget includes $788 million to support economic and democracy programs in the NIS. We also are requesting $371 million in defense funds to continue reducing the threat from the region's weapons of mass destruction. The budget gives new priority to programs that help create opportunities for American business

Table 9–1. INTERNATIONAL DISCRETIONARY PROGRAMS

(In millions of dollars)

	1993 Actual[1]	1994 Actual	1995 Estimate[2]	1996 Proposed	Change: 1995 to 1996	Change: 1993 to 1996
International Development and Humanitarian Assistance	8,900	8,720	8,739	9,146	+407	+246
International Security Assistance	6,148	5,316	5,799	6,011	+212	–138
Conduct of Foreign Affairs	4,300	4,617	4,787	4,156	–630	–143
Foreign Information and Exchange Activities	1,247	1,494	1,440	1,312	–128	+65
International Financial Programs	599	707	527	585	+58	–13
Total, International Discretionary Budget Authority	**21,194**	**20,854**	**21,291**	**21,210**	**–81**	**+16**
Total, International Discretionary Outlays	**21,570**	**20,806**	**22,144**	**21,019**	**–1,126**	**–552**

[1] 1993 budget authority level does not include $12 billion for the U.S. Quota for IMF.
[2] Includes proposed supplementals and rescissions.

Chart 9-1. 1996 PROPOSED SPENDING BY CATEGORY: INTERNATIONAL AFFAIRS

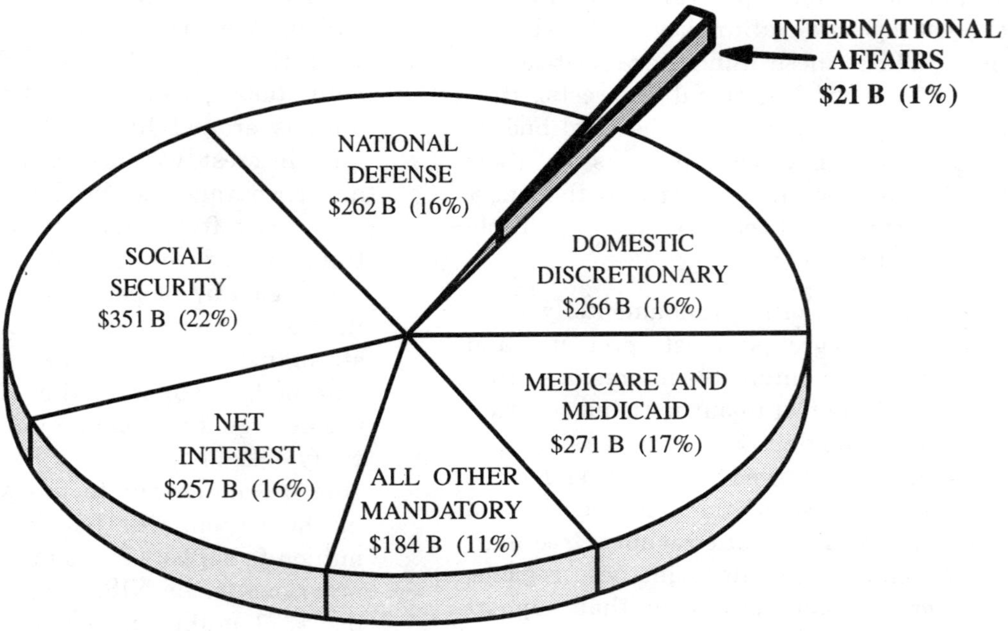

to invest, trade, and develop partnerships in the region's emerging private sectors.

- More broadly, a strong, stable, democratic Europe has been a vital U.S. national interest for generations. Once serving as the Cold War's front line against the West, the nations of Central Europe, especially those in the northern tier (Poland, the Czech Republic, Slovakia, Hungary, and the Baltic nations), are emerging as important partners with democratic, free market societies. With our assistance, these nations have made significant strides and deserve our continued support. The struggle for democracy, economic health, and peace has been more difficult in the southern tier. Support for that process is vital.

Our budget strongly supports this mission, providing $480 million in funding to help healthy, market democracies emerge. This budget includes $60 million to support the process of reconstruction in Bosnia—once the tragic struggle in the former Yugoslavia has ended. In addition, we are providing $100 million (partly from the defense budget) to strengthen military-to-military relations with, and provide military training and equipment for, Central European democracies as they move toward possible NATO membership.

- Changes in the Middle East in the past two years also have been dramatic. Our interest in peace and stability in that region has a long history, and a significant part of our international affairs budget supports this effort. Today, American diplomacy is key to continued progress in the peace process and in shaping international responses to the growing need for trade with, and investment in, the region.

The budget maintains the long continuity of our support for the peace process in the Middle East, requesting more than $5.2 billion to assist countries participating in that process. These funds provide continued strong economic and military support for Israel and Egypt and provide increased military support for Jordan, which also will benefit from additional debt relief proposed for 1995 funding. The funds also provide economic assistance for Palestinians in the West Bank area and in Gaza. At the same time, we have demonstrated our resolve to fight terrorism and to deter countries that could pose a threat to emerging regional stability. We remain strongly committed to the defense of Kuwait and the Gulf states, and to preventing the emergence of weapons of mass destruction in Iraq and Iran.

- In Asia, regional stability and strong friendships have been vital to our national security for 40 years. Our commitment to regional security is firm and was strengthened this year by our leadership in securing a new framework for our relationships with North Korea. This budget supports programs to implement that framework, which will bolster our global leadership on non-proliferation, and to take a critical step toward eliminating the last major threat to regional stability.

  Our continued military presence in the Asian region also reassures our allies that we understand the important role that they play in our national security, and it sends a clear message that we support continued peace and stability in the region.

2. Second, a strong and growing global economy that incorporates an increasing number of nations is essential to our own economic growth and job creation. As we move toward the 21st Century, the world is less and less characterized by "have" and "have not" nations, and more and more by economic partnerships. Latin America and Asia are emerging as important markets and trading partners as well as competitors in this increasingly global economy.

This Administration has brought significant new vigor to promoting an open, global trading system and expanding markets for American exports. American leadership in crafting the North American Free Trade Agreement (NAFTA) and expanding trade under the General Agreement on Tariffs and Trade (GATT) constitutes only the first step in this mission.

Our budget and programs focus on promoting U.S. economic interests and jobs by strengthening and expanding this trading system. Our budget supports this effort by:

- Ensuring our leadership in international economic and financial diplomacy through the State Department, Treasury Department, and the Office of the U.S. Trade Representative (as well as the Commerce Department), which are leading the American effort to expand free trade in Latin America, open up Asian markets, and ensure that the future global trading system provides a fair, level playing field for American exports; and

- Providing increased support for agencies that have vigorously strengthened our trade position in the global market and especially in Central Europe, Russia, and Ukraine—the Export-Import Bank, the Overseas Private Investment Corporation, and the Trade and Development Agency.

3. Third, our leadership is important in seeking to prevent and providing a humanitarian response to crises and conflicts that have so visibly divided many nations in recent years. Our support for sustainable development through bilateral and multilateral assistance (including expanded efforts to control population growth and environmental degradation), for debt forgiveness for the poorest nations, and for humanitarian relief all contribute to this important national interest. Our proposed budget supports these efforts by:

- Focusing U.S. bilateral assistance programs, for which the budget seeks $2.1 billion, on support for democracy and sustainable development in nations that seek to enter this global economy and become vigorous economic partners over the long term. Success in this effort can help prevent the crises that lead to severe humanitarian and refugee problems and regional conflicts.

- Maintaining our strong commitment to international financial institutions, such as the International Monetary Fund,

World Bank, and the regional development banks, whose expertise and loan resources help developing countries reduce poverty and achieve self-sustaining market-oriented growth. Market-based development strengthens the global economy, fosters imports of American goods and services, and advances U.S. national security interests. The budget proposes $2.3 billion for these institutions, of which $416 million will pay for U.S. arrears to them. Coupled with participation by other countries, these funds enable the multilateral banks to lend more than $40 billion for traditional infrastructure projects, social programs (health, education), privatization, and fundamental policy reform.

- Focusing attention in our development assistance on long-term environmental and population problems. Within the amounts proposed for sustainable development aid, multilateral development banks, and voluntary UN contributions, the budget provides $1.1 billion to tackle population and environmental issues. Population programs will, for example, support maternal health programs in countries such as India, Bangladesh, and Kenya.
- Providing significant U.S. leadership in efforts to reduce the burden of debt on the poorest nations and, consequently, facilitate their efforts to begin building sustainable economies. The budget would increase funding for debt reduction and buy-backs from $7 million to $42 million. This initiative would allow the U.S. to provide significant debt reduction, promote development for the poorest and most indebted countries, and increase investment in protecting the global environment.
- Continuing a strong program to respond to humanitarian crises when they occur. A spirit of generosity traditionally has marked America's global leadership. Even where our stake may not have been vital, we have led the mobilization of international responses to humanitarian crises. In the post-Cold War world, these crises are occurring with great intensity and frequency. To head off massive death and suffering among Rwandan refugees, the United States led an international relief effort, to which it contributed $194 million in foreign aid resources in 1994. Our budget will permit the continuation of strong U.S. leadership in responding to these crises, providing more than $1.7 billion for refugee, humanitarian feeding, and disaster assistance programs.

10. Maintaining a Quality Military Force

10. MAINTAINING A QUALITY MILITARY FORCE

Whether our forces are engaged in combat, acting as peacekeepers, or delivering humanitarian assistance, we must continue to review their requirements, provide adequate funding and keep our military edge ... I have repeatedly stated that our number one commitment is to the readiness and well being of our men and women in uniform.

President Clinton
December 1, 1994

This year promises a vigorous debate over our national defense. We welcome it, since we attach high priority to our military capabilities as the backbone of our national security strategy.

U.S. military forces must be able to support and act in synergy with our foreign policy. Our military must deter our adversaries and reassure our friends and allies that America is prepared to put force behind the defense of its interests. Our forces must prevail when committed to combat. They must be highly ready and technologically advanced. They must be prepared and trained for new threats, such as deterring and countering the proliferation of weapons of mass destruction, and for new contingency and humanitarian missions such as those we have asked them to perform in Haiti and Rwanda.

This Nation has built, and this Administration continues to support, a powerful military capability. Our defense budget, which is significantly higher than that of any other nation, supports one of the world's largest military forces, with a superior level of quality and talent. It continues our commitment to maintaining high levels of training and readiness of that force and to equipping it with a technology second to none.

The U.S. is today the only nation with the logistical, mobility, intelligence, and communications capabilities which allow it to conduct large-scale, effective military operations on a global basis. Our military operations of the past two years have demonstrated these capabilities. Moreover, coupled with our unique position as the security partner of choice in many regions, our military capability provides a foundation for regional stability through mutually beneficial partnerships. Our willingness and ability to play a leading role in defending common interests helps ensure that we will retain a strong leadership position in international affairs.

Our budget for national defense continues our support for this capability, one which can deploy robust and flexible forces for a variety of critical tasks:

- **Dealing with Major Regional Contingencies.**—Our forces help offset the military power of regional states with interests opposed to those of the U.S. and its allies. To do this, we must credibly deter and defeat aggression, by projecting and sustaining U.S. power in two regions if needed.

- **Providing a Credible Overseas Presence.**—U.S. forces are also deployed in key overseas regions in peacetime to deter aggression. Such overseas presence demonstrates our commitment to allies and friends, underwrites regional stability, gains us familiarity with overseas operating environments, promotes combined training among the forces of friendly countries, and provides timely initial response capabilities.

- **Countering Weapons of Mass Destruction.**—We are devoting greater efforts to stemming the proliferation of weapons of mass destruction and their delivery means. At the same time, we are improving our capabilities for deterring and preventing the use of such weapons and protecting ourselves against them.

- **Contributing to International Peace and Security.**—When our interests call for it, the U.S. is prepared to deploy unilaterally or participate in multilateral efforts to help settle internal conflicts and bolster new democratic governments. Thus, our forces are prepared for rapid overseas deployment for such activities, as well as for participating in peacekeeping, peace enforcement, and other operations to support our national security goals.

- **Supporting Other National Security Objectives.**—U.S. general purpose and specialized forces are equipped to carry out other non-combat missions, when our interests call for them, including counterterrorism operations, noncombatant evacuation, counternarcotics operations, and humanitarian and disaster relief operations.

Our defense budget is based on the Bottom-Up Review that the Department of Defense (DOD) carried out in 1993, and the Nuclear Posture Review completed in 1994, to plan for America's defense in the post-Cold War era. Those reviews have integrated a sound defense strategy with the military forces and resources to carry it out.

The military services no longer face the prospect of a world-wide war with the Soviet Union. Today, our forces are prepared for two conflicts of the size of the Gulf War that might happen almost simultaneously. These dramatic international changes of the past few years have led to a bipartisan commitment to downsize and reshape the U.S. military. We are near completion of this process, which we have carried out in a steady, careful, and sustained way. A comparison of military forces at the end of the Cold War (1989) to those that the Bottom-Up Review and the Nuclear Posture Review will achieve are summarized in Table 10–1.

Defense Budgets and the Defense Funding Initiative

The Administration is committed to providing budgets for national defense that sustain these forces. Since the President's 1994 budget, submitted in March 1993, we have increased our initial funding plan for defense three times. We have also requested and received defense supplementals three times as world events have unfolded—to ensure that our armed forces have the funds they need to carry out their missions.

First, we increased planned defense budgets by $13 billion in 1993 to cover funding shortfalls in the 1993–1998 budget that we inherited from the prior Administration. Second, we added $11.4 billion to cover the costs of the unrequested 1994 pay raise that Congress adopted.

The third increase was presented in the Defense Funding Initiative, which the President announced in December. This initiative provides for an additional increase of more than $25 billion for the defense program over the next six years. These funds will ensure that we maintain the readiness of our armed forces at high levels, that the pay and quality of life for our men and women continues to improve, and that we begin to arm our forces with the next generation of defense hardware at the end of the century. The increases made to the defense program are shown in Chart 10–1.

In addition to these increases, the Administration is proposing a $2.6 billion supplemental defense appropriation for 1995 to maintain defense readiness, to replenish accounts drawn down for our military's important and successful operations in the Adriatic, Haiti, and the Persian Gulf, and to cover the costs of these operations for the remainder of the year.

This budget requests discretionary funding of $258.3 billion in budget authority and $262.2 billion in outlays for programs in the National Defense Function (050). These outlays represent 16 percent of the proposed spending in the budget. (See Chart 10–2.) It includes the functions of the Department of Defense-Military (051), Atomic Energy Defense Activities (053), and other Defense-

Table 10–1. MILITARY FORCE TRENDS

	1989 Cold War	1995	Target Force [1]
Active Forces:			
Army Divisions	18	12	10
Navy Aircraft Carriers [2]	16	11	11
Navy Air Wings	13	10	10
Navy Surface Combatants and Attack Submarines	287	197	161
Marine Divisions and Air Wings	3	3	3
Air Force Tactical Wings	25	13	13
Reserve Forces:			
Army Combat Brigades	56	48	42
Navy Air Wings	2	1	1
Navy Aircraft Carrier	0	1	1
Other Navy Ships	26	19	16
Marine Division and Air Wing	1	1	1
Air Force Tactical Wings	12	8	7
Nuclear Deterrent:			
Intercontinental Ballistic Missiles	1,000	585	450–500
Ballistic Missile Submarines (Missiles)	34 (608)	16 (384)	14 (336)
Bombers [3,4]	268	140	About 70
Mobility Forces:			
Strategic Airlift Aircraft [4]	367	354	About 245
Sealift Ships [5]	163	149	174
Military Personnel (in thousands):			
Active Forces	2,130	1,523	1,445
Guard and Reserve Forces	1,171	965	893

[1] Steady-state force levels to be reached in some cases after 2000.
[2] Includes one non-deployable training carrier in 1989.
[3] Does not include 82 B-1 bombers in the Target Force dedicated to conventional missions.
[4] Primary Aircraft Inventory—excludes aircraft in maintenance and attrition reserve.
[5] Includes ships in the Ready Reserve Force maintained by the Department of Transportation but funded by DOD.

Related Activities (054). For DOD's military functions, we are seeking discretionary funding of $246.7 billion in budget authority and $250.9 billion in outlays for 1996. Table 10–2 shows budget authority and outlay funding levels for these functions through 2000.

Defense Priorities and Goals

Assure Continued High Levels of Readiness: The Administration continues to place its highest priority on the readiness of U.S. defense forces—ensuring their ability to mobilize, deploy, and operate effectively in the face of the varied challenges that the post-Cold War era presents. The Defense Funding Initiative supports our commitment to high levels of readiness, as does the requested defense supplemental appropriation for 1995. For 1996, the budget proposes funding of $91.9 billion for Operations and Maintenance (O&M), the principal readiness-related account.

Maintain and Improve the Quality of Life for Military Personnel: Our armed forces continue to attract, retain, and motivate people of high quality. We will provide military personnel with compensation levels that are competitive with private sector pay, and an attractive standard of living for them and their families.

This budget contains several initiatives to improve military quality of life, including:

Chart 10-1. PRESIDENT'S DEFENSE FUNDING INITIATIVE

(Department of Defense - Military, discretionary budget authority)

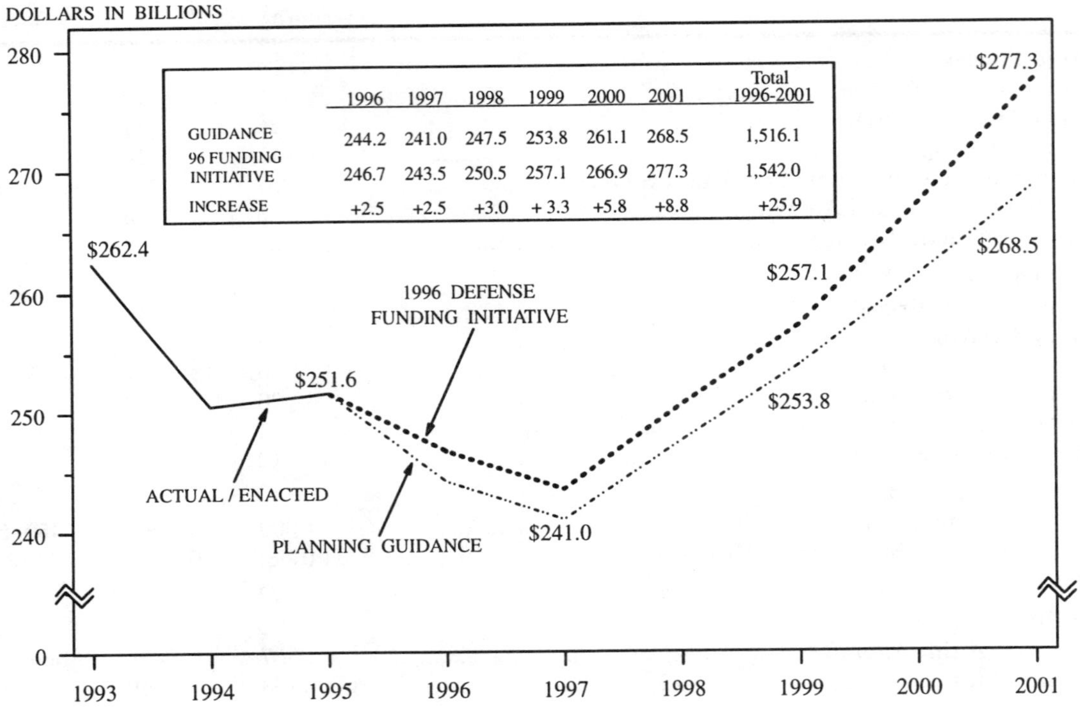

Table 10–2 FUNDING SUMMARY FOR NATIONAL DEFENSE

(Discretionary funding, in billions of dollars)

	1994 Actual	Proposed					
		1995[1]	1996	1997	1998	1999	2000
Department of Defense							
Military (051):							
Budget Authority	250.5	253.5	246.7	243.5	250.5	257.1	266.9
Outlays	269.4	260.8	250.9	246.8	245.0	250.4	258.7
Atomic Energy Defense Activities (053):							
Budget Authority	10.9	10.3	11.2	10.0	9.3	9.3	9.2
Outlays	11.9	10.5	10.8	10.3	9.7	9.4	9.3
Other Defense Related Activities (054):							
Budget Authority	0.9	0.3	0.3	0.4	0.4	0.3	0.3
Outlays	0.9	0.8	0.5	0.4	0.4	0.3	0.3
Total National Defense (050):							
Budget Authority	262.2	264.1	258.3	253.9	260.2	266.8	276.5
Outlays	282.2	272.1	262.2	257.5	255.1	260.2	268.3

[1] Includes proposed emergency supplementals and savings proposals.

Chart 10-2. 1996 PROPOSED SPENDING BY CATEGORY: NATIONAL DEFENSE

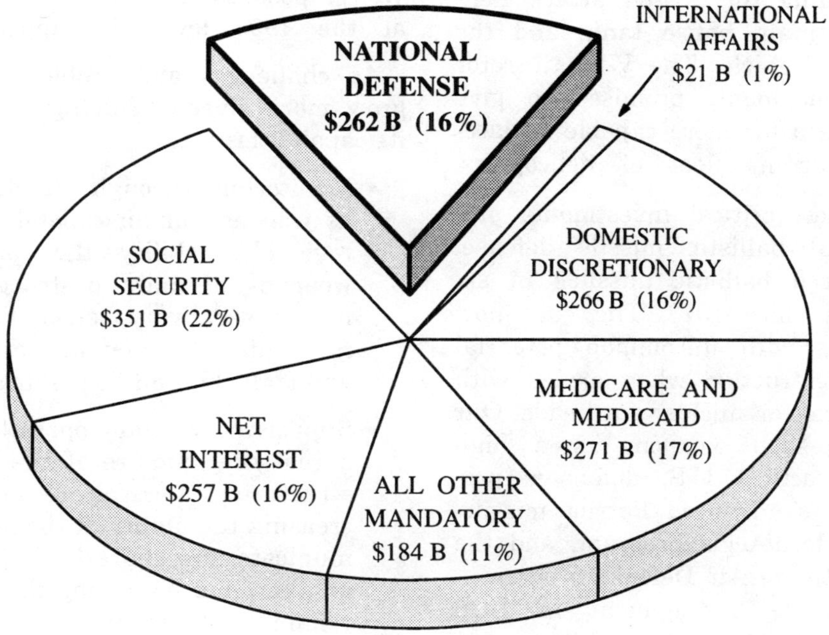

- A 2.4 percent military pay raise (effective next January), pay raises at current-law levels through the end of the century, and funding for a new cost-of-living allowance (COLA) approved for military personnel living in "high-cost" areas in the continental U.S.;
- An increase in the Basic Allowance for Quarters (BAQ) to defray the cost of housing for military members living off-base, and funding to upgrade and maintain base housing and barracks; and
- An increase in military community and family support, including more child care facilities, family counselors, and improved recreational activities.

Maintain High Technology Hardware and Plan for the Next Generation: Superior technology is the hallmark of U.S. armed forces. The investments we make are designed to maintain our technological lead into the next century. In particular, we expect investments in information technologies and sensors to give our forces major advantages in gathering, processing, and acting upon information from the battlefield. The budget proposes $7.8 billion for science and technology programs.

Previous investments in science and technology are yielding dividends. A new generation of weapons and defense systems is in early procurement or completing development. Procurement of the E–8 Joint STARS surveillance aircraft, with its ability to detect moving vehicles and provide target information to missiles and aircraft, promises to revolutionize battle management. Two advanced tactical aircraft are in development—F/A–18E/F multirole fighter for the Navy and F–22 stealth fighter for the Air Force. Also in development, for the tactical aircraft of both services, are new air-delivered precision weapons—the Joint Direct Attack Munition and the Joint Stand-Off Weapon.

Important modernization programs in other mission areas include further procurement of the C-17 strategic airlift aircraft for the

162-000 O - 95 - 5

Air Force, and DDG-51 destroyers and a Seawolf submarine for the Navy. The Army continues to upgrade systems proven in the Gulf War, including the AH-64 attack helicopter, the M-1 main battle tank, and the Bradley Fighting Vehicle. The V-22 tilt-rotor aircraft, in development, promises to give the Marine Corps a far more capable replacement for its current fleet of helicopters.

One of our most critical investments provides for tactical ballistic missile defense. Nations have used ballistic missiles in six regional conflicts since 1973. They are now common weapons with uncommon potential for terror and destruction when armed with chemical, biological, or nuclear warheads. Our defense against such weapons is a high priority. Three tactical U.S. defensive programs—the Army's advanced Patriot missile, the Navy's Standard/Aegis program, and the Theater High Altitude Air Defense program—will enter full-scale development in 1996 and 1997, with deployment to follow soon after.

Maintain Stewardship Over Our Nuclear Capability: Although nuclear forces no longer play as prominent a role in our defense capability as they once did, they remain an important part of our overall defense posture. The Energy Department's (DOE) primary post-Cold War defense mission is to maintain the safety and reliability of the nuclear weapons stockpile and ensure that our research base in nuclear technology remains advanced. The Stockpile Management Program addresses the ongoing requirements of the mission, while the Stockpile Stewardship Program seeks to improve the scientific and technical base needed to assure the long-term safety and reliability of the stockpile, without nuclear testing. The budget proposes $1.9 billion for the former program, $1.6 billion for the latter.

More broadly, the budget proposes $11.2 billion in total DOE spending on defense activities. This includes $6.2 billion for cleanup and disposal of wastes from prior nuclear weapons activities, $0.7 billion for developing nuclear reactors for Naval vessels, and $0.7 billion for nonproliferation, arms control, and other activities.

Retain and Refocus Our Intelligence Capabilities: Intelligence remains a critical ingredient of our national security posture. We propose to keep the Intelligence budget at the 1995 level to support this effort.

As challenges and problems multiply and grow more diverse, Intelligence is refocusing its capabilities:

- Monitoring, through significant technical as well as human capabilities, threats to regional stability—the proliferation of weapons of mass destruction and their means of delivery, terrorist activities, ethnic conflicts, rising militant nationalism, and trafficking in illegal drugs.
- Supporting military operations—providing a real time picture of the battlefield, restructuring tactical reconnaissance, increasing the ability of the services to communicate and share information with one another, and improving the timeliness and reliability of imagery.
- Enhancing economic security—monitoring international compliance with economic sanctions and international trading practices, including unfair foreign competition and foreign government efforts to acquire sensitive U.S. commercial information.

To plan for the future, the President and Congress established a commission of distinguished Americans that will spend the next year reviewing the roles and capabilities of the Intelligence Community. Their conclusions will help to guide future decisions on the Community's goals and resources.

Setting New Management and Streamlining Goals

Investing in Dual-Use Technology: At one time, investments in technology for defense missions set the path for commercial applications. Today, commercial developments increasingly lead the way to military uses. Wise investments in dual-use technologies support national defense. They allow defense systems to draw on leading-edge commercial developments in such areas as computers and communications, and they allow investments in defense programs to accelerate commercial progress in such areas as advanced materials and space systems. These advances, in turn, will benefit defense systems by lowering costs and providing an assured source of supply. When most successful, these advancements will permit the production of commercial and defense components on the same assembly line.

The Administration's dual-use investment strategy focuses heavily on electronics and sensors. Potentially, the payoff is enormous. Earlier applications of these technologies allowed U.S. forces to dominate the battlefield in the Gulf War.

The Technology Reinvestment Program (TRP) is a key component of this dual-use strategy. The TRP awards Federal funds competitively, on a cost-shared basis, to enable industry-led projects to create new dual-use technologies. A key to its success is its emphasis on industry partnerships—most project teams combine unique defense and commercial expertise—and cost sharing; winning projects have matched each $1 of Federal funds with about $1.30 of non-Federal funds. This cost-share ensures industry's commitment to the project and lays the foundation for industry participants to assume the total cost of product development.

Since the start of the TRP program in 1993, over 15,000 companies across America have submitted over 3,000 proposals to participate; the program has made 251 awards. This budget requests $500 million for the program. (See Chapter 7, "Investing in Science and Technology.")

Continuing Acquisition Reform: With enactment of the Federal Acquisition Streamlining Act (FASA), reform of defense procurement took a big step forward last year. This legislation, which the National Performance Review vigorously supported, is a good example of what cooperation between the Administration and Congress can produce.

FASA, discussed in greater detail in "Making Government Work," will produce real savings in the defense budget. It will greatly simplify small-dollar purchases through electronic transactions, clear away barriers to buying commercial products, and test new ideas through pilot programs. These savings will generate more military capability for the defense dollar at a time when we must make every dollar count.

FASA is just the beginning. The Administration is working on next-step legislation to continue the acquisition reform effort. The Defense Department is also making a strong effort to replace military specifications ("mil-specs") on contracts with commercial standards wherever possible. It continues to evaluate procurement methods and systems to foster continual improvement.

Shrinking the Defense Infrastructure: DOD's main challenge with its facilities is to tailor them to the downsized force structure. In this process, the next step is to close unneeded military bases. Recommendations by the Base Realignment and Closure Commission (BRAC) in 1988, 1991, and 1993 will lead to the closure of 70 major domestic bases, with annual savings of roughly $4.5 billion, by 1999. But despite this progress, base closures have not kept pace with force structure reductions; from 1985–1999, forces will shrink by about 30 percent, while closures from BRAC's first three rounds will reduce the number of bases by 15 percent.

BRAC 1995, the process of selecting the next round of bases to close, is the last round that the law allows. DOD is working to ensure that closure and realignment decisions will lead to a more efficient use of the remaining defense infrastructure. The budget provides $3.9 billion in 1996 to implement closure and realignment decisions. We must spend these funds in order to ensure the long-term savings we will achieve by right-sizing the defense infrastructure.

At the same time, DOD is committed to assisting the economic redevelopment of communities affected by base closures. The President's Five Point Plan for Revitalizing Base Closure Communities speeds the transfer of base property for economic development and provides transition assistance for communities and workers. In this effort, the budget increases funding for DOD's Office of Economic Adjustment (OEA) to $59 million, $20 million over 1995, to help BRAC 1995 communities plan for economic redevelopment.

Improving Financial Management: Reform of DOD's financial management system is a major Administration initiative. DOD's reforms include the consolidation of over 300 financial and accounting centers and accounting locations into 26 sites. These consolidations will generate productivity savings of $30 million in 1996, increasing to $100 million in 2001.

DOD also is reducing the number of automated finance and accounting systems. By 1996, it will cut, by 80 percent, not only the number of military and civilian payroll systems, but also the number of systems for retiree, contract, transportation pay, and debt management.

Streamlining the Civilian Workforce: DOD is committed to streamlining its civilian workforce to increase its efficiency and effectiveness, without sacrificing quality or compromising military readiness. DOD projects a 22-percent reduction in civilian positions from 1993–99. It has targeted headquarters, procurement, finance, and personnel staffs, according to guidance from the National Performance Review. This downsizing will not affect the military services' ability to respond quickly and effectively.

MAKING GOVERNMENT WORK

MAKING GOVERNMENT WORK

> *We can no longer afford to pay more for—and get less from—our Government. The answer for every problem cannot always be another program or more money. It is time to radically change the way Government operates—to shift from top-down bureaucracy to entrepreneurial Government that empowers citizens and communities to change our country from the bottom up. We must reward the people and ideas that work and get rid of those that don't.*
>
> *Putting People First*
>
> President Clinton
> Vice President Gore

With this budget, the President is building on his initial success in making Government work and moving out in dramatic, new directions.

Through the National Performance Review (NPR), which the President created two years ago, the Administration has improved service to Government's "customers," cut red tape, empowered Federal employees, and eliminated programs that no longer serve a useful purpose. We have sought to ensure that Federal programs achieve real results—e.g., cleaner air—rather than merely spend taxpayer dollars. We streamlined Federal agencies, cutting management layers and excessive controls while moving to reduce the Federal workforce to its smallest size since John Kennedy was President. Also, we worked with Congress to overhaul the procurement process, launched an effort to make Federal regulations more sensible, and expanded the use of such tools as information technology and electronic benefits transfer (EBT).

Streamlining puts an even higher premium than usual on recruiting and retaining a quality workforce. We are proposing $1.9 billion for 1996 civilian pay raises and will consult with employee organizations and others before deciding how to allocate it. The Defense Department's budget includes $1 billion for a 2.4 percent, across-the-board pay raise, to take effect next January.

In its first phase, the NPR, under the direction of Vice President Gore, mostly examined the "how" of Government—human resource management, procurement rules, and other processes by which the Government operates. In general, it did not focus on the more basic question of "what" the Federal Government should, and should not, do.

With this budget, the President has begun to tackle this very fundamental question. To begin, he is proposing a major restructuring of three Cabinet departments—Housing and Urban Development, Transportation, and Energy—and two major agencies—the General Services Administration and the Office of Personnel Management.

More importantly, these restructurings are the first step in a Government-wide examination of departments and agencies, which the President has asked the Vice President to lead. This effort is designed to sort out responsibilities among the Federal, State, and local levels of government, and between Government and such private sector providers as businesses, non-profits, and community groups. Working with the NPR, OMB, the President's Management Council, and the White House policy councils, Federal agencies will examine every program, find programs to eliminate or shift to the States or other providers, and design better ways to run those that will remain in Federal hands.

11. Reinventing the Federal Government—Phase I

11. REINVENTING THE FEDERAL GOVERNMENT—PHASE I

In its September 1993 report, *From Red Tape to Results: Creating a Government that Works Better and Costs Less,* the NPR articulated four key themes:

1. *Putting Customers First*—changing Government's culture by focusing on what matters to the people it serves;
2. *Empowering Employees to Get Results*—removing layers of oversight, giving frontline employees not only responsibility, but also accountability, for results;
3. *Cutting Red Tape*—eliminating unnecessary paperwork, procedures, and requirements for the Federal Government, its State and local partners, and its customers; and
4. *Cutting Back to Basics*—eliminating obsolete and duplicative programs and functions, and reengineering what's left.

The Administration already has produced impressive results from its efforts:

- By the end of 1994, Federal employment already had dropped by 102,000;
- All departments and agencies have embarked on streamlining initiatives;
- More than 100 agencies have set for themselves more than 1,500 customer service standards, pledging what each agency will strive to achieve; and
- The Administration and Congress already have enacted $63 billion of the NPR's proposed $108 billion in savings over five years.

Focusing on Performance

The NPR is part of an Administration-wide effort to make Government work—that is, to improve its "performance." Whether in implementing the 1993 Government Performance and Results Act (GPRA) or evaluating programs as it put together this budget, the Administration has worked hard to reach that goal. Only by performing better can Government regain the confidence of the American people.

These efforts include the signing of performance agreements between the President and the heads of agencies; the agencies' development of customer service standards; the use of performance data in this year's budget process; the efforts to begin reforming the intergovernmental system; the planning and performance measurement efforts under GPRA; and the reporting on financial and program performance under the 1990 Chief Financial Officers Act and the 1994 Government Management Reform Act. The aim of these efforts is for each agency and program to present a clear picture of its goals; the links between those goals and how it spends its money and organizes its personnel; and the extent to which it accomplishes its goals.

Signing Performance Agreements: The President last year signed agreements with the Secretaries of Health and Human Services, Housing and Urban Development, Interior, Labor, Transportation, and Veterans Affairs, and the Administrators of the Small Business Administration and General Services Administration. The agreements are designed to encourage agencies to improve their operations and achieve better results. They spell out the goals for each organization, including specific commitments that are accompanied by measurable performance indicators. When the goals are disseminated throughout the agencies, the agreements make it possible to link political and career employees in a top-to-bottom chain of accountability to help improve results.

In the coming year, the President will review agreements from the heads of other large agencies. Over time, the agreements will incorporate each agency's key performance-improvement initiatives, become more customer-focused, and place more emphasis on generating better results for the American people.

Creating Customer Service Standards: The more than 1,500 customer service standards, published in the NPR's September 1994 report, *Putting Customers First: Standards for Serving the American People,* are a major step toward a results-driven Government. The standards are clear, precise, and easily understandable.

- The IRS promises that taxpayers will receive their tax refunds within 40 days if they file a paper return, 21 days if they file electronically; in seven States, taxpayers can file their returns by phone.
- The Consumer Product Safety Commission promises that the public can report on, and learn about, unsafe products at any hour of the day or night, by dialing 1–800–638–2772.
- The SBA promises complete reviews of loan applications within three days, based on a one-page application.
- The Commerce Department provides the latest information on overseas markets through a compact disk that it mails within 24 hours—or the customer gets the disk free.

The effort to improve customer service is a long-term one that requires a new perspective about what Government is and what it should do. Customer service involves identifying customers, surveying them to learn their needs and concerns, and reengineering, streamlining, and often reorganizing services to better meet those needs. As illustrated in the example that follows, it also often means that an agency must work with other agencies that serve the same customers.

> The Customs Service often took days to move perishables and other cargo from other nations through Miami. Viewing shippers as its customers, Customs worked with other agencies (e.g., Immigration and Naturalization Service, Food and Drug Administration, and Fish and Wildlife Service) to find ways to move cargo more quickly. By improving the port facilities and relying on electronic filings of shipping documents, Customs discovered how to please shippers and regulators simultaneously. Now, Customs pre-approves much cargo before it reaches Miami, permitting agents to focus on inspecting higher-risk shipments.

Reforming the Intergovernmental System: The Administration has begun to change how the Federal Government interacts with State and local governments. It has used "waivers" to give States more flexibility to manage federally-funded programs, such as Medicaid. For example, the Federal Government is working with Indiana and West Virginia to consolidate their required planning for 199 Federal programs for children and families. Working with Congress, the Administration has enacted legislation to increase State and local flexibility. Examples include the Goals 2000: Educate America Act and the Empowerment Zones and Enterprise Communities Program.

In addition, a Federal inter-agency team has worked with State and local officials in Oregon to design and test a results-oriented approach to intergovernmental service delivery. Initially, the effort will focus on welfare reform, job training, and child health programs. Under the redesigned system—which will reduce red tape and administrative burdens for State and local governments—the State will set clear performance goals for government programs and hold itself accountable for achieving results.

Implementing the Government Performance and Results Act (GPRA): For too many years, Government has focused on inputs—that is, funding and staffing levels—and the rules and procedures by which to run programs. GPRA marks a shift to results, to the question: What is Government achieving by spending tax dollars, and how well are its programs meeting the goals set for them? Under the law, agencies must develop strategic plans that define their missions and general long-term goals, annual performance plans that contain specific performance targets for each year, and annual reports that compare actual performance to performance targets. The law also calls for Federal managers to receive more flexibility and discretion, in return for improved results.

Implementation is accelerating. In 1994, OMB designated 75 pilot projects covering specific programs and activities in all Cabinet departments and 13 independent agencies. The pilots cover over 400,000 civilian and military personnel and virtually every major function of Government. OMB soon will designate a second set of pilot projects that will receive more managerial flexibility in return for accountability for better results.

An example of a pilot project is the prescription drug program in the Public Health Service (PHS). One of its 1995 performance goals is to complete a review, within a year, of 70 percent of product applications for treating, diagnosing, or preventing severely debilitating or life-threatening diseases. By comparison, the PHS had a target rate of 55 percent for 1994.

GPRA's full-scale implementation will begin in the fall of 1997, when agencies will submit strategic plans to OMB and Congress. That September, agencies also will submit annual performance plans; these plans will support OMB's preparation of the first Government-wide performance plan, which it will submit to Congress as part of the President's 1999 budget.

Using Performance Information in the Budget Process: The Government must run more efficiently and effectively, especially at a time of constrained resources. In preparing this budget, the Administration began a long-term effort to broaden the use of performance information in the budget and appropriations process. We asked whether programs were achieving the results that their proponents intended and we encouraged agencies to provide information on outputs and outcomes to include in this year's budget Appendix.

For example, in OMB's budget review of the Housing and Urban Development Department (HUD), the quality of public housing compared unfavorably with private low-income housing and subsidized housing alternatives in terms of their physical condition, crime problems, and neighborhood environment. Partly due to such information, OMB agreed with HUD to "end public housing as we know it" by shifting assistance to portable vouchers by 1998.

Integrating Financial and Performance Information: To make sound decisions, Government officials must have reliable financial information—how much programs cost, how agencies are spending money, and what the American people are getting for their tax dollars. Departments and agencies are building on the laws that Congress enacted in the last few years to improve financial reporting and management, and to ensure that performance, budgeting, and accounting systems work together to increase accountability for results.

In 1990, OMB, the Treasury Department, and the General Accounting Office created the Federal Accounting Standards Advisory Board to recommend accounting standards for the Federal Government. Also in 1990, Congress passed the Chief Financial Officers Act, requiring the 14 Cabinet departments and nine of the largest agencies to prepare audited annual financial statements for selected accounts. Congress went further last year with the Government Management Reform Act, requiring these 23 agencies—rising to 24 in March, when the Social Security Administration becomes an independent agency—to prepare and audit annual financial statements that cover all of their activities, and virtually all of the Executive Branch's budget authority.

In another initiative to promote performance and accountability, we will encourage agencies to examine their budget account structures and revise them to align resources with results and organizations. In some cases, budget accounts do not collect significant costs—such as salaries and expenses which may be paid centrally or in another program; Federal employee pension costs; support services; and the costs of fixed assets. Under an initiative known as Budgeting for Accountability, agencies will examine their budget account structures and work with their Appropriations Committees to revise them. In addition, we will propose legislation to require that the full accruing cost of pensions be reflected in future agency budgets, to help link program resources with the outputs and outcomes they generate.

Streamlining

A major tool to improve performance is streamlining, which involves reductions in not just the workforce but also in the red tape and processes that interfere with good customer service. The challenge is to create a smaller workforce and better performance at the same time.

Specifically, the task is to reduce the number of employees in areas where Government expends too much effort for too little contribution to the public good. That means the multiple layers of Government, large numbers of headquarters staff, and employees devoted primarily to micromanagement. No single streamlining plan fits all agencies; each must develop a plan to address its own needs.

Developing Streamlining Plans: The President established the President's Management Council (PMC), comprising the chief operating officers of Cabinet departments and several major agencies, and it has led efforts to help agencies develop and improve their streamlining plans. In the last year, the PMC enabled members to share their concerns as well as their "best practices" across the Government.

Consulting employees' unions as well, agencies worked to develop plans that focused on delivering services critical to their missions. Streamlining was an important element in this year's budget process; in reviewing the plans, OMB sought to ensure that agencies are aligning staffing levels with program requirements and anticipated funding levels, and that agencies are restructuring their workforces to improve customer service and performance.

Shrinking the Workforce: The Administration worked successfully for congressional passage of the Federal Workforce Restructuring Act of 1994. The Act will cut the Federal workforce by 272,900 full-time equivalent positions (FTEs) by 1999, making it the smallest since John Kennedy was President—a remarkable achievement in light of the huge increase in the population, Federal budget, and Federal roles and responsibilities since 1963. The PMC worked with Congress to help insure that the legislation enabled non-defense agencies, for the first time, to offer employee "buyouts"—the tool that private organizations have used to downsize quickly.

In 1994, the Federal workforce shrank by 102,000 FTEs, more than 37,000 of which were attributable to buyouts of up to $25,000 each. Generally, agencies avoided layoffs in making their reductions, and the Administration will continue to work to minimize layoffs.

Revamping Agency Operations—Major Successes: In using the opportunity of downsizing to overhaul their operations, several agencies stand out. They include the Departments of Agriculture, Labor, and the Interior; Customs Service; Internal Revenue Service; Federal Emergency Management Agency; Small Business Administration; and Social Security Administration.

The Agriculture Department (USDA) is restructuring along six mission lines. At headquarters, the Department cut the number of separate agencies and offices from 43 to 29 while consolidating its administrative services. A new Farm Service Agency will provide commodity price and income support, farm loans, and crop insurance. A new field structure, focused on one-stop shopping for USDA customers, will streamline the Agricultural Stabilization and Conservation Service, Farmers Home Administration, and Soil Conservation Service county offices to create new USDA Service Centers. The Department will cut the number of USDA field offices by 1,100 and, through 1999, reduce Federal employment by 13,500 FTEs and non-Federal county staffing by more than 1,000.

The Labor Department plans to close or consolidate many regional and field offices by 1999. The Employment Standards Administration Wage and Hour Division will downsize field locations from eight to five regions and from 58 to 45 districts. The Office of the American Workplace will reduce program offices by a third and regional offices by half. The Mine Safety and Health Administration (MSHA) will reshape its field structure by eliminating the sub-district managerial layer, redirecting staff to enforcement priorities, and giving more authority to MSHA inspectors. The Department will lower employment by 1,700 control positions, increase the supervisor's span of control from one for every five employees to about one for every nine, and cut the number of steps in its hiring process by over half. In addition, Labor cut the Occupational Safety and Health Administration field inspector manual from 329 to 102 pages, allowing inspectors to spend more time protecting workers and less on unproductive paperwork.

The Interior Department plans to cut headquarters staff by nearly half as part of an overall effort to cut Interior's FTE levels by 9 percent by 1999. Also at Interior, the Bureau of Reclamation, which largely has achieved its original mission, is shifting its emphasis from construction of water projects, such as major dams, to resource management. Reclamation also has successfully reorganized its top-heavy Denver office and transferred decision-making authority to the lowest possible levels within its regional, area, and field offices.

The Customs Service has launched a major reorganization that will cut headquarters personnel by a third and abolish seven regional offices and 45 district offices, replacing them with 20 Customs Management Centers and 5 Strategic Trade Centers. Customs also plans major changes in the way it does business in the next few years as it implements the Customs Modernization Act, designs and implements new systems for dealing with the public, and improves its targeting and strategic response to trade violations. To improve service, it plans to redeploy one-third of its headquarters positions, along with positions in its regions and districts, to 301 ports of entry.

The IRS has announced a major restructuring to improve service and increase voluntary compliance. This "new" IRS will take full advantage of information technology to give faster, more accurate service to customers, cut taxpayer expenses, and provide better-targeted and more productive tax enforcement. The agency plans to "right-size" its field structure, redeploying financial and human resource personnel to front-line operations wherever possible. The agency will consolidate its 55 telephone operations sites into 23 Customer Service Centers with on-line access to comprehensive tax data bases; this change will enable taxpayers to resolve many issues in connection with their tax accounts in a single call. The IRS also is restructuring headquarters and regional offices.

The Federal Emergency Management Agency (FEMA), which handles Federal disaster relief, has transformed itself from a much-criticized agency to one earning praise from those it serves. To better serve disaster victims, FEMA scrapped two management layers, cut the number of supervisors by a third, empowered employees, and increased the speed and responsiveness of services.

The Small Business Administration's (SBA) streamlining plan flows from the Administrator's performance agreement and the agency's business plan. SBA is moving personnel closer to its customers—that is, from headquarters and 10 regional offices to its district offices. Since September 1992, regional office staffing has fallen from 523 to 115—223 procurement and surety bond personnel have moved from the regions to district offices, and another 157 employees have voluntarily left headquarters and the regions to fill various jobs in district offices.

The Social Security Administration's (SSA) streamlining effort is designed to enable the agency to respond to the growth in its workload, particularly in disability claims processing, and target better service to key areas, such as improved telephone service and more continuing disability reviews. SSA seeks to restructure the workforce, automate to increase efficiency, and reengineer to improve service dramatically. Thus far, SSA has allocated 1,200 buyouts to meet staff reduction goals, and employed a team concept to overcome the traditional problems of boundaries and layers.

From the "how" of Government, we now turn to the more basic question of "what."

12. Reinventing the Federal Government—Phase II

12. REINVENTING THE FEDERAL GOVERNMENT—PHASE II

For all of our success to date, reinvention is no short-term challenge. Even the most successful businesses have needed years to overhaul their operations in order to compete in the new economy. The Federal Government, which dwarfs even the largest corporations in size, also will need to continually renew its processes.

As we move ahead, we are cognizant of one very obvious fact: The American people remain deeply dissatisfied with how their Government works. Consequently, we want to accelerate our reinvention efforts, move ahead more boldly, and ask even more fundamental questions about what the Federal Government does and how it can do it better.

While preparing this budget, the President asked his senior advisors as well as the departments and agencies for bold, creative, innovative, new ideas about how to deliver services and benefits to the American people. This marked the beginning of an exciting new era for Government. Cabinet secretaries, agency heads, and other Administration officials have begun to engage actively in the next stage of reinvention.

In the reviews that produced the five major restructurings in this budget, the Administration organized its ideas around a few basic themes:

Consolidation—The Federal Government has too many categorical programs, many of which are duplicative and inefficient. Whenever possible, the Administration will work to consolidate programs in order to improve performance.

Devolution—In some cases, State or local governments can perform more effectively than the Federal Government. The Administration will consolidate these programs into fewer, more results-oriented programs, giving States and localities more flexibility about how to spend the money and accountability for achieving results.

Privatization—Government need not perform some activities at all; the private sector can perform them at least as well, and at lower cost. The Administration will turn such functions over to the private sector or establish partnerships or contractual relationships to acquire the goods or services more efficiently.

Termination—Many programs, perhaps even whole agencies, have outlived their usefulness. The Administration plans to continue targeting such programs and agencies for termination.

These concepts were central to the President's restructuring proposals for three Cabinet departments and two other agencies, as described below. Table 12–1 summarizes the savings identified to date from Phase II of the reinventing Government initiative.

Department of Housing and Urban Development (HUD)

Since its birth in 1965, HUD has struggled to reconcile and integrate multiple missions. In 1994, the National Academy of Public Administration wrote, "the current overload of programs... saps HUD's resources, muddles priorities, fragments the Department's workforce, creates unmeetable expectations, and confuses communities."

HUD's restructuring builds on the reinvention that it began in 1993. The proposal will dramatically transform a department that was too attentive to process and "top-down" solutions, and too loyal to ineffective categorical programs, into one organized to achieve real results for communities and low-income persons.

HUD's restructuring is part of the Administration's broader effort to devolve responsibilities to States and localities within a framework of national goals. Over three years, it will:

Table 12–1. SAVINGS FROM REINVENTING GOVERNMENT—PHASE II

(Deficit reduction, in millions of dollars) [1]

	Total 1996–2000
Reinventing the Department of Housing and Urban Development	770
Reinventing the Department of Energy	14,121
Reinventing the Department of Transportation	6,435
Reinventing the General Services Administration [2]	1,400
Reinventing the Office of Personnel Management [2]	30
Subtotal, Major Agency Restructuring	22,757
Performance Partnerships:	
Consolidating 108 Public Heath Service activities into 16 grant categories	215
Consolidating up to 12 Environmental Protection Agency grants	96
Combining funding for 14 rural development loan and grant programs in the Department of Agriculture	16
Terminating the Interstate Commerce Commission	123
Terminating the Chemical Safety and Hazard Investigation Board	1
Eliminating Army Corps of Engineers local projects role	837
Reinventing the Bureau of Mines	140
Privatizing the Helium Program [3]	(16)
Expanding lease authority to the National Park Service	59
Privatizing the National Weather Service	40
Mandating a State bank examination fee	1,002
Targeting Impact Aid	194
Terminating low-priority Education programs	555
Relying on the private sector for NASA communication with spacecraft	179
Subtotal, Savings from Reinventing Government—Phase II	26,198
Canceling Highway Demonstration Projects (includes 1995 outlay savings)	290
Total, Savings from Reinventing Government (including 1995 outlay savings)	**26,488**

[1] Includes transfers to other agencies.
[2] Savings shown for GSA and OPM are government-wide savings.
[3] Amounts do not include estimates of discretionary savings resulting from Federal agencies being authorized to purchase refined helium in the private market.
Note: See Summary Table S–6 for additional detail on savings from reinventing Government.

- Consolidate HUD's 60 programs into three flexible, *performance-based funds;*
- *Transform public housing* into a system that works for people and communities; and
- Create an *entrepreneurial, Government-owned Federal Housing Administration (FHA) corporation* that increases home-ownership and affordable housing opportunities.

These reforms will create new "performance partnerships" (for more on such partnerships, see the "Performance Partnership" section of this Chapter) between HUD, State and local governments, the private sector, and community-based organizations. State and local governments can strike an historic bargain: far more flexibility in how they use Federal resources in exchange for accountability to the public for meeting ambitious goals. State and local governments will better serve their residents by organizing services and funding around public needs, not red-tape and prescriptive, process-oriented regulations. HUD's workforce will shrink by over 4,000 as a direct result; and local and State governments should achieve comparable administrative savings.

Consolidate HUD's 60 Programs into Three Flexible, Performance-Based Funds:

1. Certificates for Families and Individuals

HUD will continue to help low-income renters afford housing with Housing Certificates for Families and Individuals. This proposal will bring together all current assistance for public housing, privately-owned assisted housing, and Section 8 rental assistance.

Current residents of public housing and privately owned assisted housing projects will get certificates and the freedom to use them to help pay rent in the private market. The system of tying subsidies to units rather than families will end. However, the proposal will not force families from their residence; they will be able to use their certificate to stay where they are.

State and local governments will have the responsibility for administering housing certificates. If they choose to have them administered by others, they can contract with entities other than public housing authorities. Administrators will have the flexibility to structure the assistance to meet local needs, provided they meet specific conditions, including: adherence to income targeting; compliance with Federal fair housing laws; and attention to vulnerable populations including the homeless, disabled, people with HIV/AIDS, and the frail elderly.

Localities will agree on performance benchmarks for their certificate programs, consistent with national performance goals. These goals will encourage support for families who are working to achieve self-sufficiency. A locality might, for example, focus a portion of assistance on AFDC recipients making the transition from welfare to work. A bonus pool will provide extra allocations to eligible high performers.

2. Affordable Housing Funds

A comprehensive housing policy should aim to provide a sufficient supply of decent quality housing affordable to low-income households, including populations with special needs not met by the private market. To support these local efforts, the Administration will consolidate the Home Investment Partnerships program (HOME), housing for the elderly and persons with disabilities, housing counseling, Homeownership and Opportunity for People Everywhere (HOPE), Lead-Based Paint Hazard Reduction Grants, and the National Homeownership Fund into a single, flexible Affordable Housing Funds (AHF) program.

AHF will give localities and States formula grants to support locally-designed housing production, rehabilitation, and homeownership initiatives. As with today's HOME program, 60 percent of formula funds will go to localities and 40 percent to States—with a special national set-aside for Native Americans. Jurisdictions would distribute a portion of funds to community-based organizations.

In their required consolidated plans, jurisdictions will detail how they would use their funds, consistent with national and locally established performance goals. Local performance benchmarks would be similar to those listed above for the Certificates program. A pool of bonus funding will reward high performers.

3. Community Opportunity Funds

A third performance-based program, Community Opportunity Funds (COF), will give States and localities flexible funding to help revitalize and renew distressed communities. COF will consolidate the Community Development Block Grant (CDBG) and the Economic Development Initiative.

COF will distribute funds largely by formula to local and State governments, with a national set-aside for Native Americans. As in CDBG, 70 percent of funds will go to localities and 30 percent to States. Jurisdictions will use their grants for a wide range of activities, such as assistance to community-based organizations for neighborhood revitalization; business loans to entrepreneurs to build shopping or commercial centers in distressed communities; "mobility to work" efforts that link residents in distressed communities with job opportunities elsewhere in the metropolitan area; and the environmental cleanup of "brownfield sites" to prepare for economic or housing development.

As with the other two performance funds, COF will provide a strong framework of results-oriented accountability. Communities will develop their own economic development strategies to increase opportunity for low-income residents. Performance measures, consistent with the program's statutory goals, might include the number of jobs created for low- and moderate-income residents or the amount of private resources leveraged. As with the other funds, a portion of COF funds would go to a bonus pool to reward high-performing jurisdictions.

Transforming Public Housing: Public housing, which began 60 years ago as transitional housing for working people who fell on hard times, over the years has become a trap for the poorest of the poor. While it has worked in many communities, the rigid, top-down, command-and-control system that evolved has condemned tens of thousands of people to living in squalid conditions—at a very high cost in wasted lives, ruined communities, and squandered Federal dollars. In many communities, the program also has encouraged the concentration of poor residents in specific sections, thereby exacerbating the difficulties confronting these residents.

An effort to end public housing as we know it, HUD's new approach to housing assistance for families and individuals will allow current public housing residents to stay where they are or move to rental units in the private market. It will break the monopoly that housing authorities enjoy over Federal housing resources by focusing on residents rather than "units," and by requiring housing authorities to compete for low-income residents with other providers of affordable housing. It will change the landscape of distressed inner-city neighborhoods by speeding the demolition of uninhabitable and non-viable public housing projects, and ending support for the construction of "public housing" developments exclusively occupied by the very poor.

At the outset, HUD will consolidate all public housing funding into two funds: one for operations and one for capital. In 1996, HUD will:

- Deregulate over 3,000 high-performing but mostly smaller housing authorities, allowing them to operate flexibly within a framework of national low-income housing goals and objectives, according to specific, agreed-upon performance indicators;
- Break up the worst, large, troubled housing authorities, divesting parts of their portfolios to non-profit owners and managers, including residents, where appropriate;
- Target resources to jurisdictions with the greatest need for capital reinvestments, in order to allow them to improve their housing stock for competition with private-market providers;
- Demolish thousands of severely deteriorated, mostly vacant units for which no market demand exists, and provide for site restoration and the relocation of any displaced residents using portable certificates; and
- Work aggressively with State and local governments and other entities to improve the operations of over 100 troubled housing authorities, thereby improving their longer-term prospects as low-income housing providers. HUD would move the 10-15 most troubled entities through a two-year, receiver-like process, divesting them of their properties and management control.

By 1998, no housing authority will receive funds directly from HUD. States and localities will be able to replace non-performing housing authorities with community-based and other organizations. By 1998, all formerly project-based public housing subsidies will be completely portable.

Creating a New FHA: In its 60 years, FHA has provided access to mortgage credit for 23 million working American homeowners, many of them first-time homebuyers, and has been a source of decent, affordable housing for at least 2.5 million renters. But in the last decade, while the private housing finance market grew more sophisticated, innovative, and efficient at delivering capital to housing, FHA's slow-moving bureaucracy lagged behind. Not only have fewer and fewer young American families been able to use FHA insurance to buy a home, the need to subsidize financially and physically troubled FHA-insured multifamily properties has become a growing drain on taxpayers.

The new, entrepreneurial FHA will have two principal objectives:

- To make homeownership more affordable for first-time homebuyers, residents of inner cities, and other groups now underserved by the private market by encouraging public-private partnerships and leveraging private capital; and
- To encourage a strong multifamily market by restructuring the debt on the Nation's portfolio of assisted housing, subjecting projects to competitive market forces, and improving their financial management and the conditions where people live, and by instituting timely and thorough underwriting of new projects.

The new FHA Corporation will consolidate FHA's insurance programs into two general insurance authorities: single-family and multifamily. FHA's corporate charter will include performance goals that define FHA's public purposes and ensure its safety and soundness. The HUD Secretary will set specific performance targets based on the charter.

FHA will develop new lines of business that exploit market incentives and modern mortgage finance technology. These will include innovative, risk-sharing partnerships with well-capitalized financial entities—Government-Sponsored Enterprises, the Federal Home Loan Banks, private mortgage insurance companies, State and local housing finance agencies, and community-based organizations. The Federal Government will judge FHA's performance by how well its products serve the diverse needs that the market does not meet.

Within FHA, a group will be responsible for restructuring, project by project, the debt on assisted housing to reflect current market values; this will allow HUD to stop providing excessive rent subsidies to keep projects alive. Finally, FHA will reduce its portfolio of defaulted loans. Plans call for the sale at auction of $4 billion in single-family loans in 1996, and over $6 billion in multifamily mortgages over two years. These auctions will improve the Government's financial situation. Because the private sector can manage the loans more efficiently, sale proceeds will exceed the value to the Government of continuing to hold and service the loans.

Department of Energy (DOE)

The Administration seeks to realign DOE's activities to reflect changing world conditions and changing demands on the Nation's science and technology infrastructure. It also seeks to help DOE pursue its mandate more efficiently through contract and procurement reforms, fewer layers of management and supervision, and an end to redundancies among program offices. The Administration proposes to privatize or eliminate assets and programs no longer critical to the Nation's needs.

The result will be a department that is more focused on five key missions: energy resources, science and technology, national security, environment quality, and industrial competitiveness—and one that is more streamlined and efficient in its operations. The proposal will save $14.1 billion—$8.4 billion in program savings, and $5.7 billion from selling assets over the next five years. (See Table 12–2.)

The steps described below build upon the Secretary's actions of the last two years, such as freezing contractor salaries, moving to reduce the costs of environmental cleanup, and reforming contracting practices. Now, a task force of DOE employees is conducting an intensive four-month review of activities, seeking to target for elimination redundant or unnecessary work and management layers. This team will enable DOE to overhaul or eliminate lower priority programs and identify work that could be better performed elsewhere, inside DOE or out. Also, an independent, high-level task force is examining the future of the national laboratories and plans to issue its recommendations to the Secretary and Administration in February. The Administration plans to incorporate the task force recommendations into DOE's restructuring.

Table 12–2. DEPARTMENT OF ENERGY REINVENTING GOVERNMENT—PHASE II SAVINGS

(Outlays, in billions of dollars)

	Total 1996–2000
Programmatic Reforms:	
Environmental Management	4.4
Applied Research Programs	1.2
Cost Cuts and Reorganization	2.8
Subtotal, programmatic reforms	**8.4**
Asset Sales:	
Naval Petroleum Reserve	1.6
PMAs:	
Alaska	0.1
Southeastern	0.5
Southwestern	0.5
Western	2.6
Natural and Enriched Uranium	0.4
Subtotal, asset sales	**5.7**
Total, Department of Energy savings	**14.1**

Privatize Power Marketing Administrations (PMAs): The Administration plans to privatize four PMAs—Alaska Power Administration (APA), Southeastern Power Marketing Administration, Southwestern Power Marketing Administration, and Western Power Marketing Administration, raising about $3.7 billion. The Administration proposed the sale of APA in last year's budget, but Congress did not enact legislation to permit the sale. We propose to sell the other three PMAs in subsequent years, and we will develop a specific proposal for each sale after active and careful consultation with Congress and other interested parties. The proposal will provide customer protection from significant rate increases.

Also, the Administration plans to submit legislation to turn the Bonneville Power Administration (BPA), another PMA, into a Government corporation, thus allowing BPA to operate more efficiently.

Privatize Naval Petroleum Reserves: The Administration proposes to privatize the Elk Hills, Calif. oil and gas fields in 1997, producing $1.6 billion in net sales receipts. The Government established Elk Hills in the early part of this century and it no longer serves a strategic purpose for the Navy, which now purchases almost all of its oil on the open market. During any future periods of national emergency, the Nation's Strategic Petroleum Reserve would provide the Navy with an ample supply of oil. Elk Hills is an anachronism, and the Federal Government no longer needs to own and operate such oil and gas fields.

Sell Excess Uranium: The Administration proposes to sell some of the inventory of natural and enriched uranium that DOE now controls, including highly enriched uranium (HEU) that the Nuclear Weapons Council has deemed unnecessary to our national security needs. Before the sale, the HEU would be blended with natural uranium; thus, the material sold would be useful only as an energy source for commercial reactors, not as weapons grade material. Allowing for the costs of blending, processing, safeguarding, and transportation, the material has an estimated net value of at least

$400 million. The Administration will propose legislation to authorize DOE to transfer ownership of this material to the U.S. Enrichment Corporation (USEC) which, in turn, could then market the fuel to utilities that operate nuclear power plants. The Administration also proposes to sell the USEC to the private sector.

Improve Efficiencies in Nuclear Waste Cleanup and Management: In the next five years, the DOE Environmental Management program will save an estimated $4.4 billion. The Administration proposes to achieve these savings by:

- Using site-based budgeting to give DOE management and regulators maximum flexibility to allocate resources among site priorities. DOE will continue to administer funding for technology development, the management of special nuclear materials, and certain other initiatives on a centralized basis;
- Improving resource allocation and increasing funding certainty for State and Federal regulators, by adopting multi-year funding of up to three years for sites where DOE and the other parties can agree on a specific plan and budget for that period;
- Working closely with Environmental Protection Agency and State regulators to prioritize budgets at each site—a procedure called for by the new three-year budget approach;
- Reauthorizing Superfund, particularly the land-use provisions in the Administration's Superfund proposal that are critical to these savings; and
- Generating a 20-percent productivity increase by improving management and cost controls, reducing overhead costs, and implementing more efficient practices in contractor oversight and contract reform;

Reduce Costs in DOE's Applied Research Programs: DOE conducts applied research on a wide array of energy technologies for fossil fuels, nuclear fusion and fission, solar and renewable energy, and conservation technologies—much of it in DOE's laboratories, often in conjunction with the private sector. The Administration proposes to require more non-Federal cost-sharing of applied R&D, to better target DOE's spending on efforts for which the private sector predicts the highest potential payoffs. DOE also will curtail or eliminate lower-priority programs or those thought to have achieved their program objectives. In the latter category, DOE will not commit to more new starts for clean coal projects. This proposal would save an estimated $1.2 billion in outlays over five years.

Reduce Costs of Doing Business at DOE and its Laboratories: While DOE is already operating more efficiently, it still can generate substantial cost savings in how it and its laboratories do business. The Administration proposes to cut costs by shedding lower priority work, eliminating duplication, and reducing layers of supervision and management. The DOE Strategic Alignment Initiative, scheduled for completion in April 1995, will amplify these plans. The Initiative will incorporate the work of the Galvin Task Force on the future of the national laboratories. Subsequently, DOE will choose the specific nature of cost reductions and steps. These steps will include a proposal for the private sector to develop and operate energy cogeneration plants at DOE facilities. These efforts would save an estimated $2.8 billion over five years.

Department of Transportation (DOT)

DOT's rigid structure has restricted funds to specific modes of transportation, making investments less efficient. Transportation policy is unnecessarily centralized in Washington and lacks incentives for business-like management. Finally, personnel and procurement regulations inhibit the Federal Government's ability to provide services, such as air traffic control, efficiently .

To increase State and local flexibility to invest in infrastructure, and to enable the Federal Government to provide more efficient services, DOT will consolidate programs that the Government now funds through separate modal grants into three programs: (1) a unified transportation allocation to States and localities, (2) a discretionary grant, and (3) State Infrastructure Banks. The restructuring also will transfer the Federal Aviation

162-000 O - 95 - 6

Administration's (FAA) air traffic control services to a Government corporation. (See Chart 12–1.)

The organization of the new DOT will reflect the effort to align transportation infrastructure programs more sensibly among Federal, State and local governments. Transportation programs at the Federal level will focus on enhancing interstate commerce, safety, environmental concerns, national defense, and technological progress, such as Intelligent Transportation System activities.

Unified Transportation Grants: The grants will increase State and local flexibility by consolidating 30 categorical grants into a $10 billion program for transportation infrastructure. The grants will fund a broad range of transportation investments, including construction and repair of highways, mass transit, rail, and airport facilities. The Government will honor previous commitments for specific construction projects in all modes, such as transit and airport construction projects. Highway fuel taxes and aviation ticket taxes will finance this program of formula grants to States and localities from a unified transportation trust fund.

State Infrastructure Banks (SIBs): The proposal provides $2 billion to capitalize new SIBs, enabling jurisdictions to more easily leverage public and private resources for infrastructure and encourage more business-like strategies for financing the national transportation system. SIBs would reduce the need for general taxpayer financing to support infrastructure, and would focus on projects likelier to be self-supporting. The SIBs would increase States' flexibility in using Federal funds; they could fund any type of transportation infrastructure.

Discretionary Grants: The proposal also provides $1 billion in discretionary grants to finance projects of special regional or

Chart 12-1. DOING MORE WITH LESS: REINVENTING THE DEPARTMENT OF TRANSPORTATION

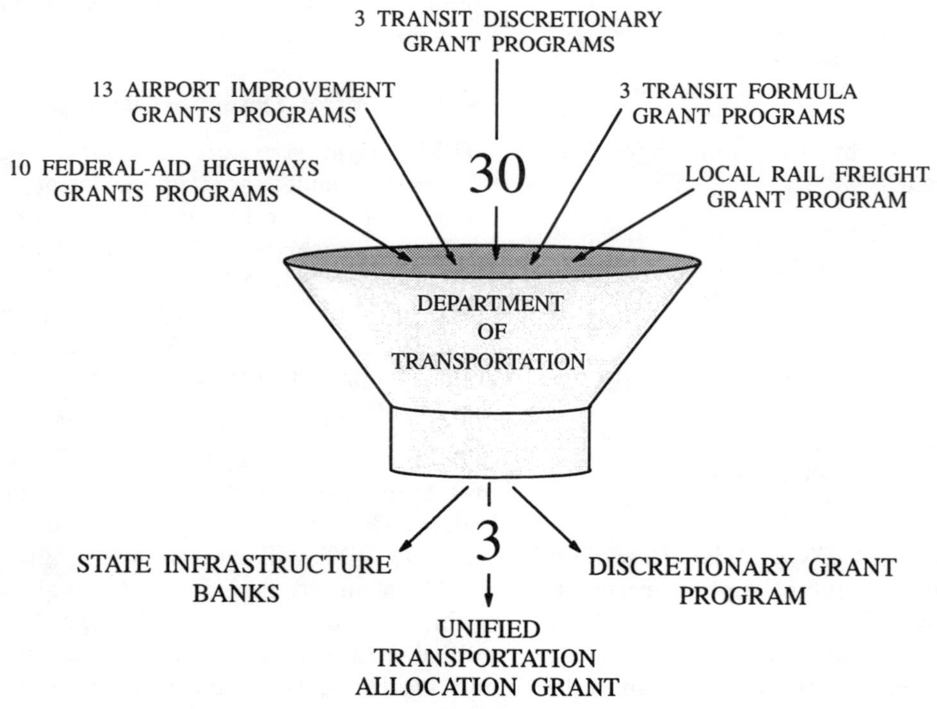

national significance that are not addressed through other mechanisms.

U.S. Air Traffic Services Corporation: A reinvented DOT no longer will perform functions for which the Federal Government is not best suited. The core Federal role in aviation is to regulate safety and encourage infrastructure investment. It need not include the day-to-day operations of the air traffic control system.

As a result, the Administration will propose legislation to transfer the FAA's air traffic control services to a wholly-owned Government Air Traffic Services Corporation. The corporation will be free of most Federal procurement, personnel, and budget restrictions, thereby giving it the flexibility to speed modernization of the air traffic system and improve its operating efficiency. This proposal implements recommendations of the National Performance Review, the President's Airline Commission, and others.

The corporation will be fully self-supporting through its own user fees, interest on those fees, and debt financing. The corporation's Board of Directors will adopt a business plan which will determine corporation spending, borrowing (subject to the Secretary's disapproval), and fees. In conjunction with the corporation, the Administration will propose that residual FAA functions, some of which are now funded out of general revenues, be fully fee-funded in 1997.

The FAA, or a successor, will retain safety and regulatory functions, overseeing the corporation as well as the air carriers, aircraft manufacturers, and other aviation entities that it already regulates.

In another effort to improve performance and cut costs, the budget proposes a significant reform of the National Passenger Rail Corporation (AMTRAK). Although the budget proposes $750 million for Amtrak in 1996, the request assumes that Amtrak will adopt substantial reform that year to become more commercially viable, and to reduce its future reliance on Federal operating subsidies.

General Services Administration (GSA)

The Government created GSA in 1949 to: (1) develop policies that would help agencies perform administrative services cost-effectively; and (2) provide selected administrative services directly to departments and agencies, taking advantage of economies of scale and avoiding duplication.

In today's market, we must challenge assumptions about economies of scale and the cost-effectiveness of our traditional means of providing goods and services.

Since its creation, GSA has focused more on its role as a central service provider and less on its policy and oversight functions. Effective exercise of GSA's policy and oversight functions could influence over $120 billion of government-wide administrative costs, far more than the $12 billion in administration services that flow through GSA programs.

This budget proposes to transform GSA into a policy and oversight organization for government-wide administrative services, except personnel. The proposal will increase agencies' accountability for results, encourage innovation and better government-wide planning, and assure responsible asset management. GSA will continue to provide services only where careful review demonstrates that that will not compromise its policy role and will serve the Government's interests.

GSA will accelerate its reinvention efforts by asking of each of its service functions, "Why can't the private sector provide this service or activity more effectively?" The reinvention process will place the burden of proof on Government to explain why it is in the business at all. If Government must perform the function, the question will be, "Why should it be done centrally; why can't other agencies do it just as well?"

The Administration will subject GSA's operations to market-driven analyses to determine the commercial feasibility and relative cost-effectiveness of several options for change—including privatization, decentralization, transfer, and termination. Where privatization is the preferred option, private experts will help to develop business plans to guide the restructuring of specific GSA services into viable businesses for sale to employees (as Employee Stock Option Plans, or ESOPs) or to private firms.

Presumably, all other service functions (and associated FTE) that are not sold will be transferred to the agencies, unless GSA's continued operation of the function would best serve the public's interest. The proposal will encourage agencies to franchise these activities to avoid duplication, promote competition, and maximize efficiency, and agencies will get the authority to acquire and manage services and assets. Over the next two to three years, we estimate that GSA's FTE will fall by more than half.

The plan will safeguard employees by giving them the opportunity to participate in the ownership of businesses, placement in service contracts, or transfers to other agencies. Employee unions will help to design and implement the details of this reinvention.

Office of Personnel Management (OPM)

The President proposes to transform OPM from an agency that primarily provides services into one that oversees a competitive system for providing most training and background investigations to agencies. We will grant agencies the authority to perform these functions themselves, or procure them from the private sector or from privatized OPM business units. This proposal would prompt the privatizing of entire OPM business units.

OPM will continue providing leadership and oversight of the 100-year-old civil service system, and ensure that the Government continues to operate with an open and competitive, merit-based, non-political civil service. OPM will provide core personnel policy and oversight functions in the areas of pay, employee benefits, labor relations policy, integrity of the merit system, hiring, and executive resources. OPM will continue to administer the Federal civilian retirement program, and oversee private sector operation of the Federal Employee Health Benefits Program and the Federal Employees Group Life Insurance Program.

All told, these changes will cut OPM's FTE workforce by about a third. Agencies may find more savings as they discover the most cost-effective ways to meet their training and investigations needs.

"Performance Partnerships"

Some of the proposals described above reflect a new concept—"performance partnerships" with States and local governments. The proposals will consolidate funding streams and eliminate overlapping authorities, create funding incentives to reward desirable results, and reduce micromanagement and wasteful paperwork. They also will begin to focus programs on outcomes and outputs, treating them as the basic measure of success. The partnerships will seek to empower communities to make their own decisions about how to address their needs, and to be held accountable for results.

With this in mind, the Administration is proposing a variety of other consolidations to provide greater flexibility and increase accountability:

- The fourth element of the President's Middle Class Bill of Rights would combine 70 education and job training programs into one system; it would provide substantial flexibility for State and local governments to develop comprehensive workforce development systems to meet their particular needs, empower individuals to choose their own training, and hold providers accountable for program performance, including job placements.
- The Public Health Service, a part of the Health and Human Services Department, proposes to consolidate 108 activities into 16 grant categories and build performance incentives into the authorizing legislation.
- The Environmental Protection Agency proposes to allow States to consolidate up to 12 media-specific grants (e.g., air, water, hazardous waste), enabling States to target resources toward their most pressing priorities while still abiding by Federal law.
- The Agriculture Department (USDA) proposes to combine funding for 14 rural development loan and grant programs and authorize USDA's State Directors to allocate funds between these programs. These Directors will work with State and local governments, other community-based organizations, and the State Rural Development Councils—whose members include

State, local, and Tribal governments, and private sector representatives—to direct funds to each State's highest rural economic development priorities. USDA's proposal will include performance measures and performance incentives.

For a picture of how the facets of these proposals relate to one another, see Table 12–3 "Performance Partnerships."

The proposals highlighted in Table 12–3 will save additional FTE (and associated administrative costs) beyond levels required by the 1994 Federal Workforce Restructuring Act. The Administration expects other FTE savings in the future as part of Phase II of the National Performance Review.

Table 12–3. "PERFORMANCE PARTNERSHIPS"

	Department of Agriculture: Rural Development Programs	Departments of Education and Labor: G.I. Bill for America's Workers	Department of Health and Human Services: Public Health Service	Department of Housing and Urban Development	Department of Transportation	Environmental Protection Agency
Number of programs consolidated.	14 existing USDA rural development loan and grant programs remain separate, but USDA State Directors would be authorized to shift funds between existing programs.	70 programs to be consolidated into one system.	108 programs to be consolidated into 16 categories.	60 statutory programs to be consolidated into 3 programs. The first stage, in 1996, consolidates into eight.	30 categorical programs would be consolidated into three broad allocations: a unified grant, State Infrastructure Banks, and a discretionary grant program.	Up to 12 media-specific State grants would be consolidated at the request of the State, although the underlying EPA programs would remain separate.
Performance incentives.	Up to 10 percent of the annual formula allocation would be withheld and awarded based on superior performance.	Increased flexibility for States and localities to use resources in ways that best meet their needs; providers that fail to meet standards or fail the market test of choice would be eliminated.	Increased funding for grantees that develop, report and show progress toward performance goals.	To keep full spending discretion, localities must meet their performance targets. Up to 10 percent of formula allocation would be withheld and distributed on performance.	Increased flexibility for recipients to use funds in ways that best meet their needs; fewer Federal requirements; ability to leverage Federal funds to generate increased total investment.	Incentives would be negotiated in work plans between EPA and the States, and could include performance-based funding and various means to encourage additional States to accept delegation of EPA programs.
Improved flexibility.	More flexibility at State level on funding priorities set by USDA in consultation with State Rural Development Councils, and State and local governments.	States and localities can design service delivery systems as they see fit to accomplish results.	Small categorical grants replaced with larger, flexible pools of funds. Grantees can decide how funds to be used.	Would remove spending restrictions from current law and replace process compliance with accountability for results.	States and localities given broader discretion to choose projects, fewer restrictions by type of mode (e.g., highways vs. transit); Infrastructure Banks allow closer aligning of expected returns with level of subsidy provided, more flexible use of contributions from State/local revenues and private fees.	Participating States would transfer funds between programs, based on agreements with EPA, without further action by Congress.

Table 12–3. "PERFORMANCE PARTNERSHIPS"—Continued

	Department of Agriculture: Rural Development Programs	Departments of Education and Labor: G.I. Bill for America's Workers	Department of Health and Human Services: Public Health Service	Department of Housing and Urban Development	Department of Transportation	Environmental Protection Agency
Improved accountability.	State-by-State work plans (embodying performance measures and accountability) would be negotiated between USDA headquarters and the USDA State Directors (in consultation with State Rural Development Councils, and State and local governments.	Improved information on jobs, labor markets, and institutional performance will empower individuals to exercise informed choice and not use poor schools; tougher quality standards on providers based on results, system goals for services and outcomes, and published performance.	Strong State planning and reporting process. Grantees will report on outcomes, and progress on broad-based public health goals as well as specific results achieved with PHS funds.	Would consolidate programs into performance-based formula grants which are accompanied by Federal conditions. Grant recipients will be accountable for locally-developed performance benchmarks.	Performance reporting will be simplified under a few large programs; Infrastructure Banks will require substantial contributions of resources from States and localities, user fee financing will assure market tests of investment decisions.	The State work plans would include an evaluation component to maintain EPA oversight while improving environmental results.
Administrative savings.	$42 million over five years with accompanying reductions in headquarters FTEs.	$31 million over five years for Federal oversight FTEs. States use savings from their program flexibility redesign for additional services.	$15 million in 1996 for 230 oversight FTEs with FTE savings more than doubling over four years for cumulative savings totalling $218 million.	$770 million over five years. Phased-in estimates of HUD administering (1) grant versus direct Federal programs; and (2) fewer grants versus the multiplicity of HUD's current grant structure.	Consolidation of grant programs would reduce grant administration costs.	Lower EPA processing costs for consolidated grants, and lower EPA implementation costs in States that accept more delegation of EPA programs.
1996 BA for Performance Partnership grants.	$988 million	$14.1 billion (Discretionary BA)	$3 billion	$26 billion	$25 billion	$634 million
Locus of decision-making.	State Directors (coordinating with the State Rural Development Councils, and State and local governments) would be able to shift resources among existing programs to meet the specific needs of each State.	Most program and administrative design responsibilities are shifted from Federal to State and local levels. Individuals empowered to select training.	Five of 16 program groups will be State grant programs, where decision-making would be left to States. States will be eligible for most of the other 11 grant clusters.	Decision-making shifted to States, cities, and communities.	Fewer Federal constraints on use of funds shifts decision-making to States and localities; Infrastructure Bank decisions reflect market viability of investments.	Participating States would be able to make funding decisions based on their priorities and to simplify their administrative procedures.

How is performance measured?

Performance measures and performance targets will be developed in consultation with State and local governments and other grantees. Performance measures will include input, output, and outcome measures for the populations served.

Restructuring Programs: Other Efforts

In a host of other areas, the Administration proposes to eliminate some programs, turn some functions over to the private sector, and better focus some activities on their proper Federal roles. The savings from these proposals also will help to finance the President's middle-class tax cut and keep the budget deficit under control.

Terminating the Interstate Commerce Commission (ICC): The budget proposes to phase out the ICC, thus removing Government controls that place costly and unnecessary burdens on industry. The proposal would eliminate the bulk of the ICC's activities, including most remaining motor carrier regulatory functions and some rail functions that have outlived their usefulness. It would transfer the remaining needed activities to the Departments of Transportation and Justice and the Federal Trade Commission. The proposal would save $123 million by 2000.

Terminating the Chemical Safety and Hazard Investigation Board: The budget would not fund the Chemical Safety and Hazard Investigation Board, created by the 1990 Clean Air Act amendments and never in operation. Its purpose, as an independent agency, is to investigate chemical accidents and provide recommendations for preventing further incidents. The board's important functions will be accomplished through increased funding for the Environmental Protection Agency, Occupational Safety and Health Administration (OSHA), and National Transportation Highway Safety Board. The board lacks authority to respond to accidental releases or develop regulations required for prevention. Its elimination would in no way compromise emergency responses to chemical accidents, subsequent investigations, or the issuance of regulations to prevent accidents. In fact, the increased funding for EPA and OSHA will provide more dollars for investigations, without an additional and costly bureaucracy.

Eliminating Army Corps of Engineers Local Projects Role: The budget proposes to focus the Corps' role on water projects that provide national benefits—commercial inland and deep-draft navigation, interstate waterways, multi-State flood control, environmental restoration, operation and maintenance of such projects, and emergency responses to floods and hurricanes. It would phase out the Corps' role on smaller projects that primarily provide local benefits (beach erosion, local flood protection, and construction and maintenance of recreational harbors), and are best left to State and local governments. The proposal would save an estimated $837 million by 2000.

Reinventing the Bureau of Mines: The budget proposes to refocus the Bureau of Mines on priority functions, such as environmental remediation and health and safety. The proposal would cut costs by streamlining bureau functions and consolidating field research centers into four "Centers of Excellence" that, in turn, would focus research efforts on environmental remediation, pollution prevention and control, health and safety, and materials research partnerships. The proposal also would save money by eliminating programs that States or the private sector would more appropriately conduct. The proposal would save an estimated $140 million by 2000.

Privatizing the Helium Program: The budget proposes that the Federal Government privatize the Federal helium program by selling the Bureau of Mines production facility in Amarillo, Texas or entering a long-term lease with a private entity. In addition, the Federal Government would begin to liquidate its crude helium reserve through annual sales to the private sector, or through the offer of contract sales in the open market. We also will seek authority to cancel the Federal debt that the helium program owes to the Treasury, a step which will not affect the deficit. By now, the Helium Conservation Program, authorized in 1960, has met its objectives. A U.S. private-sector market for crude and refined helium is well established, as are private sector suppliers of the gas. In addition, the number of known reserves of helium are far greater than 30 years ago. The proposal would save an estimated $16 million by 2000.

Expanding Lease Authority to the National Park Service: In an step that mirrors Interior Secretary Bruce Babbitt's entrepreneurial management initiative, the budget proposes to expand Federal authority to place unused National Park System (NPS) facilities under long-term leases or special concessions contracts. This proposal will build on and expand authorities like those recently provided for leasing the Letterman/LAIR complex at the Presidio in California. The proposal will allow for the productive use of now-unused NPS facilities in a business-like fashion, while maintaining the integrity of the parks. Of the estimated $80 million that the proposal would raise by 2000, half would go to "enhancing" the National Park System, the other half to the Treasury.

Privatizing the National Weather Service: The budget proposes to privatize portions of the National Weather Service—specifically, specialized weather services provided to aviation, marine, and agricultural communities. The Service will continue to provide basic warnings and forecasts to the public. This proposal permits a more active role for the commercial weather services industry, which already provides specialized weather information for aviation, marine, and agricultural users, and will save an estimated $40 million through 2000.

Mandating a State Bank Examination fee: The Office of Controller of the Currency and Office of Thrift Supervision regularly examine and assess fees to national banks and savings associations, respectively, based on their asset size. By requiring that the Federal Deposit Insurance Corp. and Federal Reserve assess fees on State-chartered banks and bank holding companies, this proposal would level the playing field among the banking regulators and eliminate an unwarranted subsidy to State banks; the proposal would exempt banks with assets of less than $100 million. Currently, the FDIC and Federal Reserve can assess fees on State-chartered banks and bank holding companies for their examinations, but do not have to. This proposal would raise $1 billion by 2000.

Targeting Impact Aid: Impact Aid makes grants to school districts for revenues deemed lost by virtue of the presence of Federal lands or facilities. The budget proposes to reduce spending by concentrating resources on compensating the two groups who represent the most lost revenue: children who live on Indian lands and children of members of the uniformed services who live on Federal property. The proposal saves an estimated $194 million by 2000.

Terminating Low-Priority Education Programs: The budget proposes to terminate 10 low-priority Education Department programs, saving $555 million through 2000. The programs provide subsidies to certain colleges, and finance a number of special scholarship and fellowship programs. Pell grants, student loans, and other student aid provide over $30 billion a year for postsecondary education, far outweighing any contribution that these small programs may make. The budget also proposes to terminate or phase out another 31 programs, saving $3.5 million through 2000.

Relying on the Private Sector for NASA communication with spacecraft: NASA's Space Network is the primary tracking, communications, and data acquisition system for low-Earth-orbiting spacecraft, including the Space Shuttle, International Space Station, and many unmanned, robotics spacecraft. For that network, NASA has begun the procurement of three replacement satellites and associated ground stations. NASA does not necessarily need to own the satellite system itself, however. To increase the efficiency of these systems, the budget proposes to let commercial firms provide part, perhaps a major part, of these services.

Canceling Highway Demonstration Projects: The budget proposes to cancel $400 million in 1995 funding for highway demonstration projects, thus reducing earmarked funding for projects that often do not meet the most critical needs of States and regions to which they are awarded.

What Next?

Phase II of our efforts to reinvent Government will build on these proposals as the Administration examines the other Federal departments and agencies, programs and functions. Most fundamentally, the Administration wants to sort out responsibilities among the Federal, State, and local levels of government, and between Government and the private sector. The departments and agencies themselves, and through the President's Management Council, will take the lead, working with NPR, OMB, and the White House policy councils.

At each agency, the process will feature a "bottom-up review," modeled on the Defense Department's effort. The Vice President has asked agencies to form teams that will consider the following questions:

1. If your agency were eliminated, who would pursue its goals—other agencies, States and localities, the private sector, or no one?
2. If we must retain a Federal role to accomplish certain goals of national importance,

how can we reach them in a way that improves customer service?

3. What do your customers—not just interest groups—think about the possible eliminations or changes?

Nor will the Administration forget the critical role of Federal workers. As the Vice President put it:

> The President and I believe absolutely in Federal workers. But these workers face uncertain times. We need to involve them in sorting out tomorrow's Government. We need to continue to cut red tape and empower them to get results. And we need to relate them in a way that values their past contribution and their role as the most important resource in the Government of the future.

The Administration views recruiting and retaining a quality workforce as a high priority, especially as we seek to streamline agencies and redefine the very role of Government. The Administration's pay policy strives to strike a balance between providing pay levels that make Government competitive with the private sector and raising pay so much that we have to resort to big cuts in employment, thus jeopardizing service.

The budget provides an estimated $1.9 billion for 1996 civilian pay raises. This funding would allow for a 2.4 percent across-the-board increase, effective next January 1. As in last year's budget, the Administration makes no assumption about how to distribute the pay raise between locality pay and a national schedule adjustment. Continuing a process that worked well last year, the Administration will consult with employee organizations and others before deciding. The Defense Department's budget includes $1.0 billion for a January 1996 across-the-board military pay raise of 2.4 percent.

13. Other Reforms

13. OTHER REFORMS

On its own or with Congress, the Administration has launched a host of other, related initiatives to make Government work better.

The Administration opened up the once-secret regulatory process to public scrutiny. It has sought to sensibly balance the public interest against the inherent dangers of unduly burdening any particular segment. In addition, the Administration has innovatively sought to use new technologies, such as information technology and electronic benefits transfer, to better deliver service to the American people.

Working with Congress, the Administration overhauled the archaic Federal procurement system. No longer will taxpayers have to endure tales about the excessive prices that Government pays for even the simplest items; Government now will buy from local retailers.

REFORMING THE REGULATORY PROCESS

Federal regulations are not *inherently* good or bad. They have the potential to be either. Well-chosen and carefully crafted, they can protect consumers from dangerous products and ensure that Americans have information to make informed choices. Such regulations can limit pollution, protect workers, discourage unfair business practices, and contribute in many other ways to a safer, healthier, more productive, and more equitable society. Excessive or poorly designed, however, regulations can cause confusion and delay, generate unreasonable compliance costs, retard innovation, reduce productivity, and accidentally distort private incentives.

Many people hear about particularly contentious regulations, such as those governing the spotted owl. But each year, under Democratic and Republican administrations, the *Federal Register* has published thousands of regulations that administer, maintain, modify, and update various Federal programs. If, for example, Federal officials offer grants and loans to students, small businesses, and others, it is generally regulations that explain who is eligible, how they can apply, and how Government will make selections.

Many regulations (or rules) grow out of statutory mandates, and require changes in the law to modify them. Others come at the discretion of agencies. Some regulations are critically important or highly visible (e.g., setting the safety criteria for airlines or nuclear power plants); some are relatively trivial (e.g., establishing the times that a draw bridge may be raised or lowered); and many are routine or administrative (e.g., allocating spectrum allowances for radio stations).

This Administration has worked hard, and successfully, to reform the regulatory process. Its goal is not only to scrap outdated, unjustified or unnecessarily costly rules. It is also to improve the quality of necessary regulations in order to serve the public good. In short, the Administration's goal has been to make rules more sensible.

Executive Order No. 12866

To this end, President Clinton issued Executive Order No. 12866 on September 30, 1993. It was designed to return the Government to the task at hand—to design sensible rules that improve the quality of life without imposing unnecessary costs, and do so in an efficient, fair, and accountable manner for the American people.

The Order articulates the President's regulatory philosophy and his view of how the regulatory process should work. Most fundamentally:

> The American people deserve a regulatory system that works for them, not against them: a regulatory system that protects and improves their health, safety, environment, and well-being and improves the performance of the economy without imposing unacceptable or unreasonable costs on society; regulatory policies that recognize that the private sector and private markets are the best engine for economic growth; regulatory approaches that respect the role of State, local, and Tribal governments; and regulations that are effective, consistent, sensible, and understandable.

Within the Executive Branch, the Order encourages OMB and the agencies to work together. With respect to the public, it stresses openness and early involvement in the rulemaking process by all interested parties, particularly State, local, and Tribal governments. It also stresses sound, timely analysis; early, frequent consultation; streamlined procedures; and reduced delay.

A year into our efforts, we have made great strides in regulatory reform. Coordination among agencies has improved dramatically; agencies now routinely consult with State, local, and Tribal governments on regulatory matters. Currently, we are working closely with the new Congress on legislation to address the problem of unfunded Federal mandates on other levels of governments.

The Administration also recognized the disproportionate burden that regulations may place on small businesses. At a recent Small Business Forum, departments and agencies pledged to act upon small business recommendations to simplify regulations and reduce unnecessary burdens.

More Sensible Regulations

In the past year, the Executive Order has helped generate "smarter," more sensible regulations. Described below are a number of instances:

- The Order calls for good data and good analysis to inform (not just justify) decisionmaking. The National Highway Traffic Safety Administration's (NHTSA) rulemaking on side-impact protection for light trucks grew out of a regulatory analysis that NHTSA's staff prepared to help guide decisionmaking.

- In the wake of Hurricane Andrew, the Department of Housing and Urban Development (HUD) moved to upgrade the safety of mobile homes. To help shape its policy choices and stimulate discussion among the stakeholders, HUD used its draft regulatory impact analysis to set out the trade-offs—and the data on which they are based—for public scrutiny.

- The Order stressed the importance of focused (or tailored) requirements and performance-based (or flexible) provisions—not across-the-board, mechanical, command-and-control approaches. The Environmental Protection Agency applied these principles to its rules on lead abatement. Its initial proposal was heavily prescriptive, required extensive paperwork, and did not distinguish between potentially high-risk and low-risk lead hazards. It then re-wrote the proposal to reduce its prescriptive character, adopt performance standards, re-focus requirements on the more important sources of health risk, and gave State and local governments more flexibility to establish lead abatement programs.

- The Department of Transportation's (DOT) alcohol and drug testing rules show how a department can approach a complex issue analytically and significantly improve its rule—reducing burdens without reducing safety—by applying the principles of the Order. In its final rule, DOT adopted a performance-based approach for determining the rate of random drug and alcohol testing. DOT also simplified and streamlined its requirements for reporting drug testing data, introducing sampling techniques and reducing the burden of information collection requirements on employers.

- In preparing its final rule to govern asbestos in the workplace, the Occupational Safety and Health Administration (OSHA) made substantial changes to improve its clarity and ensure as much flexibility as possible in process-specific standards. Thus, while the proposal might have required extensive controls for any maintenance work conducted around asbestos-containing materials, OSHA's final rule required such controls only in connection with a physical disturbance of materials.

- In designing rules for the Mammography Quality Standards Act, the Food and Drug Administration made the standards less burdensome on mammography facilities—which are nearly all small businesses—by incorporating existing industry standards as much as possible.

Lookbacks

People who must comply with Federal rules often say that what exasperates them is the accumulated burden of rules in effect—many of which appear unnecessary, redundant, outdated, or downright stupid. In response, the Order provides that agencies will review existing regulations to ensure that they are still timely, compatible, and effective, and that they do not impose unneeded burdens.

This "lookback" plants the seeds for a fundamental re-engineering of entire regulatory systems in agencies, many of which have stayed essentially unchanged for 30–50 years. Such re-engineering requires that an agency have a dedicated team with broad understanding of the program's objectives, expertise in the intricacies of the regulatory program, an intimate knowledge of the stakeholders, and resourcefulness, tenacity, resolve, and support.

The following are examples of successful lookbacks:

- Work is underway at the Commerce Department's Bureau of Export Administration to rewrite the Export Administration Regulations. This comprehensive review is designed to simplify and clarify this long, complex body of regulations that establishes licensing regimes for dual-use products—those that may have both commercial and military applications—and make the regulations more user-friendly. Promulgated first in 1949, the rules were designed to implement that year's Export Control Act. They have not been fully overhauled since then.
- The National Highway Transportation Safety Board has an institutionalized lookback program. Its rules deal primarily with automobile and light truck safety. Regularly, the agency picks rules to review, evaluating not only their effectiveness and whether any provisions are unnecessary, unduly burdensome, or otherwise need change, but also the initial analysis itself—whether the predicted costs and benefits have been realized, and, if not, why not.

While we have made much progress, we plan to focus increased attention this year on improving the regulatory system. We will work with agencies to ensure that our improvements translate into better regulatory decisions. We will focus on the adequacy of data underlying a regulatory action—the depth of analysis, particularly the evalution of alternatives to traditional regulation.

We also will reach out to those affected by a regulation, both those whom we expect to benefit and those we expect to face burdens, to assure that the proposal is likely to achieve its objective in the most cost-effective, least-intrusive way. At the same time, under the leadership of Vice President Gore, we will expore alternatives to reaching our regulatory goals in more innovative, creative ways.

EMPLOYING THE BENEFITS OF INFORMATION TECHNOLOGY

We recognize the potential of advanced communications and information technology to create jobs, improve how the Government provides services, and expand the benefits of the Nation's health and education systems. The U.S. already has the world's most advanced information infrastructure, mainly developed by the private sector.

To maintain our advantage, the private sector must continue to lead—with support from Government. The Administration has initiated various programs to promote private investment, encourage critical new technologies, improve Government efficiency and service delivery, and provide greater access to Government information.

1. Promoting Private Sector Investments: A key role for Government is to encourage fair competition in rapidly evolving industries, and ensure that all citizens have confidence in these new technologies.

Remove barriers to competition in telecommunications. The Administration supports legislation to remove legal and regulatory impediments to competition in the telecommunications industry, while safeguarding the public interest. With more competition in the cable and telephone industries, Americans will enjoy better service, more options, and lower costs, while

U.S. industry remains globally competitive.

Protect Intellectual Property Rights. The digital era promises to bring movies, music, books, games, and more to the home and workplace. Yet, writers and artists will be unwilling to make their creations available electronically unless they are sure to receive royalty payments and be protected against copyright infringement. The Administration plans to support legislation to amend the Copyright Act, in order to update intellectual property law for the electronic era.

Protect individual privacy. Americans are increasingly concerned about their personal privacy as more and more personal information is collected, stored, and distributed. While they once viewed the Federal Government as the principal threat, they are now equally concerned about commercial entities, which collect a wide variety of information about peoples' activities, such as their purchasing habits. The Administration is developing principles to serve as the basis for protecting personal information—to address the rights and responsibilities of the subjects, users, and collectors of data.

2. Encouraging New Technologies: To be effective in a global economy, the U.S. must retain its technological lead. Government has a limited role to play in stimulating technological development in order to improve national economic competitiveness, education, health care, and the environment.

Demonstrate innovative uses of technology. The USDA, the National Telecommunications and Information Administration, and the National Science Foundation are giving matching grants to enable hospitals, schools, universities, and local governments to demonstrate new ways of using advanced communications technology in the public interest. This technology is supporting a child-abuse prevention network that will let prevention professionals across the Nation communicate; a project that will collect and share environmental data about the Great Lakes with scientists and students across the Midwest; and a project that will enable tuberculosis patients to receive coordinated care at home through laptop computers.

Support research and development. Working with industry and academia, the High Performance Computing and Communications Program brings together 10 departments and agencies to support research and development of the most advanced supercomputers and networks. (See Chapter 7, "Investing in Science and Technology.") As part of the Defense Department's Technology Reinvestment Program, the Department will invest in information technologies that are applicable to defense missions but that also can help to develop commercial products. Technology also can forestall serious violations of privacy or property rights that could occur in an electronic environment. The National Institute of Standards and Technology is supporting the use of commercial technologies to enable participants to know with whom they are communicating, that information they receive comes from whom it purports to, and that information stored or transmitted has not been altered.

3. Improving Government Efficiency and Service Delivery: For a Government to "work better and cost less," it must increasingly use information technology to accomplish its missions.

Establish an International Trade Data System. Forty agencies collect and use trade data for analysis and import-export processing. We propose to integrate information about shippers, bills of lading, types of cargo, exports, imports, and duties, into a cohesive system. We are scrapping duplicative import forms and speeding the clearance of imports. Our proposal will speed cargo clearance and make the information more usable to business.

Consolidate data processing centers and networks. We are cutting the number of data facilities that process administrative services, such as payroll, and eliminating Government's duplicative communications links.

Expand electronic mail and service delivery. The Administration is developing the capacity for interagency electronic mail, permitting both effective communications within agencies and faster response to citizen inquiries. Eventually, we will reach directly to the citizen, by electronically delivering Social Security and Veterans benefits, receiving and sending tax forms electronically, and buying and selling goods over a computer. (See the sections below on electronic commerce and electronic benefits transfer.)

Establish a National Law Enforcement/ Public Safety Network. This Network will improve coordination and communication among Federal, State, and local law enforcement and public safety agencies, thus improving the response to emergency situations while cutting costs.

4. Providing Greater Access to Government Information: Government information is an important national resource, whether it is crop statistics, weather reports, economic indicators, facts about Government programs, or our Nation's laws. Information technology can provide inexpensive, quick access to citizens when and where they want it.

Promote dissemination of Government Information. The Commerce Department's "FedWorld" provides information to Americans on everything from Federal jobs to the President's weekly radio addresses to setting up a small business. FedWorld, which the National Technical Information Service operates, connects users to more than 200 Government bulletin boards and Internet servers. Over 100,000 registered users now make over 3,000 contacts daily. Also, every public document delivered to the White House press corps is published electronically over FedWorld and other Internet access sites. The Clinton Administration has published over 3,000 Federal documents electronically.

Create A National Environmental Data Index. Many Federal agencies collect environmental data and related information, including the Interior Department, Environmental Protection Agency, National Aeronautics and Space Administration, and National Oceanic and Atmospheric Administration. This information is useful to scientists, teachers, students, and the public. However, finding the right information is often very difficult. We propose to create an index that will make it easier to collect, find, and use national and world data.

Improve agency management of information resources. OMB has taken the first steps to establish a Government Information Locator Service, or GILS, to help the public locate and access all kinds of information across the Federal Government. GILS will be accessible through the Internet or by modem to identify, describe, and locate public information.

REFORMING THE PROCUREMENT SYSTEM

One important way to reinvent Government is to reform the Federal procurement system. Guided by a patchwork of cumbersome laws and regulations, the system accounts for about $200 billion in expenditures each year. Due to its complexity and its failure to let procurement officials use good business judgment, the system does not provide timely, economical support to Government programs and taxpayers.

Many problems arose from the multitude of procurement laws that the Government enacted over several decades, as its programs expanded and grew more complex. Taken separately, many of these laws sought desirable public policy goals. Others came in response to procurement "horror stories." Taken together, however, they made the system very complex, cumbersome, and expensive to administer.

In response, the Administration proposed legislation to reform the procurement system, leading to the Federal Acquisition Streamlining Act of 1994 (FASA). We expect to implement the streamlining provisions through regulation well before the maximum time allowed by the law, so we can start saving money as soon as possible.

Many agencies have participated in a new concept called "pledging," in which their leaders voluntarily pledge specific acquisitions to use as test beds for new, innovative acquisition concepts and techniques. In 1994, agencies signed five such pledges.

The major streamlining reforms and cost-saving measures underway are:

Electronic Commerce: The Administration is establishing a Government-wide electronic contracting system. Initial transactions began early in 1995. The program will transform a labor-intensive, paper-based acquisition environment to a more cost-effective one that will enable the Government to cut its acquisition processing costs, expedite transactions, receive lower prices from increased competition, and expand small business participation. Government-wide, we expect to save $123 million a year by implementing these changes for purchases of under $100,000.

To simplify the process of doing business with Government, we are working to present a single face to Government's suppliers. Any small business with a personal computer and modem will be able to learn about, and submit bids for, many Government purchases anywhere in the country; a business in El Paso, Boise, or Buffalo will be able to bid on business from a Government office in Washington.

Simplified Acquisition Threshold: The new, simplified acquisition threshold that FASA established will allow for simplified purchase procedures and shorter solicitation periods for purchases of up to $50,000—that is, 18 million separate purchases a year. FASA also set a threshold of $2,500 under which agencies may use the Government purchase card to buy from readily available sources, such as a local retailer. Agencies complete over nine million of these transactions each year. This provision will allow program officials to avoid contracting offices and saves $54 in administrative costs for each transaction.

Commercial Products: All too often, the Government has bought items specified to its unique requirements and forced suppliers to adapt to special demands. One of our priorities is to increase the Government's reliance on the commercial marketplace, enabling agencies to more easily buy commercial items. We are writing regulations to implement the new statutory preference for commercial items. They will broadly define commercial items to include products customarily purchased by the general public, certain commercial services, and products based on evolving technology which may not now be available in the commercial marketplace—as long as they are available to meet the Government's needs.

The Government will save money by eliminating from its programs costly items designed to meet unique, often outdated specifications. Additional savings will come from a substantial cut in Government's demand for extensive contractor cost or pricing data, and the elimination of many Government-unique statutory requirements from prime contracts and subcontracts for commercial items. For instance, the Defense Department is working aggressively to eliminate the inappropriate use of military specifications ("milspecs") and military standards that unnecessarily add to the cost of what the Government buys; it is moving toward relying on performance criteria or commercial standards in its contracts.

Past Performance in Contract Award: A contractor's past performance is a key indicator of future performance. We plan to make past performance a key factor in awarding competitively-negotiated contracts. Our initiative will promote competition and improve the quality and timeliness of Government's products and services. It also will save money. Better contractor performance will reduce the need for Government resources devoted to contract administration. In January 1994, 20 agencies pledged 61 contracts, with an estimated value of $2.6 billion, to a past performance pilot test program.

One major Defense Department contracting activity that used this approach has demonstrated its effectiveness. That activity experienced a cut in the value of contracts terminated for default (resulting from contractor deficiencies) in one major program area from over $133 million in 1990 to under $14 million in 1994.

Performance Based Service Contracting: Federal agencies spend over $100 billion a year on contracts for services, which have been plagued for cost overruns, delays, and performance problems. We have sought to move service contracting in a results-oriented direction, through which the Government clearly states the results it expects to achieve for taxpayers from its service contracts.

Performance-based service contracting entails defining the work in measurable, mission-related terms. With this approach, the Government should enjoy better performance and lower costs; it should pave the way for converting many costs reimbursement contracts to fixed price contacts, and it will reduce Government micromanagement. On October 13, 26 agencies volunteered to convert 87 recurring contract requirements (worth $1.2 billion) to this approach in the next year. In 1994, the new contractor at the Energy Department's Idaho National Energy Laboratory committed to $751 million in savings over five years, based on adoption of a performance-based approach.

Alternative Dispute Resolution (ADR): ADR will cut the cost and time needed to resolve contract disputes through litigation. Agencies have used ADR techniques to resolve, in days, claims and disputes that might have taken years through courts or boards of contract appeals. Of particular interest is the technique known as partnering, shown to be highly effectively in preventing disputes before they arise. Thirty-one agencies have pledged greater use of ADR techniques in contract administration and in the resolution of existing disputes for contracts with a total value of over $2.7 billion.

Better Government-Industry Communications: Complex legal restrictions on the release of sensitive procurement information have fueled an acquisition climate in which the legitimate, necessary exchange of information is often unduly restricted. Competitors for Government contracts need enough information to make intelligent business decisions with which to prepare contract proposals. Also, agencies must be able to get enough information to conduct meaningful market research, enabling them to consider the latest, best thing that industry can order to meet the Government's needs.

In response, the Administration is conducting a project to help agencies improve their communication practices through all phases of the acquisition cycle. Twenty-two agencies agreed to work together to find and eliminate obstacles to better communicating their needs to industry. In addition, 19 of the agencies made specific pledges to use the most effective communication practices in a total of 22 acquisitions, valued at over $10 billion.

EXPANDING THE USE OF ELECTRONIC BENEFITS TRANSFER (EBT)

Each year, Federal and State programs deliver nearly $500 billion in cash payments, benefits, and food assistance to individuals. While the programs deliver most of these benefits on paper, with checks or vouchers, modern banking technology such as direct deposit can transfer funds into individual bank accounts electronically. Electronic Benefit Transfer (EBT) can deliver food assistance and cash benefits to individuals who lack bank accounts.

EBT offers several advantages over paper checks and coupons. It cuts the costs of printing, mailing, and processing checks, coupons, and vouchers; cuts the number of lost and stolen check claims; creates an electronic audit trail for each transaction, making it easier to detect abuse, such as the illegal use of food stamps; reduces or eliminates check cashing fees for clients; and gives recipients better security and protection against theft of benefits.

Clients will get their Government assistance by using the Benefit Security Card, which will function much like any other credit or debt card. An interagency EBT task force will work with commercial providers to make EBT compatible with the current systems of retail and financial services electronic fund transfer. The Government will not build a separate electronic system; it will use the existing electronic commerce networks.

Currently, 38 States are working to implement EBT. Six now operate pilot systems. Maryland is operating a State-wide EBT system that delivers about $55 million a month in food stamps, AFDC, child support, and general assistance to over 200,000 recipients; clients can access their benefits anywhere in the State by using a single card. Texas will finish implementing its State-wide system in 1995, making it the largest in the Nation. In 1996, eight southern States plan to launch the first multi-State, multi-program system that uses a single card. Also that year, the Treasury Department will enter into agreements with financial institutions to provide nation-wide EBT support services to the Federal and State governments.

SUMMARY TABLES

Budget Aggregates

BUDGET AGGREGATES

Table S–1. OUTLAYS, RECEIPTS, AND DEFICIT SUMMARY
(In billions of dollars)

Category	1994 Actual	Estimate 1995	1996	1997	1998	1999	2000
Outlays:							
Discretionary:							
National defense	282.2	272.1	262.2	257.5	255.1	260.2	268.3
International	20.8	22.1	21.0	20.9	20.4	20.2	20.1
Domestic	242.6	259.6	265.8	269.3	264.9	262.8	261.1
Subtotal, discretionary	545.6	553.8	549.0	547.7	540.4	543.3	549.6
Mandatory:							
Programmatic:							
Social security	316.9	333.7	351.4	369.9	389.4	409.8	430.7
Medicare and Medicaid	223.9	242.8	270.6	295.9	322.4	349.6	380.5
Means-tested entitlements (except Medicaid)	88.4	96.1	101.1	110.3	116.5	122.6	132.1
Deposit insurance	–7.6	–12.3	–6.3	–1.4	1.2	–1.3	–3.5
Other	128.6	131.9	131.4	134.2	135.4	140.5	146.1
Subtotal, programmatic	750.2	792.2	848.2	909.0	964.9	1,021.2	1,085.9
Undistributed offsetting receipts	–37.8	–41.4	–42.1	–42.4	–43.0	–39.4	–40.0
Subtotal, mandatory	712.4	750.9	806.2	866.6	921.9	981.8	1,045.9
Net interest	203.0	234.2	257.0	270.4	282.9	297.1	309.9
Subtotal, mandatory and net interest	915.4	985.1	1,063.2	1,137.0	1,204.8	1,278.9	1,355.8
Total outlays	**1,460.9**	**1,538.9**	**1,612.1**	**1,684.7**	**1,745.2**	**1,822.2**	**1,905.3**
Receipts	**1,257.7**	**1,346.4**	**1,415.5**	**1,471.6**	**1,548.8**	**1,624.7**	**1,710.9**
Deficit	**203.2**	**192.5**	**196.7**	**213.1**	**196.4**	**197.4**	**194.4**

162-000 O - 95 - 7

Table S–2. SUMMARY OF RECEIPTS, OUTLAYS, AND SURPLUSES OR DEFICITS (–): 1789–2000

(in millions of dollars)

Year	Total			On-Budget			Off-Budget		
	Receipts	Outlays	Surplus or Deficit (–)	Receipts	Outlays	Surplus or Deficit (–)	Receipts	Outlays	Surplus or Deficit (–)
1789–1849	1,160	1,090	70	1,160	1,090	70			
1850–1900	14,462	15,453	–991	14,462	15,453	–991			
1901	588	525	63	588	525	63			
1902	562	485	77	562	485	77			
1903	562	517	45	562	517	45			
1904	541	584	–43	541	584	–43			
1905	544	567	–23	544	567	–23			
1906	595	570	25	595	570	25			
1907	666	579	87	666	579	87			
1908	602	659	–57	602	659	–57			
1909	604	694	–89	604	694	–89			
1910	676	694	–18	676	694	–18			
1911	702	691	11	702	691	11			
1912	693	690	3	693	690	3			
1913	714	715	–*	714	715	–*			
1914	725	726	–*	725	726	–*			
1915	683	746	–63	683	746	–63			
1916	761	713	48	761	713	48			
1917	1,101	1,954	–853	1,101	1,954	–853			
1918	3,645	12,677	–9,032	3,645	12,677	–9,032			
1919	5,130	18,493	–13,363	5,130	18,493	–13,363			
1920	6,649	6,358	291	6,649	6,358	291			
1921	5,571	5,062	509	5,571	5,062	509			
1922	4,026	3,289	736	4,026	3,289	736			
1923	3,853	3,140	713	3,853	3,140	713			
1924	3,871	2,908	963	3,871	2,908	963			
1925	3,641	2,924	717	3,641	2,924	717			
1926	3,795	2,930	865	3,795	2,930	865			
1927	4,013	2,857	1,155	4,013	2,857	1,155			
1928	3,900	2,961	939	3,900	2,961	939			
1929	3,862	3,127	734	3,862	3,127	734			
1930	4,058	3,320	738	4,058	3,320	738			
1931	3,116	3,577	–462	3,116	3,577	–462			
1932	1,924	4,659	–2,735	1,924	4,659	–2,735			
1933	1,997	4,598	–2,602	1,997	4,598	–2,602			
1934	2,955	6,541	–3,586	2,955	6,541	–3,586			
1935	3,609	6,412	–2,803	3,609	6,412	–2,803			
1936	3,923	8,228	–4,304	3,923	8,228	–4,304			
1937	5,387	7,580	–2,193	5,122	7,582	–2,460	265	–2	267
1938	6,751	6,840	–89	6,364	6,850	–486	387	–10	397
1939	6,295	9,141	–2,846	5,792	9,154	–3,362	503	–13	516
1940	6,548	9,468	–2,920	5,998	9,482	–3,484	550	–14	564
1941	8,712	13,653	–4,941	8,024	13,618	–5,594	688	35	653
1942	14,634	35,137	–20,503	13,738	35,071	–21,333	896	66	830
1943	24,001	78,555	–54,554	22,871	78,466	–55,595	1,130	89	1,041
1944	43,747	91,304	–47,557	42,455	91,190	–48,735	1,292	114	1,178
1945	45,159	92,712	–47,553	43,849	92,569	–48,720	1,310	143	1,167
1946	39,296	55,232	–15,936	38,057	55,022	–16,964	1,238	210	1,028
1947	38,514	34,496	4,018	37,055	34,193	2,861	1,459	303	1,157
1948	41,560	29,764	11,796	39,944	29,396	10,548	1,616	368	1,248
1949	39,415	38,835	580	37,724	38,408	–684	1,690	427	1,263
1950	39,443	42,562	–3,119	37,336	42,038	–4,702	2,106	524	1,583
1951	51,616	45,514	6,102	48,496	44,237	4,259	3,120	1,277	1,843
1952	66,167	67,686	–1,519	62,573	65,956	–3,383	3,594	1,730	1,864
1953	69,608	76,101	–6,493	65,511	73,771	–8,259	4,097	2,330	1,766
1954	69,701	70,855	–1,154	65,112	67,943	–2,831	4,589	2,912	1,677

* $500 thousand or less.

Table S–2. SUMMARY OF RECEIPTS, OUTLAYS, AND SURPLUSES OR DEFICITS (–): 1789–2000—Continued

(in millions of dollars)

Year	Total			On-Budget			Off-Budget		
	Receipts	Outlays	Surplus or Deficit (–)	Receipts	Outlays	Surplus or Deficit (–)	Receipts	Outlays	Surplus or Deficit (–)
1955	65,451	68,444	–2,993	60,370	64,461	–4,091	5,081	3,983	1,098
1956	74,587	70,640	3,947	68,162	65,668	2,494	6,425	4,972	1,452
1957	79,990	76,578	3,412	73,201	70,562	2,639	6,789	6,016	773
1958	79,636	82,405	–2,769	71,587	74,902	–3,315	8,049	7,503	546
1959	79,249	92,098	–12,849	70,953	83,102	–12,149	8,296	8,996	–700
1960	92,492	92,191	301	81,851	81,341	510	10,641	10,850	–209
1961	94,388	97,723	–3,335	82,279	86,046	–3,766	12,109	11,677	431
1962	99,676	106,821	–7,146	87,405	93,286	–5,881	12,271	13,535	–1,265
1963	106,560	111,316	–4,756	92,385	96,352	–3,966	14,175	14,964	–789
1964	112,613	118,528	–5,915	96,248	102,794	–6,546	16,366	15,734	632
1965	116,817	118,228	–1,411	100,094	101,699	–1,605	16,723	16,529	194
1966	130,835	134,532	–3,698	111,749	114,817	–3,068	19,085	19,715	–630
1967	148,822	157,464	–8,643	124,420	137,040	–12,620	24,401	20,424	3,978
1968	152,973	178,134	–25,161	128,056	155,798	–27,742	24,917	22,336	2,581
1969	186,882	183,640	3,242	157,928	158,436	–507	28,953	25,204	3,749
1970	192,807	195,649	–2,842	159,348	168,042	–8,694	33,459	27,607	5,852
1971	187,139	210,172	–23,033	151,294	177,346	–26,052	35,845	32,826	3,019
1972	207,309	230,681	–23,373	167,402	193,824	–26,423	39,907	36,857	3,050
1973	230,799	245,707	–14,908	184,715	200,118	–15,403	46,084	45,589	495
1974	263,224	269,359	–6,135	209,299	217,270	–7,971	53,925	52,089	1,836
1975	279,090	332,332	–53,242	216,633	271,892	–55,260	62,458	60,440	2,018
1976	298,060	371,792	–73,732	231,671	302,183	–70,512	66,389	69,609	–3,220
TQ	81,232	95,975	–14,744	63,216	76,555	–13,339	18,016	19,421	–1,405
1977	355,559	409,218	–53,659	278,741	328,502	–49,760	76,817	80,716	–3,899
1978	399,561	458,746	–59,186	314,169	369,089	–54,920	85,391	89,657	–4,266
1979	463,302	504,032	–40,729	365,309	404,054	–38,745	97,994	99,978	–1,984
1980	517,112	590,947	–73,835	403,903	476,618	–72,715	113,209	114,329	–1,120
1981	599,272	678,249	–78,976	469,097	543,053	–73,956	130,176	135,196	–5,020
1982	617,766	745,755	–127,989	474,299	594,351	–120,052	143,467	151,404	–7,937
1983	600,562	808,380	–207,818	453,242	661,272	–208,030	147,320	147,108	212
1984	666,457	851,846	–185,388	500,382	686,032	–185,650	166,075	165,813	262
1985	734,057	946,391	–212,334	547,886	769,584	–221,698	186,171	176,807	9,363
1986	769,091	990,336	–221,245	568,862	806,838	–237,976	200,228	183,498	16,731
1987	854,143	1,003,911	–149,769	640,741	810,079	–169,339	213,402	193,832	19,570
1988	908,954	1,064,140	–155,187	667,463	861,449	–193,986	241,491	202,691	38,800
1989	990,691	1,143,172	–152,481	727,026	932,261	–205,235	263,666	210,911	52,754
1990	1,031,321	1,252,705	–221,384	749,666	1,027,640	–277,974	281,656	225,065	56,590
1991	1,054,272	1,323,441	–269,169	760,388	1,081,754	–321,367	293,885	241,687	52,198
1992	1,090,453	1,380,856	–290,403	788,027	1,128,518	–340,490	302,426	252,339	50,087
1993	1,153,535	1,408,675	–255,140	841,601	1,142,088	–300,487	311,934	266,587	45,347
1994	1,257,745	1,460,914	–203,169	922,719	1,181,542	–258,823	335,026	279,372	55,654
1995 estimate	1,346,414	1,538,920	–192,506	995,158	1,246,936	–251,778	351,256	291,984	59,272
1996 estimate	1,415,456	1,612,128	–196,671	1,045,095	1,307,105	–262,010	370,361	305,023	65,338
1997 estimate	1,471,618	1,684,709	–213,091	1,083,607	1,368,142	–284,534	388,011	316,567	71,444
1998 estimate	1,548,809	1,745,185	–196,376	1,140,846	1,415,596	–274,750	407,963	329,589	78,374
1999 estimate	1,624,734	1,822,180	–197,446	1,195,796	1,479,121	–283,326	428,938	343,059	85,879
2000 estimate	1,710,912	1,905,338	–194,426	1,259,982	1,548,618	–288,636	450,930	356,720	94,210

1996 Budget Proposals

1996 BUDGET PROPOSALS

Table S–3. SUMMARY OF BUDGET PROPOSALS

(Deficit impact, in billions of dollars)

	Estimate						Total, 1995–2000
	1995	1996	1997	1998	1999	2000	
Proposals subject to pay-as-you-go:							
Mandatory programs:							
REGO II	....	–0.6	–3.2	–3.0	1.0	0.9	–4.8
Other	....	–0.7	–3.2	–3.3	–7.1	–9.6	–23.9
Subtotal, mandatory (see Table S–5 for detail)	....	–1.3	–6.3	–6.3	–6.1	–8.7	–28.7
Revenues:							
REGO II	....	–0.1	–0.1	–0.1	–0.1	–0.1	–0.4
Middle class tax cut and empowerment zones	0.1	3.9	11.9	12.5	15.2	19.8	63.3
Other	–0.1	–1.0	–1.6	–1.8	–2.0	–2.2	–8.6
Subtotal, revenues (see Table S–6 for detail)	–*	3.0	10.3	10.7	13.2	17.6	54.7
Subtotal, mandatory and revenues	–*	1.6	4.0	4.4	7.1	9.0	26.0
Discretionary:							
REGO II (see Table S–6 for detail)	....	–0.7	–4.0	–5.0	–5.6	–5.6	–20.9
Other (see Table S–4 for detail)	....	–5.1	–4.4	–11.8	–24.1	–35.0	–80.5
Subtotal, discretionary [1]	....	–5.8	–8.5	–16.8	–29.7	–40.6	–101.4
Total, pay-as-you-go	–*	–4.1	–4.5	–12.5	–22.6	–31.6	–75.4
Proposals not subject to pay-as-you-go:							
Employee retirement contributions (effect of pay raise):							
Employer share	....	0.2	0.4	0.7	1.0	1.3	3.5
Employee share	....	0.1	0.2	0.3	0.4	0.5	1.3
Discretionary	–0.3	–0.1	....	....	....	....	–0.4
Other proposals (largely credit program interest)	*	–0.3	–0.2	–0.3	–0.4	–0.6	–1.8
Debt service	–*	–0.2	–0.4	–1.0	–2.2	–4.1	–7.9
Total, not subject to pay-as-you-go	–0.3	–0.3	–0.1	–0.4	–1.3	–2.9	–5.3
Total, all proposals	**–0.3**	**–4.5**	**–4.6**	**–12.8**	**–23.9**	**–34.5**	**–80.6**

* Less than $50 million.

[1] The Administration proposes to reduce the existing 1996 through 1998 discretionary caps by these amounts. Consistent with the scorekeeping provisions of the Budget Enforcement Act, this reduction in the caps will be scored for pay-as-you-go purposes.

Table S–4. PROPOSED DISCRETIONARY SPENDING RELATIVE TO THE CAPS

(In billions of dollars)

	1996		1997		1998		1999		2000	
	BA	OL	BA	OL	BA	OL	BA	OL	BA	OL
Caps:										
End-of-session caps [1]	518.6	549.6	527.6	548.1	530.1	547.3	537.5	555.8	537.5	555.8
Adjustments for:										
Inflation [2]	3.0	1.8	7.2	5.1	11.5	8.9	20.3	17.2	37.1	34.4
Emergencies and other	–*	3.4	0.1	3.0	*	1.0	*	*	*	*
Transportation budget authority	24.8	....	25.6	....	26.4	....	27.2	....	28.1	....
Adjusted caps	546.5	554.9	560.6	556.2	568.0	557.2	585.0	573.0	602.7	590.2
Proposed levels:										
Discretionary proposals other than the Department of Defense	290.8	298.0	285.2	300.9	292.1	295.4	281.5	292.9	279.1	290.9
Department of Defense	246.7	251.0	243.5	246.8	250.5	245.0	257.1	250.4	266.9	258.7
Total discretionary proposals	537.5	549.0	528.7	547.7	542.6	540.4	538.6	543.3	546.0	549.6
Discretionary proposals compared to caps	**–9.0**	**–5.9**	**–31.9**	**–8.5**	**–25.4**	**–16.8**	**–46.4**	**–29.7**	**–56.7**	**–40.6**
Savings in the President's Budget:										
Reinventing Government—Phase II	–3.5	–0.7	–3.8	–4.0	–5.3	–5.0	–9.8	–5.6	–11.3	–5.6
Other savings	–5.5	–5.1	–28.0	–4.4	–20.1	–11.8	–36.6	–24.1	–45.3	–35.0
Memorandum:										
Exon-Grassley savings in the 1994 Congressional Budget Resolution	–4.0	–5.4	–10.7	–2.4	–4.1	–0.5	....	....	....	....

* Less than $50 million.

[1] The end-of-session caps for 1999 and 2000 were calculated using the 1998 caps after adjustments for inflation and Exon-Grassley.

[2] The inflation adjustments for 1996 through 1998 are the result of applying the provisions of Sec. 251(b)(l)(B)(iii) of the Budget Enforcement Act of 1990, as amended, to the discretionary caps for those years. The adjustments shown for 1999 and 2000 are the result of extending the 1998 caps into those years and adjusting them for inflation with an across-the-board increase in budget authority and outlays of 3 percent per year.

Total savings from discretionary proposals, 1996–2000:	*Outlays*
Reinventing Government—Phase II	–20.9
Other savings	–80.5
Total savings	–101.4

Table S–5. MANDATORY PAY-AS-YOU-GO PROPOSALS

(Outlays, in millions of dollars)

	Estimate 1995	1996	1997	1998	1999	2000	Total, 1995–2000
Agriculture:							
Recover costs for oversight of marketing agreements and orders	....	–9	–10	–10	–10	–10	–49
Reduce spending on farm programs	....	....	....	–500	–500	–500	–1,500
Department of Commerce:							
Expand fisheries management program	....	–10	–10	–10	–10	–10	–50
Increase fisheries management and fund Columbia River hatcheries from Bonneville Power Administration (BPA)	....	9	22	23	24	24	102
Department of Defense-Civil:							
Shift military retirement cost-of-living adjustment to April, consistent with timing for civilians	....	385	....	....	....	....	385
Department of Education:							
Eliminate the mandatory appropriation under the Smith-Hughes Act of 1918	....	–1	–6	–7	–7	–7	–28
Accelerate shift to direct student loans	....	–299	–745	–1,006	–949	–1,113	–4,112
Recover guarantee agency reserves in the family education loan program	....	–350	–250	–250	–150	–100	–1,100
Department of Energy/USEC:							
Provide permanent funding from nuclear waste disposal fund for Yucca Mountain	....	216	486	572	636	590	2,500
Sell USEC stock	....	–400	–1,100	....	....	....	–1,500
Sell excess uranium with USEC	....	–400	....	....	....	....	–400
Save costs of continued USEC operations	....	150	8	–10	–88	–159	–99
Privatize Naval Petroleum Reserves	....	....	–2,152	439	417	395	–901
Sell Power Marketing Administrations	....	–85	–898	–3,294	671	678	–2,928
Increase BPA revenues or efficiencies to finance Mitchell Act hatcheries [1]	....	–14	–15	–15	–15	–15	–74
Department of Health and Human Services:							
Medicaid—impact of purchase cost of PHS proposal to reduce vaccine excise	....	–47	–52	–57	–62	–64	–282
Medicare:							
Extend Medicare secondary payer	....	....	....	....	–1,230	–1,740	–2,970
Extend supplementary medical insurance premiums at 25% of costs	....	....	....	....	–1,154	–2,857	–4,011
Extend freeze on skilled nursing facilities cost limits	....	–130	–250	–280	–300	–320	–1,280
Extend freeze on home health agencies cost limits	....	–10	–280	–390	–420	–450	–1,550
Impact of above extensions on:							
Medicaid	....	....	....	....	90	230	320
Premiums for otherwise uninsured (HI)	....	1	4	6	14	17	42
Department of Housing and Urban Development:							
Reform FHA's multifamily programs to provide more flexibility in the disposition of property	....	....	....	....	....	....	....
Department of Interior:							
Increase commercial operations fees for Delaware Water Gap	....	–*	–*	–*	–*	–*	–2
Spend funds for operation of Rt 209 within Delaware Water Gap NRA	....	*	*	*	*	*	2
Privatize helium fund [2]	....	–4	5	5	5	5	16
Expand National Park Service lease authority	....	–8	–10	–11	–13	–17	–59
Department of Justice:							
Border services:							
Impose user fee at land border ports	....	–100	–213	–219	–226	–233	–991
Spend fees on services	....	100	213	219	226	233	991

Table S–5. MANDATORY PAY-AS-YOU-GO PROPOSALS—Continued

(Outlays, in millions of dollars)

	Estimate						Total, 1995–2000
	1995	1996	1997	1998	1999	2000	
Department of Transportation:							
Extend rail safety user fees	....	–45	–47	–49	–51	–53	–245
Department of the Treasury:							
Modify earned income tax credit eligibility rules:							
Deny EITC to undocumented workers and related compliance measures	....	....	–346	–366	–371	–375	–1,458
Impose interest and dividend test on recipients	....	–12	–241	–257	–269	–286	–1,065
Border services:							
Impose user fee at land border ports	....	–100	–213	–219	–226	–233	–991
Spend fees on services	....	100	213	219	226	233	991
Create revolving fund to finance circulating coin production at the US mint	....	58	60	61	63	65	307
Department of Veterans Affairs:							
Extend rounding down compensation cost-of-living adjustment (COLA) and 1/2 COLA for certain survivor benefits	....	–30	–74	–123	–160	–194	–581
Extend authority to limit pension benefits to $90 for certain beneficiaries	....	....	....	....	–497	–506	–1,003
Extend authority to verify income of pension beneficiaries	....	....	....	....	–26	–63	–89
Maintain GI Bill benefit COLA at 50%	....	–13	–27	–40	–55	–68	–203
Eliminate statutory restrictions on the collection of deficiency judgments in housing program	....	–90	....	....	....	....	–90
Increase fees for manufactured housing program	....	–*	–*	–*	–*	–*	–*
Extend expiring OBRA provisions in order to maintain higher loan fees and reduce resale losses	....	....	....	–187	–185	–372	
Extend authority to recover certain costs from health insurers	....	....	....	....	–312	–319	–631
Extend authority to collect per diems and copayments for certain veterans	....	....	....	....	–39	–39	–78
Extend authority to verify income of veterans receiving medical care	....	....	....	....	–43	–46	–89
Environmental Protection Agency:							
Superfund "Orphan Share" spending	....	....	52	112	144	162	470
Extend pesticide re-registration fee	....	–9	–8	–15	–15	....	–47
Use fees to administer program	....	7	7	14	14	2	44
Farm Credit System Insurance Corporation:							
Reduce administrative expenses by reformulating Corporation's board of directors	....	–1	....	....	....	....	–1
Federal Communications Commission:							
Institute royalty fees and/or additional auction authority for spectrum use	....	–300	–600	–1,000	–1,400	–1,500	–4,800
Federal Deposit Insurance Corporation:							
Assess examination fee for FDIC-insured banks (outlay component)	....	–105	–110	–115	–119	–124	–573
General Services Administration:							
Allow agencies to charge a commercial equivalent fee for parking provided to employees	....	–45	–45	–45	–45	–45	–225
Spend fees for employee transit benefit programs	....	45	45	45	45	45	225
Securities and Exchange Commission:							
Reform fees collected under securities laws to provide SEC with a sound and stable funding structure (costs offset in revenues)	....	216	259	271	284	298	1,328
Small Business Administration:							
Impose loan servicing fee on loans made under section 7(a) program	....	–9	–9	–9	–8	–8	–43

Table S–5. MANDATORY PAY-AS-YOU-GO PROPOSALS—Continued

(Outlays, in millions of dollars)

	Estimate						Total, 1995–2000
	1995	1996	1997	1998	1999	2000	
Use fees for administrative expenses	....	9	9	9	8	8	43
Total, mandatory pay-as-you-go proposals	....	**–1,329**	**–6,328**	**–6,301**	**–6,089**	**–8,653**	**–28,703**

* Less than $500 thousand.

[1] Detailed database mistakenly includes these amounts in current law.

[2] Amounts do not include estimates of discretionary savings resulting from Federal agencies being authorized to purchase refined helium in the private sector.

Table S–6. REINVENTING GOVERNMENT—PHASE II

(In millions of dollars)

		Estimate					Total 1996–2000
		1996	1997	1998	1999	2000	
MAJOR AGENCY RESTRUCTURING							
Energy/USEC:							
Realign Department of Energy along the five business lines in the DOE strategic plan	BA	–145	–1,849	–2,679	–2,688	–2,797	–10,158
	OL	–70	–1,006	–2,016	–2,570	–2,803	–8,464
Sell shares in USEC	BA	–400					–400
	OL	–400					–400
Privatize the Naval Petroleum Reserves	BA		–2,354	259	250	237	–1,608
	OL		–2,297	254	238	229	–1,576
Sell Power Marketing Administrations	BA	–85	–903	–3,325	313	319	–3,680
	OL	–85	–903	–3,325	313	319	–3,681
Sell Weeks Island Oil	BA	–100					–100
	OL	–100					–100
SPR decommissioning fund	BA	100					100
	OL	100					100
Total, Department of Energy	BA	–630	–5,106	–5,745	–2,125	–2,241	–15,846
	OL	–555	–4,205	–5,087	–2,020	–2,255	–14,121
Transportation:							
Consolidate 30 Transportation grant programs into 3 programs: unified transportation growth, state infrastructure banks, and discretionary grants	BA	–3,902	–893	–1,127	–909	–1,388	–7,409
	OL	–517	–2,198	–1,609	–1,215	–897	–6,435
Housing and Urban Development:							
Consolidate 60 housing programs into three flexible performance grants	BA		–150	–225	–225	–225	–825
	OL		–120	–200	–225	–225	–770
General Services Administration:							
Transform GSA into a policy and oversight organization for administrative services, except personnel (government-wide savings)	BA		–200	–400	–400	–400	–1,400
	OL		–200	–400	–400	–400	–1,400
Office of Personnel Management:							
Restructure and downsize OPM while retaining essential policy and oversight functions (government-wide savings)	BA		–7	–7	–8	–8	–30
	OL		–7	–7	–8	–8	–30
Total, Major Agency Restructuring	BA	–3,721	–6,356	–7,504	–3,667	–4,262	–25,509
	OL	–1,072	–6,730	–7,302	–3,868	–3,785	–22,757
OTHER RESTRUCTURING							
Interstate Commerce Commission:							
Eliminate the ICC and transfer residual functions to Transportation, Justice and the Federal Trade Commission [1]	BA	–4	–32	–32	–31	–30	–129
	OL	–2	–28	–32	–31	–30	–123
Commerce:							
Privatize portions of the National Weather Service of NOAA	BA	–3	–13	–11	–10	–9	–47
	OL	–2	–8	–10	–10	–10	–40
Federal Deposit Insurance Corporation:							
Assess user fees for examination of FDIC-insured banks and bank holding companies	OL	–105	–110	–115	–119	–124	–573
	GR	–79	–83	–86	–89	–92	–429

Table S–6. REINVENTING GOVERNMENT—PHASE II—Continued

(In millions of dollars)

		Estimate 1996	1997	1998	1999	2000	Total 1996–2000
Interior:							
Reinvent the Bureau of Mines by emphasizing priority functions	BA	–20	–30	–30	–30	–30	–140
	OL	–20	–30	–30	–30	–30	–140
Total, Other Restructuring	BA	–28	–75	–73	–71	–70	–316
	OL	–129	–176	–187	–190	–194	–876
	GR	–79	–83	–86	–89	–92	–429
PRIVATIZATIONS							
Allowances:							
Privatize collection of receivables (not paygo scorable)	BA	(–156)					(–156)
	OL	(–156)					(–156)
National Aeronautics and Space Administration:							
Rely on private sector for communications with space craft	BA	....	–50	–50	–50	–50	–200
	OL	....	–33	–47	–50	–50	–179
Interior:							
Expand National Park Service lease authority to allow the productive use of currently unused NPS facilities	BA	–8	–8	–10	–12	–16	–54
	OL	–8	–10	–11	–13	–17	–59
Privatize the helium program since it has accomplished its purpose in supporting the development of a private U.S. helium industry [2]	BA						
	OL	–4	5	5	5	5	16
Total, Privatizations	BA	–8	–58	–60	–62	–66	–254
	OL	–12	–38	–53	–58	–62	–222
PROGRAM ELIMINATIONS							
Education:							
Phase out all impact aid payments except for children who live on Indian lands or children of members of the uniformed services who live on Federal property	BA	–31	–51	–88	–15	–15	–200
	OL	–25	–47	–80	–26	–16	–194
Terminate 10 small Education grant programs that are duplicative of other programs	BA	–113	–153	–153	–153	–153	–723
	OL	–14	–95	–142	–152	–153	–555
Corps of Engineers:							
Eliminate Army Corps of Engineers local project role and focus on water projects that would provide national benefits	BA	–29	–77	–178	–290	–386	–960
	OL	–8	–53	–157	–261	–358	–837
Total, Program Eliminations	BA	–173	–281	–419	–458	–554	–1,883
	OL	–47	–195	–379	–439	–527	–1,587
PERFORMANCE PARTNERSHIPS							
Health and Human Services:							
Administrative savings from consolidating many small Public Health Service grants into larger, more flexible grants, which continue in total at 1995 levels	BA	–15	–38	–44	–56	–65	–218
	OL	–14	–37	–44	–55	–65	–215
Agriculture:							
Streamline the delivery of USDA Rural Development Programs	BA	–18	–10	–12	–13	–15	–68
	OL	–1	3	–3	–6	–9	–16

Table S–6. REINVENTING GOVERNMENT—PHASE II—Continued

(In millions of dollars)

		Estimate 1996	1997	1998	1999	2000	Total 1996–2000
Environmental Protection Agency:							
Consolidate media-specific grants (e.g. air, water) into performance partnerships	BA	....	–19	–28	–28	–28	–103
	OL	....	–16	–25	–27	–28	–96
Total, Performance Partnerships	BA	–33	–67	–84	–97	–108	–389
	OL	–16	–50	–71	–89	–101	–327
TOTAL, REGO II proposals	BA	–3,962	–6,837	–8,139	–4,355	–5,059	–28,351
	OL	–1,275	–7,189	–7,992	–4,643	–4,669	–25,769
	GR	–79	–83	–86	–89	–92	–429
Memorandum							
Discretionary Budget Authority		–3,469	–3,778	–5,274	–5,432	–6,116	–24,070
Discretionary Outlays		–673	–4,023	–5,017	–5,605	–5,607	–20,925
Mandatory Outlays [3]		–602	–3,165	–2,976	962	938	–4,843
Discretionary Asset Sales		....	–145	–185	–179	–166	–675
Mandatory Asset Sales		–485	–3,050	–2,854	1,089	1,074	–4,227
Governmental Receipts (GR)		–79	–83	–86	–89	–92	–429

[1] Includes transfers to other agencies.

[2] Amounts do not include estimates of discretionary savings resulting from Federal agencies being authorized to purchase refined helium in the private market.

[3] Excludes $156 million that is not paygo scorable.

Table S–7. PROGRAM CONSOLIDATIONS

This table lists 271 existing programs by Department that are being consolidated into 27 new programs

Agency and Program	1995 BA	1995 OL	1996 BA	1996 OL	Number
Departments of Education, Labor, Agriculture, and Housing and Urban Development					
New program:					
G.I. Bill For America's Workers[1]	13,186	11,887	14,202	12,947	

Programs Being Consolidated:
Department of Education
Vocational Education Act:
- Basic State Programs [basic grants]
- Community-based organizations
- Consumer and homemaking education
- Tech-prep education
- Tribally controlled postsecondary vocational institutions
- State councils
- Demo: integration of vocational and academic learning
- Cooperative demonstration
- National Occupational Information Coordinating Committee (ED share)
- Smith-Hughes Act
- Education programs for Federal correctional institutions
- Comprehensive career guidance and counseling
- Blue Ribbon vocational education programs
- Model programs for regional training, skill trades
- Business/Education/Labor partnerships
- State Programs and Activities
- Single parents, homemakers, and pregnant women
- Sex equity
- Programs for criminal offenders
- Opportunities for Indian and Hawaiian Natives
- Demonstration centers for dislocated workers
- Workplace transition training for incarcerated youth offenders
- Native Hawaiian education—Community-based education Learning Centers
- School-to-work opportunities Act (DoED share)
- Adult education:
  - State-administered basic grant
  - National adult education discretionary program
  - State literacy resource centers
  - National workplace literacy program
  - Workplace literacy partnerships
  - Adult Education for the Homeless
  - Literacy training for homeless adults
  - Literacy for incarcerated adults
  - Literacy programs for prisoners
- Even Start—State grants
- Even Start—grants for migrants
- Library literacy
- Federal Pell grant program
- State postsecondary review program
- Federal Family Education Loan program (mandatory)
- Federal Direct Loan program (mandatory)

Department of Labor
Job Training partnership Act:
- Grants to service delivery areas for adults
- State education Grants
- State older workers grants
- Youth incentive grants
- Summer youth grants
- Summer youth grants to Indian entities
- Dislocated workers grants to local areas
- Dislocated worker Governors' 50% grants
- Dislocated worker Secretary's Reserve Account
- Defense conversion adjustment program
- Defense diversification program
- Clean Air Employment
- National Research and Evaluation
- Pilots and Demonstrations
- Youth Fair Chance
- American Samoans training grants
- Rural CEPs
- National Occupational Information Coordinating Committee (DOL share)
- Labor market information
- Women in Apprenticeship
- Youth innovations

School-to-Work Opportunities Act (DOL share)
State employment service (ES)
- ES Wagner-Peyser State Grants
- ES Governor's Discretionary Funds
- Interstate Job Bank

Alien Labor Certification
One-Stop Career Centers

Department of Housing and Urban Development
Youthbuild

Department of Agriculture
Food Stamp Employment and Training (mandatory)

Table S–7. PROGRAM CONSOLIDATIONS

(In millions of dollars)

Agency and Program	1995 BA	1995 OL	1996 BA	1996 OL	Number
Departments of Education, Labor, Agriculture, and Housing and Urban Development—Continued					
Net Impact, G.I. Bill for America's Workers[1]	**13,186**	**11,887**	**14,202**	**12,947**	**–69**

As a key component of the Middle Class Bill of Rights, the President proposes to combine nearly 70 programs in four agencies—primarily the Labor and Education Departments—into one workforce development system for adults and youth. Adults would receive resources and high quality labor market information directly, and make their own choices for training or further education. Adult services and youth services would be organized by the States and localities whatever manner best meets their needs, consistent with accountability for results in accord with national goals.

Note on program list: The General Accounting Office has identified 163 programs as job training. Most of those identified are not general job training or placement. Some provide special services, such as medical rehabilitation; others serve only certain populations in unique ways, such as certain migrant workers or veterans. Many were never funded. Some programs that clearly are general job training-related are not on GAO's list. The listing above includes all programs on the GAO list that are general job training and related programs, including those not funded, as well as the other programs that belong in an integrated system.

[1] Funds shown are the discretionary BA and OL.

Department of Housing and Urban Development

Agency and Program	1995 BA	1995 OL	1996 BA	1996 OL	Number
New Program:					
Housing Certificates for Families and Individuals Performance Funds	....	....	7,665	780	
Programs Being Consolidated:					
Section 8 Certificates	2,386	(1)	....	(1)	
Section 8 Vouchers	(5)	(1)	....	(1)	
Section 8 Contract Renewals	3,336	(3)	....	(3)	
Section 8 Family Unification	76	(1)	....	(1)	
Section 8 Certificates for Persons with Disabilities	(5)	(1)	....	(1)	
Section 8 Certificates for Persons with AIDS	(5)	(1)	....	(1)	
Section 8 Certificates for Homeless	(5)	(1)	....	(1)	
Section 8 Opt Outs	83	(1)	....	(1)	
Section 8 Counseling	[171]	(1)	....	(1)	
Lease Adjustments	22	(1)	....	(1)	
Family Self Sufficiency Coordinators	17	(1)	....	(1)	
Flexible Subsidy	50	128	....	17	
Preservation	175	(1)	....	(1)	
Section 8 Property Disposition	555	(1)	....	(1)	
Section 8 Loan Management	150	(1)	....	(1)	
Elderly Service Coordinators	22	(1)	....	(1)	
Project-Based Service Coordinators	30	(1)	....	(1)	
Congregate Housing	25	6	....	9	
Net Impact of Housing Certificates for Families and Individuals	**6,927**	**134**	**7,665**	**806**	**–17**

1996 Budget proposes consolidation of all rental assistance programs into one that provides Housing Certificates for Families and Individuals. Certificates would provide recipients with subsidies to help them afford rental housing in the private housing market.

Agency and Program	1995 BA	1995 OL	1996 BA	1996 OL	Number
New Program:					
Public and Indian Housing Operation Performance Funds	....	....	3,220	1,223	
Programs Being Consolidated:					
Public Housing Operating Subsidies	2,900	2,707	....	1,537	
Drug Elimination Grants	290	179	....	259	

Table S–7. PROGRAM CONSOLIDATIONS—Continued

(In millions of dollars)

Agency and Program	1995 BA	1995 OL	1996 BA	1996 OL	Number
Service Coordinators	30	(1)	....	(1)	
Net Impact of Public and Indian Housing Operation	**3,220**	**2,886**	**3,220**	**3,019**	**–2**
1996 Budget proposes to consolidate operating subsidies for public housing into a single Public and Indian Housing Operation Performance Funds program. A portion of these funds will be awarded competitively to States and local governments and to private and non-profit entities who are proven performers.					
New Program:					
Public and Indian Housing Capital Performance Funds	....	....	4,884	13	
Programs Being Consolidated:					
Public Housing Development	598	(1)	....	(1)	
Public/Indian Housing Amendments	50	(1)	....	(1)	
Indian Housing Development	282	(1)	....	(1)	
Severely Distressed Public Housing	500	20	....	20	
Public Housing Coordinators	30	(1)	....	(1)	
Tenant Opportunity Program	[25]	(1)	....	(1)	
Urban Youth Corps	[10]	(1)	....	(1)	
Public Housing Major Reconstruction	....	(1)	[287]	(1)	
Family Investment Centers	26	(1)	....	(1)	
Public/Indian Housing Modernization	3,700	(1)	....	(1)	
Net Impact of Public and Indian Housing Capital [7]	5,186	20	5,171	33	–9
1996 Budget proposes to consolidate all current public housing capital programs into a single Public and Indian Housing Capital Performance Funds program. This program would provide Federal resources to rehabilitate and restore viable public housing in need of modernization, demolish uninhabitable and non-viable public housing projects, and construct replacement housing where feasible.					
New Program:					
Community Opportunity Performance Funds	....	....	4,850	175	
Programs Being Consolidated:					
Community Development Grants (CDBG)	4,622	4,330	....	4,564	
Economic Development Initiative (EDI)	300	(1)	....	(1)	
UDAG Recaptures	–100	35	....	30	
Youthbuild [6]	50	16	....	25	
Colonias	(2)	(2)	....	(2)	
Historically Black Colleges	(2)	(2)	....	(2)	
Work Study Program	(2)	(2)	....	(2)	
Joint Community Development	(2)	(2)	....	(2)	
Community Outreach	(2)	(2)	....	(2)	
Early Childhood Development	(2)	(2)	....	(2)	
Insular Areas	(2)	(2)	....	(2)	
Technical Assistance	(2)	(2)	....	(2)	
Neighborhood Development	(2)	(2)	....	(2)	
Community Adjustment Planning	(2)	(2)	....	(2)	
Net Impact of Community Opportunity	**4,872**	**4,381**	**4,850**	**4,794**	**–13**
1996 Budget proposes to consolidate current HUD grants for community and economic development into a single Community Opportunity Performance Funds program. The consolidated program would provide localities and States with flexible funding for the economic revitalization and renewal of distressed communities.					
New Program:					
Affordable Housing Performance Funds	....	....	3,339	60	
Programs Being Consolidated:					
HOME Investment Partnerships	1,400	1,213	....	1,222	

Table S–7. PROGRAM CONSOLIDATIONS—Continued

(In millions of dollars)

Agency and Program	1995 BA	1995 OL	1996 BA	1996 OL	Number
Homeownership Demonstration	50	....	....	17	
Housing Counseling	50	13	....	38	
Elderly Housing	1,279	(1)	....	(1)	
Housing for Disabled	387	(1)	....	(1)	
HOPE Grants	62	87	....	63	
EZ Homes	50	(1)			
Pension Fund Partnerships	[350]	(1)	....	(1)	
Lead-Based Paint	100	(1)	....	....	
Net Impact of Affordable Housing	**3,378**	**1,313**	**3,339**	**1,400**	**–8**

1996 Budget proposes to consolidate current grants for housing production and rehabilitation, including homeownership initiatives, into a single Affordable Housing Performance Funds program. Funds would provide localities and States with flexible funding for the development of affordabble housing.

Agency and Program	1995 BA	1995 OL	1996 BA	1996 OL	Number
New Program:					
Homeless Assistance Performance Funds	....	....	1,120	50	
Programs Being Consolidated:					
Shelter Plus Care	....	50	....	50	
Section 8 SRO	....	36	....	43	
Emergency Shelter Grants	157	110	....	123	
Supportive Housing	34	114	....	121	
Innovative Homeless Initiative	25	41	....	35	
Homeless Assistance Grants	905	45	....	90	
Net Impact of Homeless Assistance	**1,121**	**396**	**1,120**	**512**	**–5**

1996 Budget proposes to create a single Homeless Assistance Performance Funds program to provide flexible support on a formula basis to States, local governments, nonprofit organizations, and Indian tribes.

Agency and Program	1995 BA	1995 OL	1996 BA	1996 OL	Number
MEMO: Annual Contributions	10,731	20,273	....	19,726	
Net Impact, Housing and Urban Development Consolidations	**24,704**	**29,403**	**25,365**	**30,290**	**–54**

NOTES:

[1] Outlays are shown under Annual Contributions For Assisted Housing total.

[2] Budget authority and outlays are shown under Community Development Block Grants total.

[3] Outlays from Contract Renewals prior to 1996 are included in the Annual Contributions total.

[4] Subtotal excludes outlays from Annual Contributions for Assisted Housing account.

[5] BA included under Section 8 certificates.

[6] Proposed transfer to Administration's job training initiative starting in 1996.

[7] 1996 Total program level includes $287 million in recaptured Public Housing Major Reconstruction (MROP) funds, which is not scored as new budget authority.

Department of Transportation

Agency and Program	1995 BA	1995 OL	1996 BA	1996 OL	Number
New Programs:					
State Infrastructure Bank	....	....	2,000	256	
Unified Transportation Infrastructure Investment Program	....	....	19,498	2,624	
Transportation Discretionary Grants	....	....	1,000	20	
Programs Being Consolidated:					
Federal-Aid Highways [1]	13,503	11,494			
Surface Transportation Program	3,522	(3)	....	(3)	
Sur Trans Enhancement Set-aside	440	(3)	....	(3)	
Sur Trans Safety Set-aside	440	(3)	....	(3)	
Bridge Program	2,446	(3)	....	(3)	
Interstate Completion	1,575	(3)	....	(3)	

Table S–7. PROGRAM CONSOLIDATIONS—Continued

(In millions of dollars)

Agency and Program	1995 BA	1995 OL	1996 BA	1996 OL	Number
Interstate Maintenance	2,580	(3)	....	(3)	
Interstate Substitution	212	(3)	....	(3)	
Congestion Mitigation	910	(3)	....	(3)	
Minimum Allocation	1,460	(3)	....	(3)	
Donor state bonus	455	(3)	....	(3)	
Grants-in-Aid to Airports [1]	1,785	1,324			
Primary Airports	412	(3)	....	(3)	
Cargo Airports	39	(3)	....	(3)	
Alaska Supplemental	11	(3)	....	(3)	
States	150	(3)	....	(3)	
Return Entitlements	147	(3)	....	(3)	
Noise	157	(3)	....	(3)	
Reliever	63	(3)	....	(3)	
Commercial Service	19	(3)	....	(3)	
System Planning	9	(3)	....	(3)	
Military Airports	31	(3)	....	(3)	
Small Airports/Hubs	88	(3)	....	(3)	
Capacity/safety/security/noise	244	(3)	....	(3)	
Remaining Discretionary	81	(3)	....	(3)	
Transit Formula Capital Grants [2]	1,237	1,263			
Urban Capital Grants	1,574	(3)	....	(3)	
Rural Capital Grants	133	(3)	....	(3)	
Elderly and Disabled Capital Grants	59	(3)	....	(3)	
Transit Discretionary Grants [1]	1,431	1,576			
Bus	353	(3)	....	(3)	
Rail Modernization	725	(3)	....	(3)	
New Starts	647	(3)	....	(3)	
Local Rail Freight Assistance	17	25	....	19	
Net Impact, Transportation Consolidations	**18,999**	**17,981**	**22,498**	**18,576**	**–27**

1996 Budget proposes to consolidate 30 different highway, aviation, rail and transit programs into 3 broad Federal funding mechanisms: a unified infrastructure grant program; Federal support for revolving funds to support State credit programs for infrastructure financing; and a discretionary grant program to allow the Department of Transportation to fund transportation projects of national or regional importance. There are several other programs (e.g., the National Highway System) that will be part of the Unified Transportation Infrastructure Investment account but for which funding will be reserved separately.

NOTES:

[1] Data in BA columns represent obligation limitations.

[2] In 1995, includes $1.15 billion obligation limitation plus $616 million in discretionary BA, for total new budgetary resources of $1,766 million.

[3] Outlays available only for category as a whole, not by separate programs.

[4] Outlays are for category as a whole and represent a pro-rata share of total outlays of the Federal-aid highways account.

Department of Health and Human Services—Public Health Service Performance Partnerships

Agency and Program	1995 BA	1995 OL	1996 BA	1996 OL	Number
New Program:					
HIV/STD/TB Performance Partnership	....	....	488	471	
Programs Being Consolidated:					
HIV Counseling, Testing and Partner Notification	178	(1)	....	....	
TB Prevention Control and Elimination Grants	83	(1)	....	....	
STD Prevention and Control Grants	72	(1)	....	....	
Similar Activities Being Consolidated	138	(1)	....	....	

Table S–7. PROGRAM CONSOLIDATIONS—Continued

(In millions of dollars)

Agency and Program	1995 BA	1995 OL	1996 BA	1996 OL	Number
Net Impact of HIV/STD/TB Partnership	**471**	**453**	**488**	**471**	**–19**
Consolidates twenty programs for HIV, STD, and TB into a single Performance Partnership with States in which funds are granted by formula according to need and performance. (2)					
New Program:					
Chronic Disease and Disability Performance Partnership	....	....	118	114	
Programs Being Consolidated:					
Disability Grants	6	(1)	....	....	
Diabetes Control Grants	12	(1)	....	....	
Breast and Cervical Cancer Screening Grants	80	(1)	....	....	
Similar Activities Being Conssolidated	20	(1)	....	....	
Net Impact of Chronic Disease and Disability Partnership	**118**	**114**	**118**	**114**	**–5**
Consolidates six programs in chronic disease into a single Performance Partnership with States in which funds are granted by formula according to need and performance. (2)					
New Program:					
Immunization Performance Partnership	....	....	177	171	
Programs Being Consolidated:					
State Operations Grants	24	(1)	....	....	
Infrastructure Grants	108	(1)	....	....	
Surveillance and Response Grants	5	(1)	....	....	
Similar Activities Being Conssolidated	39	(1)	....	....	
Net Impact of Immunization Partnership	**177**	**170**	**177**	**171**	**–5**
Consolidates six programs in immunizations into a single Performance Partnership with States in which funds are granted by formula according to need and performance. (2)					
New Program:					
Health Center Cluster	....	....	757	730	
Activities Being Consolidated:					
Community Health Center Grants	617	(1)	....	....	
Migrant Health Center Grants	65	(1)	....	....	
Health Care for the Homeless	65	(1)	....	....	
Health Care for Residents of Public Housing Grants	10	(1)	....	....	
Net Impact of Health Center Cluster	**757**	**717**	**757**	**730**	**–3**
Clusters four grants for health centers which assist the disadvantaged into clusters of Federally-administered grants, which will share a common application and review process. (2)					
New Program:					
Five Health Professions Clusters	....	....	387	373	
(1) Health Professions Workforce Development Cluster					
Activities Being Consolidated:					
National Health Service Corps Field	45	(1)	....	....	
National Health Service Corps Recruitment	80	(1)	....	....	
Nursing Loan Repayment	2	(1)	....	....	
Similar Activities Consolidated	3	(1)	....	....	
Subtotal, HP Workforce Cluster	130	123	....	....	
(2) Enhanced AHEC Cluster					
Activities Being Consolidated:					
Area Health Education and Training Centers Grants	21	(1)	....	....	

Table S–7. PROGRAM CONSOLIDATIONS—Continued
(In millions of dollars)

Agency and Program	1995 BA	1995 OL	1996 BA	1996 OL	Number
Health Education and Training Centers Grants	3	(1)	....	....	
General Dentistry Grants	2	(1)	....	....	
Allied Health Special Project Grants	2	(1)	....	....	
Geriatric Education Centers Grants	7	(1)	....	....	
Rural Health Interdisciplinary Training Grants	4	(1)	....	....	
Subtotal, Enhanced AHEC Cluster	39	37	....	....	
(3) Minority Disadvantaged HP Cluster					
Activities Being Consolidated:					
Exceptional Financial Need Scholarships	10	(1)	....	....	
Financial Assistance to Disadvantaged HP	6	(1)	....	....	
Loans for Disadvantaged Students	8	(1)	....	....	
Scholarships for Disadvantaged Students	17	(1)	....	....	
Centers of Excellence Grants	23	(1)	....	....	
Similar Activities Consolidated	25	(1)	....	....	
Subtotal, Minority Disadvantaged HP Cluster	89	84	....	....	
(4) Primary Care and Public Health Training Cluster					
Activities Being Consolidated:					
Family Medicine Grants	43	(1)	....	....	
General Medicine/Pediatrics Grants	17	(1)	....	....	
Physician Assistants Grants	6	(1)	....	....	
Similar Activities Consolidated	10	(1)	....	....	
Subtotal, Primary Care and Public Health Cluster	76	72	....	....	
(5) Nursing Education/Practice Cluster					
Activities Being Consolidated:					
Advanced Nurse Education Grants	11	(1)	....	....	
Nurse Practioner/Midwife Grants	16	(1)	....	....	
Nurse Anesthetists Grants	3	(1)	....	....	
Similar Activities Consolidated	27	(1)	....	....	
Subtotal, Nursing Education Practice Cluster	57	54	....	....	
Net Impact of HP Clusters	**390**	**369**	**387**	**373**	**–32**

Clusters thirty-four health professions curriculum assistance activities and three other health professions programs into five clusters of Federally-administered grants and programs which will share a common application and review process. (2)

Agency and Program	1995 BA	1995 OL	1996 BA	1996 OL	Number
New Program:					
Emergency Medical Services (EMS) Cluster	....	....	15	14	
Activities Being Consolidated:					
Trauma Care Grants	5	(1)	....	....	
Emergency Medical Services for Children Grant	10	(1)	....	....	
Net Impact of EMS Cluster	**15**	**14**	**15**	**14**	**–1**

Clusters two emergency medical grants into one cluster of Federally-administered grants which will share a common application and review process. (2)

Agency and Program	1995 BA	1995 OL	1996 BA	1996 OL	Number
New Program:					
Rural Health Cluster	....	....	29	27	
Activities Being Consolidated:					
Rural Health Outreach Grants	27	(1)	....	....	
State Offices of Rural Health Grants	4	(1)	....	....	
Net Impact of EMS Cluster	**31**	**29**	**29**	**27**	**–1**

Table S–7. PROGRAM CONSOLIDATIONS—Continued

(In millions of dollars)

Agency and Program	1995 BA	1995 OL	1996 BA	1996 OL	Number

Clusters two rural health grants into one cluster of Federally-administered grants which will share a common application and review process. (2)

Agency and Program	1995 BA	1995 OL	1996 BA	1996 OL	Number
New Program:					
Special Populations Cluster	....	....	19	18	
Activities Being Consolidated:					
Black Lung Clinic Grants	4	(1)	....	....	
Alzheimer's Disease Demonstration Grants	5	(1)	....	....	
Payment to Hawaii Grants	3	(1)	....	....	
Pacific Basin Grants	1	(1)	....	....	
Native Hawaiian Health Care Grants	5	(1)	....	....	
Net Impact of EMS Cluster	**18**	**17**	**19**	**18**	**–4**

Clusters five grants serving special populations into one cluster of Federally-administered grants which will share a common application and review process. (2)

Agency and Program	1995 BA	1995 OL	1996 BA	1996 OL	Number
New Program:					
Mental Health Performance Partnership	....	....	326	322	
Programs Being Consolidated:					
Mental Health Block Grant	275	(1)	....	....	
Projects for Assistance in Transition from Homelessness Grants	29	(1)	....	....	
Protection and Advocacy Grants	22	(1)	....	....	
Net Impact of Mental Health Performance Partnership	**327**	**367**	**326**	**322**	**–2**

Consolidates the Mental Health Block Grant with two small formula grants into one State formula Performance Partnership.(2)

Agency and Program	1995 BA	1995 OL	1996 BA	1996 OL	Number
New Program:					
Mental Health Training and Demonstration Cluster	....	....	113	111	
Programs Being Consolidated:					
Community Support Program	24	(1)	....	....	
Homeless Demonstrations	21	(1)	....	....	
AIDS Demonstrations	1	(1)	....	....	
Clinical and AIDS Training	5	(1)	....	....	
Similar Activities Being Consolidated	60				
Net Impact of Mental Health Training and Demonstration Cluster	**112**	**126**	**113**	**111**	**–5**

Consolidates six categorical, demonstration and training grants for mental health into one Federally-administered demonstration and training cluster which will share a common application and review process. (2)

Agency and Program	1995 BA	1995 OL	1996 BA	1996 OL	Number
New Program:					
Substance Abuse Performance Partnership	....	....	1,294	1,277	
Programs Being Consolidated:					
Substance Abuse Block Grant	1,234	(1)	....	....	
Treatment Capacity Expansion Program	7	(1)	....	....	
Net Impact of Substance Abuse Performance Partnership	**1,241**	**1,392**	**1,294**	**1,277**	**–1**

Consolidates the Substance Abuse Block Grant with a categorical substance abuse grant into one State formula Performance Partnership. (2)

Agency and Program	1995 BA	1995 OL	1996 BA	1996 OL	Number
New Program:					
Substance Abuse Training and Demonstration Cluster	....	....	453	447	

Table S–7. PROGRAM CONSOLIDATIONS—Continued
(In millions of dollars)

Agency and Program	1995 BA	1995 OL	1996 BA	1996 OL	Number
Programs Being Consolidated:					
High Risk Youth Program	67	(1)	....	....	
Community Prevention Program	115	(1)	....	....	
Target Cities Program	36	(1)	....	....	
Criminal Justice Program	38	(1)	....	....	
Similar Activities Being Consolidated	200	(1)	....	....	
Net Impact of Substance Abuse Training and Demonstration	**454**	**510**	**453**	**447**	**–14**

Consolidates fifteen categorical, demonstration and training grants for substance abuse into one Federally-administered demonstration and training cluster which will share a common application and review process. (2)

Agency and Program	1995 BA	1995 OL	1996 BA	1996 OL	Number
Adjustment to Reflect Existing Block Grants:					
Total Block Grants	**–1,510**	**–1,693**	**–1,570**	**–1,549**	
Net Impact, Public Health Service Consolidations	**2,601**	**2,585**	**2,606**	**2,526**	**–92**

NOTES:
(1) Outlays available only for category as a whole, not by separate programs.
(2) Outlay estimates approximate.

Department of Health and Human Services—Administration for Children and Families

Agency and Program	1995 BA	1995 OL	1996 BA	1996 OL	Number
New Program:					
Comprehensive Runaway and Homeless Youth Program	....	....	69	61	
Programs Being Consolidated:					
Runaway and Homeless Youth	41	38	....	(1)	
Runaway Youth Transitional Living	14	13	....	(1)	
Runaway Youth Activities—Drug Prevention Program	14	15	....	(1)	
Net Impact, HHS Administration for Children and Families Consolidations	69	66	69	61	–2

[1] The 1996 Budget proposes consolidation of Runaway and Homeless Youth Programs into one formula grant to States to promote flexibility in crafting programs to address problems facing these youth.

Agency and Program	1995 BA	1995 OL	1996 BA	1996 OL	Number
Total, Programs Being Consolidated	**59,559**	**61,922**	**12,919**	**55,063**	**271**
Total, New Programs	....	....	**51,821**	**9,337**	**27**
Total, Net Impact	**59,559**	**61,922**	**64,740**	**64,400**	**–244**

Table S–8. PROGRAM TERMINATIONS

(In millions of dollars)

Agency and Program	1995		1996		Change: 1995 to 1996		Number
	BA	OL	BA	OL	BA	OL	
Department of Agriculture							
Cooperative State Research Service:							
Building and Facilities	63	55		56	–63	1	
Agricultural Stabilization and Conservation Service:							
Water Bank Program	1	10		10		–*	
Rural Electrification Administration:							
Rural Telephone Bank	10	10			–10	–10	
Food Stamp Program:							
Cattle Tick Eradication	12	12			–12	–12	
Subtotal, Agriculture	85	88		66	–85	–22	4
Department of Commerce							
National Oceanic and Atmospheric Administration:							
29 small projects in Operations, Research, and Facilities	48	27			–48	–27	
12 small projects in Construction	51	10			–51	–10	
International Trade Administration:							
Elimination of grant programs	18	18			–18	–18	
Subtotal, Commerce	117	55			–117	–55	47
Department of Defense—Military							
Defense Health Program:							
Uniformed Services University of the Health Sciences (USUHS)	96	*95	84	86	–12	–9	
*Plans for USUHS include phase-out beginning in 1997 and ending in 1999. Decrease in 1996 reflects additional programs added by Congress in 1995 to USUHS.							
Procurement:							
AH-1W Helicopter	141	106	11	110	–130	4	
Air Force T-1 Trainer	155	95	4	117	–151	21	
RDT&E:							
Navy Advanced Rocket System	15	12		6	–15	–6	
Tri-Service Standoff Attack Missile (TSSAM)	222	288		155	–222	–133	
Subtotal, Defense—Military	629	597	99	473	–530	–123	5
Department of Energy							
Fossil R&D:							
Coal R&D Program	9	9		6	–9	–3	
Power Marketing Administration (PMA):							
Privatize Alaska PMA	7	6	4	*5	–3	–1	
*Net sales proceeds from privatization in late-1996 estimated at $85 million.							
Privatize Southeastern PMA	22	23	20	29	–2	6	
*Net sales proceeds from privatization in 1997 estimated at $0.5 billion.							
Privatize Southwestern PMA	21	26	30	27	9	1	
*Net sales proceeds from privatization in 1998 estimated at $0.5 billion.							
Privatize Western Area PMA	220	251	302	257	82	6	
*Net sales proceeds from privatization in 1998 estimated at $2.6 billion.							
Elk Hills:							
Naval Petroleum Reserves	191	210	174	189	–17	–21	
Subtotal, Energy	470	525	530	513	60	–12	6

Table S–8. PROGRAM TERMINATIONS—Continued

(In millions of dollars)

Agency and Program	1995 BA	1995 OL	1996 BA	1996 OL	Change: 1995 to 1996 BA	Change: 1995 to 1996 OL	Number
Department of Education							
Impact Aid:							
Payments for Federally Connected Children: Payments for Children with Disabilities	40	38	40	39	....	1	
Payments for Federal Property	16	22	....	3	–16	–19	
Education for the Disadvantaged:							
Migrant Education: High School Equivalency Program	8	7	....	6	–8	–1	
Migrant Education: College Assistance Migrant Program	2	2	....	2	–2	–*	
Higher Education:							
Olympic Scholarships	1	*	....	1	–1	1	
Bethune-Cookman College	4	3	....	1	–4	–3	
National Academy of Science, Space, and Technology	2	*	....	1	–2	1	
Eisenhower Leadership Program	4	4	....	3	–4	–*	
Cooperative Education	7	13	....	7	–7	–6	
National Early Intervention Scholarships and Partnerships	3	2	....	2	–3	1	
Teacher Corps	2	2	....	2	–2	–*	
Native Hawaiian/Alaskan Native Culture and Arts Development	1	*	....	1	–1	1	
Law School Clinical Experience	15	15	....	13	–15	–2	
Aid for Institutional Development:							
Strengthening Institutions	80	86	40	69	–40	–17	
Endowment Challenge Grants (non-Historically Black Colleges and Universities portion)	6	9	....	9	–6	–*	
Innovative Projects for Community Service	1	1	....	1	–1	–*	
Urban Community Service	13	11	....	11	–13	–*	
Student Financial Aid Database and Information Line	*	1	....	*	–*	–*	
National Science Scholars	4	4	....	4	–4	–1	
Douglas teacher scholarships	15	14	....	12	–15	–2	
Harris Fellowships	20	20	....	17	–20	–3	
Javits Fellowships	8	8	....	7	–8	–1	
Legal Training for the Disadvantaged	3	3	....	3	–3	–*	
College Housing and Academic Facilities Loans:							
Loan subsidies	*	2	....	....	–*	–2	
Student Financial Assistance:							
State Student Incentive Grants	63	71	31	57	–32	–14	
School Improvement Programs:							
Education Infrastructure	100	12	....	68	–100	56	
Dropout Prevention Demonstrations	28	36	....	10	–28	–26	
Ellender Fellowships	4	5	....	4	–4	–1	
Education for Native Hawaiians	12	9	....	10	–12	1	
Law-Related Education (renamed Instruction in Civics, Government, and the Law)	6	7	....	6	–6	–1	
Innovative Education Program:							
Strategies State Grants	347	432	....	297	–347	–135	
Christa McAuliffe Fellowships	2	2	....	2	–2	–*	
Training in Early Childhood Education and Violence counseling	14	12	10	13	–4	2	
Education Research, Statistics, and Improvement:							
21st Century Community Learning Centers	1	*	....	1	–1	*	
National Writing Project	3	3	....	3	–3	–*	
Libraries:							
Inter-Library Cooperation	24	23	....	13	–24	–10	
Library Education and Training	5	5	....	3	–5	–3	
Library Research and Demonstrations	7	5	....	3	–7	–2	
Subtotal, Education	872	888	121	703	–751	–185	38

Table S–8. PROGRAM TERMINATIONS—Continued

(In millions of dollars)

Agency and Program	1995 BA	1995 OL	1996 BA	1996 OL	Change: 1995 to 1996 BA	Change: 1995 to 1996 OL	Number
Department of Health and Human Services (HHS)							
Community Services Programs:							
Community Economic Development	24	21	....	17	–24	–4	
National Youth Sports	12	11	....	9	–12	–2	
Rural Housing and Community Facilities Development	6	5	....	4	–6	–1	
Migrant and Seasonal Farmworker Assistance	3	3	....	2	–3	–1	
Demonstration Partnerships	8	7	....	6	–8	–1	
Subtotal, HHS	53	46	....	38	–53	–8	5
Department of Housing and Urban Development (HUD)							
Special Purpose Grants	290	N/A	....	N/A	–290	N/A	
Subtotal, HUD	290	N/A	....	N/A	–290	N/A	1
Department of the Interior							
U.S. Geological Survey:							
Water Resources Research Institute	5	5	....	1	–5	–4	
Bureau of Mines:							
Privatize the Helium Program	....	–9	....	–13	....	–4	
Office of Surface Mining:							
Rural Abandoned Mine Program (RAMP)	8	7	....	7	–8	....	
Territorial and International Affairs:							
Trust Territory Office/Palau Operations	20	19	....	....	–20	–19	
Bureau of Indian Affairs:							
Direct loan program and six additional small programs	7	7	....	....	–7	–7	
Subtotal, Interior	39	29	....	–5	–39	–34	11
Department of Labor							
Training and Employment Services:							
National Center for the Workplace	1	2	....	1	–1	–1	
Microenterprise grants	2	2	....	2	–2	–*	
Subtotal, Labor	3	4	....	3	–3	–1	2
Department of Transportation							
Federal Transit Administration:							
Interstate Transfer Grants	48	43	....	37	–48	–6	
Office of the Secretary:							
Essential Air Service	....	*26	....	13	....	–13	
Subtotal, Transportation	48	69	....	50	–48	–19	2

*Does not reflect proposed rescission of $3 million in 1995 outlays and $2 million in 1996 outlays.

Agency and Program	1995 BA	1995 OL	1996 BA	1996 OL	Change: 1995 to 1996 BA	Change: 1995 to 1996 OL	Number
Department of Veterans Affairs							
Grants to the Republic of the Philippines	1	1	....	1	–1	....	
Subtotal, Veterans Affairs	1	1	....	1	–1	....	1
DOD—Civil (Army Corps of Engineers)							
No follow-on funding for uneconomic projects. Additional savings would result from reinvention of the Corps' role in planning, constructing, and operating local water projects. Most reinvention savings would occur in the outyears	46	25	....	21	–46	–4	
Subtotal, DOD—Civil	46	25	....	21	–46	–4	1

Table S–8. PROGRAM TERMINATIONS—Continued

(In millions of dollars)

Agency and Program	1995		1996		Change: 1995 to 1996		Number
	BA	OL	BA	OL	BA	OL	
Environmental Protection Agency (EPA)							
Clean Lakes Program	3	3		2	–3	–1	
Technical Assistance	9	7		6	–9	–1	
Subtotal, EPA	12	10		8	–12	–2	2
Small Business Administration (SBA)							
Tree Planting Program	15	16			–15	–16	
Handicapped Access Direct Loan	2	2			–2	–2	
Subtotal, SBA	17	18			–17	–18	2
Other Independent Agencies (OIAs)							
Chemical Safety and Hazard Investigations Board	1	*		*	–1	–*	
Interstate Commerce Commission (ICC)	33	35	29	31	–4	–4	
Office of Nuclear Waste Negotiator	1	1			–1	–1	
Pennsylvania Avenue Development Corporation (to be terminated by end of 1997)	5	159	7	187	2	28	
Subtotal, OIAs	40	195	36	218	–4	23	4
Total, Terminations in 1996 budget	**2,722**	**2,550**	**786**	**2,090**	**–1,936**	**–460**	**131**

* Less than $500 thousand.

Table S–9. PROGRAM REDUCTIONS
(In millions of dollars)

Agency and Program	1995 BA	1995 OL	1996 BA	1996 OL	Change: 1995 to 1996 BA	Change: 1995 to 1996 OL	Number
Department of Agriculture							
Agricultural Research Service Buildings and Facilities: Buildings and Facilities	44	56	30	45	–14	–11	
Forest Service: Construction	203	224	193	203	–10	–20	
Food Safety and Inspection Service—Salaries and Expenses: Meat, Poultry, and Egg Inspection (effect of proposed user fee)	527	512	488	482	–39	–30	
Farm Service Agency: Agricultural Conservation Program	100	175	50	104	–50	–71	
Animal and Plant Health Inspection Service (APHIS) (including effect of proposed user fee)	451	448	441	442	–10	–6	
Grain Inspection Packers and Stockyards Administration (including effect of proposed user fee)	23	23	11	11	–12	–12	
The Emergency Food Assistance Program (TEFAP): TEFAP	65	72	40	40	–25	–32	
P.L. 480 Loan Program Account	239	297	134	165	–105	–131	
P.L. 480—Title III	157	215	50	71	–107	–144	
Subtotal, Agriculture	1,808	2,021	1,436	1,563	–372	–458	9
Department of Commerce							
National Oceanic and Atmospheric Administration (NOAA): four small projects in Operations, Research, and Facilities	35	20	24	14	–11	–6	4
National Telecommunications and Information Administration: Public Broadcasting Facilities, Planning and Construction (PBFP&C)	29	*30	8	*28	–21	–2	1
Subtotal, Commerce	64	50	32	42	–32	–8	5

*Does not reflect proposed rescission of $18 million in 1995 budget authority and $2 million in 1995 outlays.

Agency and Program	1995 BA	1995 OL	1996 BA	1996 OL	Change: 1995 to 1996 BA	Change: 1995 to 1996 OL	Number
Department of Defense							
Environmental Restoration, Defense	1,780	....	1,622	....	–158	....	
Civilian Personnel	42,145	42,165	41,088	41,141	–1,057	–1,024	
Active and Reserve Personnel	70,389	70,546	68,697	66,181	–1,692	–4,365	
Procurement:							
Army Multiple Launch Rocket System Launchers	143	138	49	134	–94	–4	
Army Reserve Component Automation Systems	164	139	83	139	–80	1	
Army Family of Medium Tactical Vehicles	386	131	40	198	–346	68	
Navy F/A-18C/D Aircraft	1,016	1,077	610	1,110	–406	32	
Navy Tomahawk Cruise Missile	302	264	162	260	–140	–4	
Navy Aerial Targets	122	104	69	107	–54	3	
Fleet Satellite Communications—Navy	125	160	52	140	–73	–20	
AN/SQQ-89 Surface ASW Combat System—Navy	85	78	30	73	–55	–5	
Air Force AMRAAM Air-to-Air Missile	290	289	191	354	–99	65	
Defense Support Program	361	180	103	228	–259	48	
RDT&E:							
Comanche Helicopter	489	424	199	306	–290	–118	
Ship Concept Design—Navy	156	101	18	65	–138	–36	
Air Force Electronic Warfare	118	113	50	85	–68	–28	
NORAD Cheyenne Mountain Upgrade	133	127	61	97	–72	–30	
Subtotal, Defense	118,203	116,035	113,123	110,619	–5,081	–5,417	17
Department of Education							
Education for the Disadvantaged: Capital Expenses for Private School Children	41	42	20	38	–21	–4	

Table S–9. PROGRAM REDUCTIONS—Continued

(In millions of dollars)

Agency and Program	1995 BA	1995 OL	1996 BA	1996 OL	Change: 1995 to 1996 BA	Change: 1995 to 1996 OL	Number
Impact Aid:							
Payments for Federally-Connected Children: Basic Support	632	518	550	552	–82	34	
Payments for Federally-Connected Children: Payments for Heavily Impacted Districts	40	33	20	23	–20	–10	
School Improvement Program:							
Arts in Education	12	10	10	12	–2	2	
Training and Advisory Services	21	24	14	22	–7	–1	
Student Loans: Federal Family Education Loan Program: Federal Administration	62	60	30	42	–32	–18	
Subtotal, Education	809	686	644	689	–165	3	6
Department of Energy							
Fossil Energy R&D:							
Advanced clean fuels research	39	42	17	31	–22	–11	
Advanced clean power systems	91	97	73	85	–18	–12	
Energy Supply R&D:							
In-House Energy Management	31	27	28	29	–3	2	
Civilian Energy Management	723	699	690	701	–33	2	
Biological and Environmental Research	445	411	426	429	–19	18	
Advanced Neutron Source	21	16	8	14	–13	–2	
University and Science Education	66	52	59	61	–7	9	
Magnetic Fusion	373	350	361	361	–12	11	
Uranium Enrichment Program	73	100	42	58	–31	–42	
Economic Regulation	12	13	11	12	–1	–1	
Strategic Petroleum Reserve	244	224	213	223	–31	–1	
Subtotal, Energy	2,118	2,031	1,928	2,004	–190	–27	11
Department of Health and Human Services (HHS)							
Community Services: Community Food and Nutrition	9	7	6	8	–3	*	
Health Care Financing Administration: Program Management: Research	89	78	65	72	–25	–6	
Departmental Management	124	201	121	122	–3	–79	
Subtotal, HHS	222	286	192	202	–30	–85	3
Department of the Interior							
Bureau of Indian Affairs (BIA), Fish and Wildlife Service (FWS), Bureau of Land Management (BLM): Construction	107	125	66	99	–41	–26	
Bureau of Mines (BOM): Reinvent the Bureau of Mines (including Mineral Institutes phase-out)	152	161	132	139	–20	–22	
Bureau of Reclamation: Construction	433	545	376	382	–57	–163	
Subtotal, Interior	692	831	574	620	–118	–211	5
Department of Justice							
U.S. Parole Commission	7	8	7	7	–1	–1	
Support of U.S. Prisoners	297	250	295	302	–1	52	
Subtotal, Justice	304	258	302	310	–2	51	2
Department of Labor							
Training and Employment Services:							
JTPA Training grants for low-income youth	550	607	290	624	–260	18	

Table S–9. PROGRAM REDUCTIONS—Continued

(In millions of dollars)

Agency and Program	1995		1996		Change: 1995 to 1996		Number
	BA	OL	BA	OL	BA	OL	
Other Job Training Partnership Act programs	156	171	145	164	–11	–7	
Employment Service State Grants	846	835	806	838	–40	3	
Subtotal, Labor	1,552	1,613	1,241	1,626	–311	14	6
Department of State							
Salaries and Expenses	376	437	372	370	–4	–68	
Emergencies in the Diplomatic and Consular Service	7	7	6	6	–1	–1	
Protection of Foreign Missions and Officials	10	10	9	10	–1	–1	
Contributions to International Peacekeeping Activities	533	538	445	445	–88	–93	
Contribution to The Asia Foundation Program Grant	15	15	10	11	–5	–4	
Anti-terrorism Assistance	15	15	15	15	–*	–*	
Subtotal, State	956	1,023	857	856	–99	–167	6
Department of Transportation							
Grants to the National Railroad Passenger Corporation Program	772	735	750	694	–22	–41	
Formula Grants: Transit Formula Operating Grants	710	747	500	593	–210	–154	
Subtotal, Transportation	1,482	1,482	1,250	1,287	–232	–195	2
Department of the Treasury							
U.S. Customs Service: Operation and Maintenance: Air Interdiction	88	83	61	66	–27	–17	
Federal Law Enforcement Training Center: Acquisition, Construction, Improvements, and related expenses	17	13	–3	9	–20	–4	
Bureau of Public Debt	180	182	172	173	–8	–9	
Subtotal, Treasury	285	278	230	248	–55	–30	3
Department of Veterans Affairs							
Parking Garage Revolving Fund	16	7	....	4	–16	–3	
Grants for construction of State extended care facilities	47	59	44	41	–3	–18	
Grants for construction of State veterans cemeteries	5	5	1	2	–4	–3	
Subtotal, Veterans Affairs	68	71	45	47	–23	–24	3
Environmental Protection Agency (EPA)							
Water Infrastructure Financing: Targeted Wastewater Assistance	834	412	265	506	–569	94	
Subtotal, EPA	834	412	265	506	–569	94	1
National Science Foundation (NSF)							
Academic Research Infrastructure	250	116	100	151	–150	35	
Proposed rescission of 1995 funds	132	....	....	39	–132	39	
Academic Research Infrastructure (net)	118	116	100	112	–18	–4	
Major Research Equipment	126	55	70	57	–56	2	
Subtotal, NSF	244	171	170	169	–74	–2	2
Other Independent Agencies (OIAs)							
Appalachian Regional Commission	282	164	183	202	–99	38	
State Justice Institute	14	14	7	12	–7	–2	
United States Information Agency (USIA):							
East-West Center Program Grant	25	25	20	20	–5	–4	

Table S–9. PROGRAM REDUCTIONS—Continued

(In millions of dollars)

Agency and Program	1995		1996		Change: 1995 to 1996		Number
	BA	OL	BA	OL	BA	OL	
North/South Center Program Grant	4	12	1	7	–3	–5	
International Broadcasting Operations—International Broadcasting	468	393	395	403	–73	10	
Subtotal, USIA	497	429	416	430	–80	1	3
Subtotal, OIAs	792	607	606	644	–186	37	5
Total, Reductions in 1996 Budget	**130,433**	**127,856**	**122,895**	**121,431**	**–7,538**	**–6,425**	**86**

* Less than $500 thousand.

Table S–10. PROPOSED INVESTMENTS

(Budget authority, dollar amounts in millions)

	Enacted 1993	Enacted 1995	1996 Estimate	Dollar Change: 1993 to 1996	Percent Change: 1993 to 1996	Dollar Change: 1995 to 1996	Percent Change: 1995 to 1996
Agriculture Department:							
Rural development initiative:							
Grant levels	877	1,096	1,250	373	43	154	14
Loan levels (subsidy budget authority)	384	459	570	186	48	111	24
(Loans)	(3,119)	(4,029)	(4,589)	(1,470)	47	(560)	14
WIC (Special supplemental nutrition program for women, infants and children)	2,860	3,470	3,820	960	34	350	10
Food safety	494	526	595	101	20	69	13
Food safety research	16	28	39	23	144	11	39
Enhanced natural resource protection and environmental infrastructure	625	632	649	24	4	17	3
National research initiative	98	103	130	32	33	27	26
Climate change action plan	....	8	12	12	N/A	4	50
Pacific Northwest Forest Plan implementation	....	98	107	107	N/A	9	9
Commerce Department:							
Economic Development Administration, defense conversion	....	120	120	120	N/A	....	....
National Institute of Standards and Technology: Growth/High performance computing/National Science and Technology Council (NSTC)	381	855	1,023	642	169	168	20
Information highways	....	61	100	100	N/A	39	64
NOAA: rebuild US fisheries	246	269	316	70	28	47	17
NOAA NSTC	53	85	113	60	113	28	33
Pacific Northwest Forest Plan (EDA)	....	3	3	3	N/A	....	....
Defense Department:							
ARPA technology reinvestment project	472	443	500	28	6	57	13
Office of Economic Adjustment	30	39	59	29	97	20	51
Education Department:							
School-to-work (Education Department share)	....	125	200	200	N/A	75	60
Goals 2000	....	403	750	750	N/A	347	86
Title I, education for the disadvantaged	6,709	7,233	7,441	732	11	208	3
Safe and drug free schools	598	482	500	–98	–16	18	4
Immigration Initiative (Immigrant Education)	29	50	100	71	245	50	100
Energy Department:							
Alternative fuels vehicles	28	53	56	28	100	3	6
Conservation R&D/EPAct	346	512	643	297	86	131	26
Conservation: weatherization assistance grants	185	226	229	44	24	3	1
Federal facility energy efficiency (FFEE)	5	24	26	21	420	2	8
Renewable energy programs	251	388	423	172	69	35	9
Cooperative R&D agreements	151	274	296	145	96	22	8
Advanced neutron source construction	12	21	....	–12	–100	–21	–100
Linear accelerator "B-Factory" construction	....	44	52	52	N/A	8	18
Climate change action plan	....	101	188	188	N/A	87	86
Partnership for a New Generation of Vehicles	107	168	251	144	135	83	49
Science facilities utilization	....	....	100	100	N/A	100	N/A
Health and Human Services:							
Head Start	2,776	3,535	3,935	1,159	42	400	11
Immigration initiative (HHS share)	....	....	150	150	N/A	150	N/A
Public Health Service:							
NIH	10,326	11,321	11,788	1,462	14	467	4
Ryan White Act AIDS treatment	348	633	723	375	108	90	14
Immunizations [1]	511	843	844	333	65	1	*
High performance computing	47	78	78	31	66	....	....
Drug treatment	....	....	100	100	N/A	100	N/A
Housing and Urban Development:							
Multifamily property disposition [2]	93	555	777	684	735	222	40
Community partnerships against crime	175	290	290	115	66	....	....

Table S–10. PROPOSED INVESTMENTS—Continued

(Budget authority, dollar amounts in millions)

	Enacted 1993	Enacted 1995	1996 Estimate	Dollar Change: 1993 to 1996	Percent Change: 1993 to 1996	Dollar Change: 1995 to 1996	Percent Change: 1995 to 1996
Incremental housing vouchers	1,307	2,386	1,645	338	26	–741	–31
Homeless programs: homeless assistance block grants and innovative homeless initiatives program	572	1,120	1,120	548	96	....	....
Choice in Residency	....	....	150	150	N/A	150	N/A
Interior Department:							
Enhanced natural resource protection and environmental infrastructure	1,783	1,873	2,012	229	13	139	7
Pacific Northwest Forest Plan implementation	....	56	80	80	N/A	24	43
South Florida ecosystem restoration	26	44	64	38	146	20	45
National Biological Survey	....	167	173	173	N/A	6	4
National spatial data infrastructure initiative	....	4	7	7	N/A	3	75
Wastewater reuse pilot program	....	18	23	23	N/A	5	28
Justice Department:							
Community Oriented Policing Services (COPS) (violent crime reduction programs)	150	1,300	1,882	1,732	1,155	582	45
Other violent crime reduction programs (including other agencies)	....	1,122	2,405	2,405	N/A	1,283	114
Immigration initiative (excluding violent crime reduction programs)[3]	1,493	1,776	2,252	759	51	476	27
Labor Department:							
Immigration (targeted enforcement)	95	101	117	22	23	16	16
Dislocated Worker Assistance Act	602	1,296	1,396	794	132	100	8
School-to-work (DOL share)	....	125	200	200	N/A	75	60
One-stop career shopping	....	120	200	200	N/A	80	67
Job Corps	966	1,099	1,228	262	27	129	12
Pacific Northwest Forest Plan (JTPA-III)	....	12	12	12	N/A	....	....
Transportation Department:							
Unified Transportation Infrastructure Investment[4]	....	....	21,555	N/A	N/A	N/A	N/A
Federal-aid highways (obligations)	(16,457)	(18,616)	(4)	N/A	N/A	N/A	N/A
Mass transit formula capital grants:							
Budget authority	54	616	(4)	N/A	N/A	N/A	N/A
Obligation limitation	(844)	(1,150)	(4)	N/A	N/A	N/A	N/A
Intelligent vehicle highway system (obligation limitation)	(153)	(238)	(356)	(203)	133	(118)	50
Next generation high speed rail:							
Budget authority	....	20	59	59	N/A	39	195
Obligation limitation	....	(5)	(5)	(5)	N/A	....	....
Penn Station redevelopment	....	40	50	50	N/A	10	25
Treasury Department:							
IRS: Tax system modernization	572	622	1,032	460	80	410	66
Immigration (Customs inspection and border management)[5]	270	283	387	117	43	104	37
Corps of Engineers:							
President's August 1993 wetlands plan	86	101	112	26	30	11	11
Climate change action plan	....	1	1	1	N/A	....	....
Environmental Protection Agency:							
Clean water state revolving funds	1,928	1,236	1,600	–328	–17	364	29
Safe drinking water state revolving funds	....	700	500	500	N/A	–200	–29
Watershed restoration grants	50	100	100	50	100	....	....
Environmental technology	67	139	192	125	187	53	38
Climate change action plan	....	116	136	136	N/A	20	17
Montreal protocol	10	17	24	14	140	7	41
NAFTA environmental commitments	154	174	180	26	17	6	3
Needy cities	100	100	100	....	....	....	....
Wetlands initiative	32	36	37	5	16	1	3

162-000 O - 95 - 8

Table S–10. PROPOSED INVESTMENTS—Continued

(Budget authority, dollar amounts in millions)

	Enacted		1996 Estimate	Dollar Change: 1993 to 1996	Percent Change: 1993 to 1996	Dollar Change: 1995 to 1996	Percent Change: 1995 to 1996
	1993	1995					
Pacific Northwest Forest Plan implementation	....	5	5	5	N/A	....	....
National Aeronautics and Space Administration:							
Space Station	2,262	2,113	2,115	–147	–6	2	*
Mission to Planet Earth	917	1,338	1,337	420	46	–1	–*
Aeronautics initiatives	129	347	434	305	236	87	25
High performance computing	30	76	75	45	150	–1	–1
New Millennium initiative	67	392	495	428	639	103	26
Small Business Administration:							
Section 7(a) loan guarantees	(6,410)	(7,850)	(9,441)	(3,031)	47	(1,591)	20
One Stop Capital Shops (Empowerment zones)	....	2	3	3	N/A	1	50
Small Business Investment Company guarantees	13	44	51	38	292	7	16
(Loans)	(74)	(366)	(437)	(363)	491	(71)	19
Social Security Administration:							
Disability processing and automation investments:							
Budget authority	....	347	405	405	N/A	58	17
Obligation limitations	....	(70)	(486)	(486)	N/A	(416)	594
Community Development Financial Institutions	....	125	144	144	N/A	19	15
(Loans)	....	(24)	(56)	(56)	N/A	(32)	133
Legal Services Corporation:							
Payment to the Legal Services Corporation	357	415	440	83	23	25	6
National Science Foundation:							
NSF research and education	2,535	2,851	3,053	518	20	202	7
Equipment and facilities	84	244	170	86	102	–74	–30
National Service Initiative [6]	279	792	1,082	803	288	290	37
Labor and Education Departments:							
G.I. Bill for America's Workers [7]	12,426	13,186	14,202	1,776	14	1,016	8
Total proposed investments: Total budgetary resources [8]	**75,157**	**92,510**	**102,192**	**27,035**	**36**	**9,682**	**10**

[1] Amounts for Immunizations include mandatory spending of $170 million, $377 million, and $365 million in 1993, 1995, and 1996, respectively.

[2] Amounts for Multifamily property disposition are mandatory spending starting in 1996.

[3] Amounts for the Immigration initiative in Justice include mandatory spending of $526 million, $672 million, and $799 million in 1993, 1995, and 1996, respectively.

[4] Amounts for Transportation investment items affected by Reinventing Government-Phase II are included under "Unified Transportation Infrastructure Investment." This program will consolidate over 30 categorial infrastructure grant programs, including, but not limited to, programs from within the Federal-aid highways and mass transit formula capital programs.

[5] Amounts for Immigration in the Department of the Treasury include $100 million in 1996 for Border services user fee mandatory spending.

[6] The 1993 enacted column for National Service Initiative includes funding for ACTION and the Commission on National and Community Service. The first official year of the National Service Initiative was 1994.

[7] Also includes one program each in the Departments of Agriculture and Housing and Urban Development.

[8] Totals have been adjusted to exclude investment amounts that are included in more than one investment item.

Table S–11. SUMMARY OF SUPPLEMENTAL AND RESCISSION PROPOSALS
(In millions of dollars)

	1995 Budget Authority	Outlays					
		1995	1996	1997	1998	1999	2000
Discretionary Supplementals:							
Department of Agriculture	9	9					
Department of Education		4					
Department of the Interior	7	1	2	2	1	1	
Department of Justice (transfer)	–2	–2					
Department of Transportation		1	*				
National Aeronautics and Space Administration			1	300	99		
International Security Assistance	384	314	31	15	10	6	4
Agency for International Development	18	1	13	3	1	*	*
Other Independent Agencies	9	6	2	*			
Total, Increases in Discretionary Programs	**426**	**335**	**49**	**319**	**111**	**7**	**4**
Decreases in Discretionary Programs: [1]							
Department of Agriculture	–145	–59	–78	–9			
Department of Commerce	–18	–2	–8	–4	–4		
Department of Defense-Military	–703	–200	–204	–114	–56	–24	–11
Department of Education	–223	–30	–147	–41	–4	–*	–*
Department of Health and Human Service	–51	–13	–24	–12	–2	–1	
Department of Housing and Urban Development	–476	–54	–118	–92	–64	–52	–32
Department of Labor	–5	–5	–*				
Department of Transportation	–421	–26	–718	–136	–72	–51	–40
Environmental Protection Agency	–12	–4	–5	–2	–*	–*	
National Aeronautics and Space Administration	–28	–4	–15	–5	–2	–1	–*
Small Business Administration	–15	–12	–3				
Other Independent Agencies	–132	–*	–40	–53	–40		
Subtotal, Decreases in Discretionary Programs	**–2,230**	**–409**	**–821**	**–467**	**–243**	**–129**	**–83**
Total, Changes in Discretionary Programs	**–1,804**	**–74**	**–772**	**–148**	**–132**	**–122**	**–79**
Emergency Supplementals:							
Department of Defense-Military	2,557	1,956	459	81	27	13	6
Department of State	672	672					
Department of Transportation	28	23	3	2			
Other Independent Agencies	6,700	670	2,680	2,680	670		
Total, Emergency Supplementals	**9,957**	**3,321**	**3,142**	**2,764**	**697**	**13**	**6**
Mandatory Supplementals:							
Department of Health and Human Service	26	22	4				
Office of Personnel Management	9	9					
Other Independent Agencies		–3	3				
Total, Mandatory Supplementals	**35**	**28**	**7**				
Total, All Proposals	**8,188**	**3,275**	**2,377**	**2,616**	**565**	**–108**	**–73**

* Less than $500 thousand.
[1] In addition to rescissions, this includes provisions that require the Secretaries of Defense, Health and Human Services, Labor, and Transportation to reduce 1995 budget authority by specified amounts.

Table S–12. EFFECT OF PROPOSALS ON RECEIPTS

(In millions of dollars)

	Estimate						Total, 1995–2000
	1995	1996	1997	1998	1999	2000	
Provide tax relief to middle-income families:							
Provide tax credit for dependent children	....	–3,493	–6,820	–6,595	–8,343	–10,142	–35,393
Provide tax incentive for education and training	....	–686	–4,651	–4,941	–5,711	–7,529	–23,518
Expand individual retirement accounts (IRAs)	....	361	–323	–814	–1,006	–1,978	–3,760
Subtotal, middle-income tax relief	....	**–3,818**	**–11,794**	**–12,350**	**–15,060**	**–19,649**	**–62,671**
Other proposals:							
Modify earned income tax credit (EITC) eligibility rules:							
Deny EITC to undocumented workers/related compliance measures	....	....	96	103	106	108	413
Impose interest and dividend test on EITC recipients	....	4	77	82	82	90	335
Subtotal, modify EITC eligibility rules	....	4	173	185	188	198	748
Deter expatriation tax avoidance	....	60	200	300	410	530	1,500
Tighten rules for taxing foreign trusts	....	276	388	421	459	498	2,042
Increase the number of empowerment zones	–53	–100	–116	–128	–137	–144	–678
Reduce excise taxes on certain vaccines [1]	....	–70	–61	–61	–61	–61	–314
Expand fees collected under the securities laws	81	310	325	341	358	376	1,791
Assess fees for examination of FDIC-insured banks and bank holding companies (receipt effect)	....	79	83	86	89	92	429
Modify Federal pay raise (receipt effect)	....	–75	–157	–257	–358	–453	–1,300
Extend environmental tax on corporate taxable income [2]	....	307	520	530	536	540	2,433
Subtotal, other proposals [1]	**28**	**791**	**1,355**	**1,417**	**1,484**	**1,576**	**6,651**
Total effect of proposals [1]	**28**	**–3,028**	**–10,439**	**–10,933**	**–13,576**	**–18,074**	**–56,022**
(PAYGO proposals) [1]	(28)	(–2,953)	(–10,282)	(–10,676)	(–13,218)	(–17,621)	(–54,722)
(Non-PAYGO proposals)	(—)	(–75)	(–157)	(–257)	(–358)	(–453)	**(–1,300)**

[1] Net of income offsets.
[2] Net of deductibility for income tax purposes.

Table S–13. DISCRETIONARY PROPOSALS BY APPROPRIATIONS SUBCOMMITTEE

(In millions of dollars)

Appropriations Subcommittee	1995 Enacted		1995 Proposed [1]		1996 Proposed		Change: 1995 Enacted to 1996 Proposed	
	BA	Outlays	BA	Outlays	BA	Outlays	BA	Outlays
General Purpose Discretionary								
Agriculture and Rural Development	13,850	14,714	13,714	14,664	14,241	14,188	391	–526
Commerce, Justice, State and the Judiciary	24,087	25,627	24,061	25,618	26,039	25,818	1,952	191
National Security	242,842	250,222	242,139	250,022	236,108	241,056	–6,734	–9,166
District of Columbia	712	714	712	714	712	712	....	–2
Energy and Water Development	20,519	21,389	20,519	21,389	20,650	20,592	131	–797
Foreign Operations	13,559	14,028	13,961	14,344	14,747	14,361	1,188	333
Interior and Related Agencies	13,725	13,856	13,731	13,857	13,916	14,365	191	509
Labor, HHS, and Education	70,084	71,000	69,805	70,956	73,320	73,869	3,236	2,869
Legislative	2,361	2,425	2,361	2,425	2,611	2,592	250	167
Military Construction	8,850	9,077	8,850	9,077	10,698	9,585	1,848	508
Transportation and Related Agencies [2]	37,934	36,944	37,518	36,919	35,507	36,552	–2,427	–392
Treasury-Postal Service, and General Government	11,735	12,557	11,736	12,557	13,039	12,651	1,304	94
Veterans Affairs, HUD, Independent Agencies	71,126	77,336	70,477	77,274	71,853	77,425	727	89
Allowances	....	....	....	....	–250	–224	–250	–224
Subtotal, General Purpose Discretionary	531,385	549,889	529,584	549,815	533,191	543,540	1,806	–6,349
Violent Crime Reduction Trust Fund (VCRTF)								
Commerce, Justice, State and the Judiciary	2,345	663	2,345	663	4,010	2,144	1,665	1,481
Interior and Related Agencies	....	....	....	....	15	6	15	6
Labor, HHS, and Education	38	12	38	12	175	72	137	60
Transportation and Related Agencies	....	....	....	....	5	....	5	....
Treasury, Postal Service, and General Government	39	30	39	30	78	58	39	28
Veterans Affairs, HUD, Independent Agencies	....	....	....	....	3	3	3	3
Subtotal, VCRTF [3]	2,422	705	2,422	705	4,286	2,283	1,864	1,578
Total, Discretionary	**533,807**	**550,594**	**532,006**	**550,520**	**537,478**	**545,825**	**3,671**	**–4,769**

Memorandum: Amounts Excluded From Budget Resolution Allocations And Not Included Above

	1995 Enacted BA	1995 Enacted Outlays	1995 Proposed BA	1995 Proposed Outlays	1996 Proposed BA	1996 Proposed Outlays
Proposed Emergency Supplementals:						
Commerce, Justice, State and the Judiciary	....	....	672	672	....	....
Defense	....	....	2,539	1,954	....	452
Military Construction	....	....	18	2	....	7
Transportation and Related Agencies	....	....	28	23	....	3
Veterans Affairs, HUD, Independent Agencies	....	....	6,700	670	....	2,680
Total, Proposed Emergencies	....	....	**9,957**	**3,321**	....	**3,142**

[1] The 1995 proposed level includes enacted appropriations plus supplementals and rescissions proposed in the 1996 budget. It excludes proposed emergency spending.

[2] For comparability with 1996, Transportation budget authority in 1995 has been adjusted upward to show obligations defined as budget authority

[3] Totals have been adjusted to include transfers (of $204 million in 1995 and $15 million in 1996), from VCRTF to administrative accounts in the Department of Justice as crime spending.

Summaries by Agency/Function

SUMMARIES BY AGENCY/FUNCTION

Table S–14. DISCRETIONARY BUDGET AUTHORITY BY AGENCY

(in billions of dollars)

Agency	1994 Actual	Estimate					
		1995	1996	1997	1998	1999	2000
Legislative Branch	2.3	2.4	2.6	2.7	2.7	2.8	2.8
The Judiciary	2.5	2.7	3.1	3.1	3.2	3.3	3.4
Executive Office Of the President	0.2	0.2	0.2	0.2	0.2	0.2	0.2
Funds Appropriated to the President	11.5	12.4	13.2	12.8	12.6	12.4	12.1
Agriculture	16.8	15.3	15.8	15.5	15.2	15.0	14.7
Commerce	3.9	4.2	4.7	4.6	4.5	4.4	7.2
Defense—Military	250.5	253.5	246.7	243.5	251.6	257.9	267.5
Defense—Civil	4.0	3.5	3.4	3.3	3.4	3.3	3.2
Education [1]	24.5	24.9	24.1	23.8	23.4	23.0	22.5
Energy	18.7	17.5	17.8	16.0	15.1	14.8	14.7
Health and Human Services	33.0	33.3	35.0	34.0	33.5	32.9	32.3
Housing and Urban Development [2]	26.3	25.6	25.7	25.2	36.0	31.3	30.3
Interior	7.5	7.3	7.6	7.3	7.2	7.0	6.9
Justice	9.5	12.1	14.8	15.6	16.4	17.5	17.8
Labor [1]	10.6	11.0	14.1	13.9	13.7	13.5	13.3
State	5.4	5.6	5.0	4.9	4.8	4.7	4.6
Transportation [3]	39.3	37.4	35.7	36.8	36.5	33.3	32.7
Treasury	10.3	10.5	11.3	10.9	10.7	10.5	10.2
Veterans Affairs	17.7	18.2	19.2	18.7	18.3	17.9	17.5
Environmental Protection Agency	6.6	7.2	7.4	7.1	7.0	6.9	6.7
General Services Administration	0.6	0.4	1.0	0.8	0.8	0.8	0.6
National Aeronautics and Space Administration	14.6	14.4	14.3	13.9	13.7	13.4	13.2
Office of Personnel Management	0.1	0.1	0.1	0.1	0.1	0.1	0.1
Small Business Administration	1.9	0.8	0.7	0.7	0.7	0.7	0.7
Social Security Administration [4]	1.8	2.4	2.1	2.1	1.8	1.8	1.7
Other Independent Agencies	16.7	18.7	12.3	11.8	11.5	11.2	10.8
Allowances	....	....	–0.2	–0.5	–0.8	–0.9	–1.0
Total	**536.8**	**541.8**	**537.5**	**528.7**	**543.7**	**539.4**	**546.6**

[1] Beginning in 1996, almost 70 programs, primarily in the Education and Labor Departments, are proposed to be integrated into a workforce development system for adults and youths, administered by the States. As a result, certain funds are transferred between the two Departments. The net change results in a higher Labor budget, but the sum of the two Departments reflects a net increase of $1 billion for these activities.

[2] HUD budget authority fluctuates from year to year with the number of expiring multi-year low-income housing subsidy commitments to be made each year.

[3] Transportation budget authority for 1994 and 1995 has been adjusted to be comparable to the treatment proposed for 1996–2000.

[4] Amounts reflect only SSA-administered sources of discretionary budget authority. HHS-administered sources of funding for SSA administrative expenses are included in the HHS line item. SSA's administrative resources increase by $611 million from 1995 to 1996.

Table S–15. DISCRETIONARY OUTLAYS BY AGENCY

(in billions of dollars)

Agency	1994 Actual	Estimate					
		1995	1996	1997	1998	1999	2000
Legislative Branch	2.3	2.5	2.6	2.6	2.7	2.7	2.8
The Judiciary	2.5	2.7	3.0	3.1	3.1	3.2	3.3
Executive Office Of the President	0.2	0.2	0.2	0.2	0.2	0.2	0.2
Funds Appropriated to the President	12.1	13.0	13.0	13.2	12.9	12.8	12.9
Agriculture	15.9	16.0	15.6	15.5	15.2	15.0	14.8
Commerce	3.0	3.7	4.2	4.5	4.7	4.7	7.1
Defense—Military	269.4	260.9	251.0	246.6	246.1	251.2	259.3
Defense—Civil	3.7	3.9	3.6	3.6	3.4	3.3	3.2
Education	22.9	24.9	24.2	24.1	23.8	23.4	23.0
Energy	19.3	18.2	17.9	16.9	16.0	15.1	14.8
Health and Human Services	31.1	33.0	34.0	33.9	33.5	33.0	32.4
Housing and Urban Development	27.6	31.0	31.8	33.6	33.8	35.2	34.6
Interior	7.3	7.4	7.5	7.4	7.3	7.1	7.0
Justice	9.4	10.9	12.8	14.8	16.0	16.8	17.6
Labor	9.8	10.1	12.3	14.3	13.8	13.6	13.3
State	5.3	5.8	5.1	5.0	4.9	4.8	4.6
Transportation	36.8	37.5	36.9	36.3	36.1	36.1	35.0
Treasury	10.1	10.7	11.2	10.8	10.7	10.5	10.3
Veterans Affairs	17.2	18.1	19.0	18.7	18.3	18.0	17.6
Environmental Protection Agency	6.1	6.5	6.8	7.1	7.3	7.1	6.9
General Services Administration	0.3	1.1	0.6	0.6	0.7	0.8	0.7
National Aeronautics and Space Administration	13.7	14.2	14.1	14.0	13.7	13.5	13.3
Office of Personnel Management	0.2	0.2	0.2	0.2	0.2	0.2	0.2
Small Business Administration	1.3	1.5	1.0	0.8	0.7	0.7	0.7
Social Security Administration	4.4	4.8	5.3	5.3	5.0	4.9	4.7
Other Independent Agencies	13.5	14.8	15.2	15.0	12.3	11.2	11.0
Allowances	....	....	–0.2	–0.5	–0.8	–0.9	–1.0
Total	**545.6**	**553.8**	**549.0**	**547.4**	**541.5**	**544.1**	**550.2**

Table S–16. BUDGET AUTHORITY BY AGENCY

(in billions of dollars)

Agency	1994 Actual	Estimate					
		1995	1996	1997	1998	1999	2000
Legislative Branch	2.6	2.7	3.0	3.0	3.1	3.1	3.2
The Judiciary	2.8	3.0	3.4	3.5	3.6	3.7	3.8
Executive Office Of the President	0.2	0.2	0.2	0.2	0.2	0.2	0.2
Funds Appropriated to the President	9.6	11.5	11.3	10.4	9.9	9.3	10.5
Agriculture	65.6	61.9	64.0	64.0	62.2	63.8	64.6
Commerce	3.8	4.1	4.6	4.5	4.4	4.5	7.2
Defense—Military	251.4	252.6	246.0	242.8	249.7	256.3	266.1
Defense—Civil	30.9	30.9	31.8	32.4	33.7	35.4	36.5
Education	27.0	33.5	30.4	28.8	28.3	28.3	28.2
Energy	17.2	15.5	15.9	14.6	14.1	14.3	14.0
Health and Human Services	307.7	302.7	318.9	357.4	384.5	413.1	443.9
Housing and Urban Development	26.3	25.8	26.3	25.4	36.1	31.4	30.4
Interior	7.5	7.5	7.5	7.2	7.0	6.9	6.7
Justice	10.2	12.8	15.5	16.3	17.1	18.2	18.5
Labor	38.2	33.8	38.7	38.3	38.9	39.4	39.9
State	5.8	6.0	5.5	5.4	5.3	5.2	5.2
Transportation	42.3	40.4	37.6	38.9	37.4	34.3	33.7
Treasury	309.3	353.1	387.6	407.9	427.2	448.6	468.2
Veterans Affairs	36.8	38.2	39.5	39.6	39.6	39.6	39.6
Environmental Protection Agency	6.4	7.0	7.3	7.1	7.0	6.9	6.8
General Services Administration	0.6	0.4	1.0	0.8	0.8	0.8	0.6
National Aeronautics and Space Administration	14.6	14.4	14.3	13.9	13.7	13.4	13.2
Office of Personnel Management	40.4	42.3	43.6	46.4	49.0	51.3	53.9
Small Business Administration	2.1	0.8	0.7	0.7	0.7	0.7	0.7
Social Security Administration	348.6	366.7	380.3	406.3	428.3	451.0	477.2
On-Budget	(33.1)	(32.6)	(30.7)	(38.8)	(41.5)	(44.4)	(50.3)
Off-Budget	(315.5)	(334.1)	(349.6)	(367.6)	(386.8)	(406.6)	(426.9)
Other Independent Agencies	43.9	28.7	21.0	18.9	19.0	18.1	16.7
On-Budget	(41.2)	(24.8)	(16.6)	(17.1)	(17.0)	(16.7)	(16.6)
Off-Budget	(2.7)	(4.0)	(4.3)	(1.7)	(1.9)	(1.4)	(0.1)
Allowances	....	....	–0.4	–0.5	–0.8	–0.9	–1.0
Undistributed Offsetting Receipts	–123.5	–132.9	–141.5	–147.8	–154.7	–157.9	–164.3
On-Budget	(–87.9)	(–92.8)	(–96.6)	(–98.1)	(–99.8)	(–97.3)	(–97.5)
Off-Budget	(–35.6)	(–40.0)	(–45.0)	(–49.7)	(–54.9)	(–60.6)	(–66.8)
Total	**1,528.4**	**1,563.8**	**1,613.8**	**1,686.4**	**1,765.2**	**1,839.1**	**1,924.0**
On-budget	(1,245.8)	(1,265.8)	(1,304.8)	(1,366.8)	(1,431.4)	(1,491.7)	(1,563.8)
Off-budget	(282.6)	(298.0)	(309.0)	(319.6)	(333.8)	(347.5)	(360.2)

Table S–17. OUTLAYS BY AGENCY

(in billions of dollars)

Agency	1994 Actual	Estimate					
		1995	1996	1997	1998	1999	2000
Legislative Branch	2.6	2.8	3.0	3.0	3.0	3.0	3.1
The Judiciary	2.7	3.1	3.3	3.4	3.4	3.5	3.6
Executive Office Of the President	0.2	0.2	0.2	0.2	0.2	0.2	0.2
Funds Appropriated to the President	10.5	10.9	10.8	10.8	10.7	10.7	11.1
Agriculture	60.8	62.3	62.3	62.7	61.3	62.5	63.4
Commerce	2.9	3.6	4.1	4.4	4.6	4.7	7.1
Defense—Military	268.6	260.3	250.0	246.1	244.2	249.6	257.9
Defense—Civil	30.4	31.2	31.9	32.6	33.6	35.4	36.3
Education	24.7	32.9	30.7	29.3	28.5	28.6	28.4
Energy	17.8	16.1	15.8	15.5	14.5	14.2	13.9
Health and Human Services	278.9	301.4	331.4	357.5	384.6	412.4	444.2
Housing and Urban Development	25.8	26.9	26.3	29.6	30.1	30.6	29.3
Interior	6.9	7.3	7.3	7.2	7.1	6.9	6.7
Justice	10.0	11.8	13.5	15.5	16.7	17.5	18.3
Labor	37.0	31.9	35.9	37.5	37.8	38.3	39.1
State	5.7	6.3	5.5	5.5	5.4	5.3	5.2
Transportation	37.2	38.0	37.3	36.8	36.5	36.6	35.5
Treasury	307.6	351.8	386.1	406.1	425.5	447.0	466.5
Veterans Affairs	37.4	38.2	38.0	39.5	39.7	39.8	41.6
Environmental Protection Agency	5.9	6.3	6.6	7.0	7.2	7.1	6.9
General Services Administration	0.3	1.1	0.6	0.6	0.7	0.8	0.7
National Aeronautics and Space Administration	13.7	14.2	14.1	14.0	13.7	13.5	13.3
Office of Personnel Management	38.6	40.3	42.8	44.8	47.5	50.0	52.2
Small Business Administration	0.8	0.7	0.4	0.5	0.1	0.2	0.5
Social Security Administration	345.8	363.4	381.7	404.6	426.5	449.1	475.2
On-Budget	(31.9)	(32.1)	(32.4)	(38.7)	(41.5)	(44.4)	(50.3)
Off-Budget	(313.9)	(331.3)	(349.4)	(365.9)	(384.9)	(404.7)	(424.9)
Other Independent Agencies	11.5	8.6	14.3	18.2	17.5	13.5	10.6
On-Budget	(10.4)	(7.9)	(13.7)	(17.8)	(18.0)	(14.5)	(12.0)
Off-Budget	(1.1)	(0.7)	(0.6)	(0.4)	(–0.4)	(–1.0)	(–1.4)
Allowances	....	....	–0.4	–0.5	–0.8	–0.9	–1.0
Undistributed Offsetting Receipts	–123.5	–132.9	–141.5	–147.8	–154.7	–157.9	–164.3
On-Budget	(–87.9)	(–92.8)	(–96.6)	(–98.1)	(–99.8)	(–97.3)	(–97.5)
Off-Budget	(–35.6)	(–40.0)	(–45.0)	(–49.7)	(–54.9)	(–60.6)	(–66.8)
Total	**1,460.9**	**1,538.9**	**1,612.1**	**1,684.7**	**1,745.2**	**1,822.2**	**1,905.3**
On-budget	(1,181.5)	(1,246.9)	(1,307.1)	(1,368.1)	(1,415.6)	(1,479.1)	(1,548.6)
Off-budget	(279.4)	(292.0)	(305.0)	(316.6)	(329.6)	(343.1)	(356.7)

Table S–18. BUDGET AUTHORITY BY FUNCTION

(in billions of dollars)

Function	1994 Actual	Estimate					
		1995	1996	1997	1998	1999	2000
National defense:							
Department of Defense—Military	251.4	252.6	246.0	242.8	249.7	256.3	266.1
Other	11.9	10.9	11.8	10.6	9.9	9.9	9.9
Total National defense	263.3	263.5	257.8	253.4	259.6	266.3	276.0
International affairs	17.7	19.4	18.5	17.4	16.8	15.9	17.3
General science, space, and technology	17.6	16.9	17.3	16.7	16.4	16.1	15.7
Energy	4.7	4.3	3.7	3.7	3.8	4.1	3.7
Natural resources and environment	22.7	22.0	22.6	22.0	21.7	21.2	20.8
Agriculture	17.1	13.2	13.1	11.8	9.1	9.3	8.9
Commerce and housing credit	26.4	9.4	8.3	6.0	5.5	4.6	5.7
On-Budget	(23.7)	(5.5)	(4.0)	(4.3)	(3.5)	(3.2)	(5.7)
Off-Budget	(2.7)	(4.0)	(4.3)	(1.7)	(1.9)	(1.4)	(0.1)
Transportation	43.5	42.1	38.9	40.2	38.6	35.4	34.8
Community and regional development	15.6	15.7	9.6	9.5	9.4	9.3	8.7
Education, training, employment, and social services	51.6	58.7	59.3	57.6	57.4	57.5	57.7
Health	116.5	117.0	110.3	132.6	142.5	152.4	164.1
Medicare	162.7	157.1	178.3	194.2	210.8	228.6	246.8
Income security	217.8	221.8	230.4	243.4	263.8	270.0	282.2
Social security	321.1	338.9	354.8	374.7	394.4	414.8	435.7
On-Budget	(5.7)	(4.9)	(5.2)	(7.2)	(7.7)	(8.2)	(8.8)
Off-Budget	(315.5)	(334.1)	(349.6)	(367.6)	(386.8)	(406.6)	(426.9)
Veterans benefits and services	37.1	38.3	39.6	39.7	39.8	39.8	39.8
Administration of justice	15.7	18.7	22.0	22.5	23.3	24.5	24.7
General government	12.1	13.7	15.1	14.7	14.5	14.3	14.0
Net interest	203.0	234.2	257.0	270.4	282.9	297.1	309.9
On-Budget	(232.2)	(267.8)	(295.1)	(313.0)	(330.2)	(349.6)	(367.9)
Off-Budget	(–29.2)	(–33.6)	(–38.1)	(–42.6)	(–47.3)	(–52.5)	(–58.1)
Allowances	....	....	–0.2	–0.5	–0.8	–0.9	–1.0
Undistributed offsetting receipts:							
Employer share, employee retirement (on-budget)	–28.4	–27.9	–27.1	–26.8	–27.7	–28.0	–28.9
Employer share, employee retirement (off-budget)	–6.4	–6.4	–6.9	–7.1	–7.5	–8.1	–8.7
Rents and royalties on the Outer Continental Shelf	–3.0	–2.7	–3.0	–2.5	–2.4	–2.4	–2.4
Sale of major assets	....	....	–0.9	–2.0	–3.5	....	....
Other undistributed offsetting receipts	....	–4.4	–4.6	–4.9	–3.1	–2.6	–1.5
Total Undistributed offsetting receipts	–37.8	–41.4	–42.4	–43.3	–44.2	–41.0	–41.5
On-Budget	(–31.4)	(–35.0)	(–35.6)	(–36.2)	(–36.7)	(–33.0)	(–32.8)
Off-Budget	(–6.4)	(–6.4)	(–6.9)	(–7.1)	(–7.5)	(–8.1)	(–8.7)
Total	**1,528.4**	**1,563.8**	**1,613.8**	**1,686.4**	**1,765.2**	**1,839.1**	**1,924.0**
On-budget	(1,245.8)	(1,265.8)	(1,304.8)	(1,366.8)	(1,431.4)	(1,491.7)	(1,563.8)
Off-budget	(282.6)	(298.0)	(309.0)	(319.6)	(333.8)	(347.5)	(360.2)

Table S–19. OUTLAYS BY FUNCTION

(in billions of dollars)

Function	1994 Actual	Estimate 1995	1996	1997	1998	1999	2000
National defense:							
Department of Defense—Military	268.6	260.2	250.0	246.1	244.2	249.6	257.9
Other	13.0	11.4	11.4	10.9	10.3	10.0	9.9
Total National defense	281.6	271.6	261.4	257.0	254.5	259.7	267.8
International affairs	17.1	18.7	16.7	16.2	16.0	15.8	15.9
General science, space, and technology	16.2	17.0	16.9	16.4	16.4	16.2	15.9
Energy	5.2	4.6	4.4	4.0	3.5	3.5	3.1
Natural resources and environment	21.1	21.9	21.8	22.2	22.0	21.4	20.8
Agriculture	15.1	14.4	13.6	12.7	10.6	10.6	10.1
Commerce and housing credit	–5.1	–12.0	–7.6	–0.9	0.7	–3.4	–4.6
On-Budget	(–6.2)	(–12.7)	(–8.2)	(–1.2)	(1.2)	(–2.4)	(–3.2)
Off-Budget	(1.1)	(0.7)	(0.6)	(0.4)	(–0.4)	(–1.0)	(–1.4)
Transportation	38.1	39.2	38.6	38.4	37.9	37.8	36.7
Community and regional development	10.5	12.6	12.8	12.7	9.4	8.6	8.7
Education, training, employment, and social services	46.3	56.1	57.2	58.4	57.6	57.8	57.9
Health	107.1	115.1	124.0	132.1	142.1	152.1	163.6
Medicare	144.7	157.3	177.8	194.4	211.0	228.1	247.0
Income security	214.0	223.0	233.2	246.2	256.4	268.5	281.5
Social security	319.6	336.1	354.5	373.1	392.6	412.9	433.7
On-Budget	(5.7)	(4.9)	(5.2)	(7.2)	(7.7)	(8.2)	(8.8)
Off-Budget	(313.9)	(331.3)	(349.4)	(365.9)	(384.9)	(404.7)	(424.9)
Veterans benefits and services	37.6	38.4	38.1	39.7	39.9	40.0	41.7
Administration of justice	15.3	17.6	19.7	21.3	22.5	23.3	24.1
General government	11.3	14.5	14.6	14.3	14.2	14.3	14.0
Net interest	203.0	234.2	257.0	270.4	282.9	297.1	309.9
On-Budget	(232.2)	(267.8)	(295.1)	(313.0)	(330.2)	(349.6)	(367.9)
Off-Budget	(–29.2)	(–33.6)	(–38.1)	(–42.6)	(–47.3)	(–52.5)	(–58.1)
Allowances	....	....	–0.2	–0.5	–0.8	–0.9	–1.0
Undistributed offsetting receipts:							
Employer share, employee retirement (on-budget)	–28.4	–27.9	–27.1	–26.8	–27.7	–28.0	–28.9
Employer share, employee retirement (off-budget)	–6.4	–6.4	–6.9	–7.1	–7.5	–8.1	–8.7
Rents and royalties on the Outer Continental Shelf	–3.0	–2.7	–3.0	–2.5	–2.4	–2.4	–2.4
Sale of major assets	....	....	–0.9	–2.0	–3.5	....	....
Other undistributed offsetting receipts	....	–4.4	–4.6	–4.9	–3.1	–2.6	–1.5
Total Undistributed offsetting receipts	–37.8	–41.4	–42.4	–43.3	–44.2	–41.0	–41.5
On-Budget	(–31.4)	(–35.0)	(–35.6)	(–36.2)	(–36.7)	(–33.0)	(–32.8)
Off-Budget	(–6.4)	(–6.4)	(–6.9)	(–7.1)	(–7.5)	(–8.1)	(–8.7)
Total	**1,460.9**	**1,538.9**	**1,612.1**	**1,684.7**	**1,745.2**	**1,822.2**	**1,905.3**
On-budget	(1,181.5)	(1,246.9)	(1,307.1)	(1,368.1)	(1,415.6)	(1,479.1)	(1,548.6)
Off-budget	(279.4)	(292.0)	(305.0)	(316.6)	(329.6)	(343.1)	(356.7)

* $50 million or less.

Other Summary Tables

OTHER SUMMARY TABLES

Table S–20. RECEIPTS BY SOURCE—SUMMARY

(In billions of dollars)

Source	1994 Actual	Estimate 1995	1996	1997	1998	1999	2000
Individual income taxes	543.1	588.5	623.4	642.5	680.5	717.3	756.4
Corporation income taxes	140.4	150.9	157.4	166.1	173.2	179.2	190.5
Social insurance taxes and contributions	461.5	484.4	509.3	532.7	559.2	585.9	614.3
On-budget	(126.4)	(133.2)	(139.0)	(144.7)	(151.2)	(157.0)	(163.4)
Off-budget	(335.0)	(351.3)	(370.4)	(388.0)	(408.0)	(428.9)	(450.9)
Excise taxes	55.2	57.6	57.2	58.4	59.3	60.7	61.8
Estate and gift taxes	15.2	15.6	16.8	18.0	19.4	20.9	22.5
Customs duties	20.1	20.9	22.3	24.1	26.1	28.0	31.2
Miscellaneous receipts	22.3	28.6	29.0	29.8	31.2	32.7	34.3
Total receipts	**1,257.7**	**1,346.4**	**1,415.5**	**1,471.6**	**1,548.8**	**1,624.7**	**1,710.9**
On-budget	*(922.7)*	*(995.2)*	*(1,045.1)*	*(1,083.6)*	*(1,140.8)*	*(1,195.8)*	*(1,260.0)*
Off-budget	*(335.0)*	*(351.3)*	*(370.4)*	*(388.0)*	*(408.0)*	*(428.9)*	*(450.9)*

Table S–21. FEDERAL EMPLOYMENT IN THE EXECUTIVE BRANCH

(Civilian employment as measured by Full-Time Equivalents, in thousands)

Agency	1993 Base	1993 Actual	1994 Actual	Estimate		Change: 1993 base to 1996	
				1995[4]	1996	FTE's	Percent
Cabinet agencies:							
Agriculture	115.6	114.4	109.8	108.9	108.1	–7.6	–6.6%
Commerce	36.7	36.1	36.0	36.0	35.7	–1.0	–2.8%
Defense—military functions	931.3	931.8	868.3	834.1	800.6	–130.8	–14.0%
Education	5.0	4.9	4.8	5.1	5.1	*	0.7%
Energy	20.6	20.3	19.8	20.5	20.8	0.2	1.0%
Health and Human Services[1]	64.5	65.6	62.9	62.3	61.4	–3.1	–4.8%
Health and Human Services, exempt FTEs	0.5	0.5	0.5	0.5	0.4	*	–4.1%
Social Security Administration[2]	65.4	64.8	64.5	64.9	64.0	–1.4	–2.1%
Housing and Urban Development	13.6	13.3	13.1	12.9	12.6	–1.0	–7.2%
Interior	79.3	78.1	76.3	76.3	76.2	–3.2	–4.0%
Justice	99.4	95.4	95.3	102.0	109.2	9.8	9.9%
Labor	18.3	18.0	17.5	17.6	17.9	–0.4	–2.2%
State	26.0	25.6	25.2	25.0	24.8	–1.3	–4.8%
Transportation	70.3	69.1	66.4	65.2	64.4	–5.9	–8.4%
Treasury	166.1	161.1	157.3	161.4	162.2	–3.9	–2.4%
Veterans Affairs[1]	227.0	229.1	227.7	224.4	224.4	–2.7	–1.2%
Veterans Affairs, exempt FTEs	5.4	5.1	5.4	5.5	5.7	0.3	6.3%
Other agencies (excluding Postal Service):							
Agency for International Development[1]	4.4	4.1	3.9	3.8	3.8	–0.6	–13.1%
Agency for International Development, exempt FTEs	....	....	*	*	*	....	....
Corps of Engineers	29.2	28.4	27.9	27.7	27.4	–1.9	–6.3%
Environmental Protection Agency	18.6	17.9	17.6	18.9	18.9	0.3	1.7%
Equal Employment Opportunity Commission	2.9	2.8	2.8	2.9	3.2	0.4	12.7%
Federal Emergency Management Agency	2.7	4.0	4.9	3.9	4.0	1.3	46.4%
Federal Deposit Insurance Corp./Resolution Trust Corp.	21.6	21.9	20.0	16.3	12.3	–9.3	–43.1%
General Services Administration	20.6	20.2	19.5	16.9	15.5	–5.1	–24.9%
National Aeronautics and Space Administration	25.7	24.9	23.9	23.3	23.2	–2.5	–9.7%
National Archives and Records Administration	2.8	2.6	2.6	2.5	2.5	–0.3	–10.4%
National Labor Relations Board	2.1	2.1	2.1	2.1	2.1	*	–1.4%
National Science Foundation	1.3	1.2	1.2	1.3	1.3	–0.1	–5.7%
Nuclear Regulatory Commission	3.4	3.4	3.3	3.2	3.2	–0.2	–6.4%
Office of Personnel Management	6.2	5.9	5.3	5.5	5.5	–0.7	–11.9%
Panama Canal Commission	8.7	8.5	8.5	8.8	8.9	0.2	2.8%
Peace Corps	1.3	1.2	1.2	1.2	1.2	–0.1	–2.0%
Railroad Retirement Board	1.9	1.8	1.7	1.6	1.5	–0.3	–17.4%
Securities and Exchange Commission	2.7	2.7	2.7	2.9	3.1	0.4	14.4%
Small Business Administration	4.0	5.6	6.3	6.1	4.8	0.7	18.5%
Smithsonian Institution	5.9	5.5	5.4	5.5	5.5	–0.3	–5.7%
Tennessee Valley Authority	19.1	17.3	18.6	16.6	16.4	–2.7	–14.1%
United States Information Agency	8.7	8.3	8.1	8.0	8.1	–0.6	–7.1%
All other small agencies	16.1	15.4	14.4	16.0	15.9	–0.2	–1.3%
Total, Executive Branch civilian employment	**2,155.2**	**2,138.8**	**2,052.7**	**2,017.8**	**1,981.9**	**–173.3**	**–8.0%**
Total, Defense	931.3	931.8	868.3	834.1	800.6	–130.7	–14.0%
Total, Non-Defense	1,223.9	1,207.1	1,184.4	1,183.7	1,181.3	–42.6	–3.5%
FTEs exempt from Ceiling	....	....	5.9	6.0	6.1	....	....
Total, Executive Branch subject to Ceiling	....	....	2,047.0	2,011.8	1,975.8	....	....
FTE Ceiling[3]	....	....	2,084.6	2,043.3	2,003.3	....	....
Total FTE reduction from the 1993 base	....	–16.4	–102.5	–137.5	–173.3	....	

* Less than 50 FTEs.

[1] The Departments of Health and Human Services, Veterans Affairs, and the Agency for International Development have components that are exempt from FTE controls.

[2] The Social Security Administration will become a separate agency in 1995.

[3] FTE limitations are set for the Executive Branch in the Federal Workforce Restructuring Act of 1994 (P.L. 103–226).

[4] FTE data are reported to OPM by pay period, and allocated to fiscal year based on the period end date. 1995 FTE numbers have been adjusted to represent the same number of pay periods (26) as in 1993, 1994, and 1996. Without this adjustment for the September 18 to October 1, 1994 pay period, the 1995 total would have been higher by approximately 41,000 FTEs.

Table S–22. FEDERAL GOVERNMENT FINANCING AND DEBT [1]

(In billions of dollars)

	1994 Actual	Estimate 1995	1996	1997	1998	1999	2000
FINANCING							
Surplus or deficit (–)	–203.2	–192.5	–196.7	–213.1	–196.4	–197.4	–194.4
(On-budget)	–258.8	–251.8	–262.0	–284.5	–274.7	–283.3	–288.6
(Off-budget)	55.7	59.3	65.3	71.4	78.4	85.9	94.2
Means of financing other than borrowing from the public:							
Change in: [2]							
Treasury operating cash balance	16.6	–4.1	....	....	....	....	....
Checks outstanding, etc. [3]	2.5	–2.1	0.3	....	....	....	....
Deposit fund balances	1.1	0.1	–1.4	....	....	....	....
Seigniorage on coins	0.7	0.6	0.7	0.6	0.6	0.6	0.6
Less: Net financing disbursements:							
Direct loan financing accounts	–5.8	–11.3	–21.8	–30.7	–36.3	–38.0	–39.5
Guaranteed loan financing accounts	3.4	1.4	1.7	–0.7	–1.7	–1.4	–1.0
Total, means of financing other than borrowing from the public	18.4	–15.4	–20.5	–30.8	–37.4	–38.8	–39.8
Total, requirement for borrowing from the public	–184.7	–207.9	–217.2	–243.9	–233.8	–236.2	–234.3
Change in debt held by the public	184.7	207.9	217.2	243.9	233.8	236.2	234.3
DEBT, END OF YEAR [1]							
Gross Federal debt:							
Debt issued by Treasury	4,615.5	4,934.7	5,272.3	5,630.1	5,978.7	6,331.4	6,685.8
Debt issued by other agencies	28.3	26.8	27.3	26.3	26.3	26.3	26.3
Total, gross Federal debt	4,643.7	4,961.5	5,299.6	5,656.3	6,004.9	6,357.8	6,712.1
Held by:							
Government accounts	1,211.5	1,321.4	1,442.3	1,555.2	1,670.0	1,786.6	1,906.7
The public	3,432.2	3,640.1	3,857.3	4,101.2	4,334.9	4,571.2	4,805.4
(Federal Reserve Banks)	355.2	....	....	....	....	....	....
(Other)	3,077.1	....	....	....	....	....	....
DEBT SUBJECT TO STATUTORY LIMITATION, END OF YEAR							
Debt issued by Treasury	4,615.5	4,934.7	5,272.3	5,630.1	5,978.7	6,331.4	6,685.8
Less: Treasury debt not subject to limitation [4]	–15.6	–15.6	–15.6	–15.6	–15.6	–15.6	–15.6
Agency debt subject to limitation	0.1	0.1	0.1	0.1	0.1	0.1	0.1
Adjustment for discount and premium [5]	5.4	5.4	5.4	5.4	5.4	5.4	5.4
Total, debt subject to statutory limitation [6]	4,605.3	4,924.6	5,262.2	5,619.9	5,968.6	6,321.3	6,675.7

[1] Treasury securities held by the public and zero-coupon bonds held by Government accounts are almost entirely measured at sales price plus amortized discount or less amortized premium. Agency debt is almost entirely measured at face value. Treasury securities in the Government account series are measured at face value less unrealized discount (if any).

[2] A decrease in the Treasury operating cash balance (which is an asset) is a means of financing the deficit. It therefore has a positive sign, which is opposite to the sign of the deficit. An increase in checks outstanding or deposit fund balances (which are liabilities) is also a means of financing the deficit and therefore also has a positive sign.

[3] Besides checks outstanding, includes accrued interest payable on Treasury debt, miscellaneous liability accounts, allocations of special drawing rights, and, as an offset, cash and monetary assets other than the Treasury operating cash balance, miscellaneous asset accounts, and profit on sale of gold.

[4] Consists primarily of Federal Financing Bank debt.

[5] Consists of unamortized discount (less premium) on public issues of Treasury notes and bonds (other than zero-coupon bonds) and unrealized discounts on Government account series securities.

[6] The statutory debt limit is $4,900 billion.

List of Charts and Tables

LIST OF CHARTS AND TABLES

LIST OF CHARTS

Page

The Budget Message of the President

The Federal Government Dollar Fiscal Year 1996 Estimates 2

Promoting a Rising Standard of Living for All Americans

Sharing the Benefits of Economic Growth:

1–1. 32 Thousand New Head Start Opportunities for Children in 1996 18

1–2. Student Loan Program Costs Would be Reduced 12 Billion Dollars over Six Years, 1995–2000 21

1–3. 1.6 Million More Grants and Loans for People to Make Their Own Choices of Training and Education 22

1–4. How Long Does the Average AFDC Recipient Stay Continuously on Welfare? . 26

1–5. Out–of–Wedlock Birth Rates in the U.S. Nearly Tripled Between 1970 and 1991 27

1–6. Most Poor Women Receive No Child Support 28

Building on our Economic Record:

2–1. Federal Budget Deficit 34

2–2. Changes in Payroll Employment 36

2–3. Civilian Unemployment Rate 36

2–4. Consumer Sentiment 38

2–5. Real Business Fixed Investment 38

2–6. Inflation Trends 39

2–7. The Impact of Medicare and Medicaid on the Federal Budget Deficit 42

2–8. Annual Average Earnings of Workers 44

2–9. 1996 Proposed Spending by Category 49

Creating Opportunity and Encouraging Responsibility

Controlling Violent Crime and Drug Abuse:

4–1. 1996 Budget Reflects the Administration's Plan for Federal, State and Local Partnerships to Fight Crime 65

Reforming the Nation's Immigration System:

5–1. Immigration and Naturalization Service Budget History 74

5–2. Immigration and Naturalization Service Southwest Border Staffing Levels 76

Ensuring a Clean Environment:

6–1. Reductions of U.S. National Ambient Concentrations of Criteria Air Pollutants 86

6–2. U.S. Population Served by Secondary Treatment or Better 86

6–3. Major Progress in Superfund Cleanups 87

6–4. Impact of USDA's Wetland Reserve Program (WRP) 89

Continuing the Commitment to Health Security:

8–1. 1996 Proposed Spending by Category: Medicare and Medicaid 105

Projecting American Leadership Around the World

Strengthening the U.S. Role in International Affairs:

9–1. 1996 Proposed Spending by Category: International Affairs 116

LIST OF CHARTS—Continued

Page

Maintaining a Quality Military Force:
10–1. President's Defense Funding Initiative 124
10–2. 1996 Proposed Spending by Category: National Defense 125

Making Government Work

Reinventing the Federal Government—Phase II:
12–1. Doing More with Less: Reinventing the Department of Transportation 150

LIST OF TABLES

Page

The Budget Message of the President

Receipts, Outlays, and Deficits 2

Promoting a Rising Standard of Living for All Americans

Sharing the Benefits of Economic Growth:
1–1. Average Household Income, by Quintile 13
1–2. Percentage Distribution of the President's Middle-Class Tax Cut Proposal 15
1–3. The Budget Increases Investment in Major Programs for Lifelong Learning by $2.5 Billion Over 1995, an Increase of $5.2 Billion, or 23 Percent Over the 1993 Level 17
1–4. The G.I. Bill for America's Workers Combines 70 Programs into One Workforce Development System, and Increases Funding $1 Billion Over 1995 23

Building on Our Economic Record:
2–1. Funding the Middle-Class Tax Cut and Deficit Reduction 40
2–2. Major Federal Investment Outlays 43

Creating Opportunity and Encouraging Responsibility

Restoring the American Community:
3–1. Government-wide Native American Program Funding 59

Controlling Violent Crime and Drug Abuse:
4–1. Law Enforcement Spending by Agency 64
4–2. Violent Crime Reduction Trust Fund (VCRTF) 64
4–3. Major Violent Crime Control Initiatives 66
4–4. Drug Control Spending Increases by $1.3 Billion 67

Reforming the Nation's Immigration System:
5–1. Additional Spending Requested to Secure the Border and Manage Immigration, and to Assist States with the Costs of Illegal Immigration 73
5–2. New Spending Initiatives in the President's Immigration Management and Border Security Plan 75
5–3. Initiatives in the President's Program for Assistance to States for Illegal Immigration Costs 78

Ensuring a Clean Environment:
6–1. Targeting Resources to High-Priority Environment and Natural Resources Programs 84
6–2. Priority Investments and Other Major Environment and Natural Resource Programs 85

LIST OF TABLES—Continued

	Page
Investing in Science and Technology:	
7–1. Funding of Research and Developnment Activities	94
7–2. Funding of Selected Science and Technology Highlights	95
Projecting American Leadership Around the World	
Strengthening the U.S. Role in International Affairs:	
9–1. International Discretionary Programs	115
Maintaining a Quality Military Force:	
10–1. Military Force Trends	123
10–2. Funding Summary for National Defense	124
Making Government Work	
Reinventing the Federal Government—Phase II:	
12–1. Savings from Reinventing Government—Phase II	144
12–2. Department of Energy Reinventing Government—Phase II Savings	148
12–3. "Performance Partnerships"	153
Summary Tables	
Budget Aggregates:	
S–1. Outlays, Receipts, and Deficit Summary	173
S–2. Summary of Receipts, Outlays, and Surpluses or Deficits(-): 1789–2000	174
1996 Budget Proposals:	
S–3. Summary of Budget Proposals	179
S–4. Proposed Discretionary Spending Relative to the Caps	180
S–5. Mandatory Pay-As-You-Go Proposals	181
S–6. Reinventing Government—Phase II	184
S–7. Program Consolidations	187
S–8. Program Terminations	196
S–9. Program Reductions	200
S–10. Proposed Investments	204
S–11. Summary of Supplemental and Rescission Proposals	207
S–12. Effect of Proposals on Receipts	208
S–13. Discretionary Proposals by Appropriations Subcommittee	209
Summaries by Agency/Function:	
S–14. Discretionary Budget Authority by Agency	213
S–15. Discretionary Outlays by Agency	214
S–16. Budget Authority by Agency	215
S–17. Outlays by Agency	216
S–18. Budget Authority by Function	217
S–19. Outlays by Function	218
Other Summary Tables:	
S–20. Receipts by Source—Summary	221
S–21. Federal Employment in the Executive Branch	222
S–22. Federal Government Financing and Debt	223

OMB CONTRIBUTORS TO THE 1996 BUDGET

The following Office of Management and Budget personnel contributed to the preparation of this publication. Hundreds, perhaps thousands, of others throughout the Government also deserve credit for their valuable contributions.

A

Gordon Adams
Marsha D. Adams
Gordon P. Agress
Steven D. Aitken
Rehema B. Allen
Richard M. Allen
Timothy C. Allen
Robert A. Allison
Ahmad Al-Samarrie
Lois E. Altoft
Wayne S. Amchin
Barry B. Anderson
James L. Anderson
Robert B. Anderson
Donald R. Arbuckle
John B. Arthur
Jeffrey H. Ashford
Renee Austin
Dionel M. Aviles

B

Renata Babuska
Patricia A. Baker
Sharon A. Barkeloo
Robert E. Barker
Christina Barnes
Pamela S. Barr
Mary C. Barth
Shireif M. Battat
Richard B. Bavier
Jean D. Baxter
Bruce D. Beard
Sonja V. Bedon
Richard B. Belzer
Gary L. Bennethum
Deborah L. Benoit
Rodney G. Bent
Dorothy E. Bergamaschi
Leon J. Bernal
Maya A. Bernstein
Pamela L. Beverly
Keith B. Bickel
Angela R. Billerbeck
Harold E. Blackwell II
Jill M. Blickstein
Mathew C. Blum
James Boden
Constance J. Bowers
Yvonne T. Bowlding
Jacqueline Boykin
James Bradford, Jr.
Betty I. Bradshaw
Denise M. Bray
Godula E. Brendel
Jonathan D. Breul
Anna M. Briatico
Hazel W. Briggs
Paul W. Brower
Allan E. Brown
Christopher N. Brown
James A. Brown
Mary H. Brown
Thomas M. Brown
Paul Bugg
Ann M. Burget
Kim H. Burke
John D. Burnim
Katherine A. Byse

C

Scott J. Cameron
Debra Cammer
Annette H. Candelaria
Susan M. Carr
Matthew J. Carter
Lester D. Cash
Mary I. Cassell
Cherlyn D. Castaldo
Winifred Y. Chang
Jocelyn W. Chapman
Edward H. Chase
Antonio E. Chavez
Anita Chellaraj
Daniel J. Chenok
David C. Childs
Alice S. Cho
Dennis R. Christmas
James P. Christopoulos
Mary M. Chuckerel
Zach Church
Robert L. Civiak
Edward H. Clarke
Barry T. Clendenin
Jerry L. Coffey
Ron Cogswell
Andrea G. Cohen
Shannon Cole
William S. Coleman Jr.
Debra M. Collins
Teresa L. Collins
Nani A. Coloretti
Sheila Conley
Stephen M. Connair
Melissa Y. Cook
Robert M. Cooper
Dionne M. Copper
Daniel J. Corbett
Darlene E. Cornelius
Jacqueline A. Corsetty
Daniel W. Costello
Douglas A. Criscitello
Michael F. Crowley
James C. Crutchfield
Philip H. Cullom
William P. Curtis
Kathy D. Cutler

D

Josie R. Dade
Rosemarie W. Dale
Philip R. Dame
Robert G. Damus
Alice R. Davis
Caroline B. Davis
Margaret B. Davis
Peter O. Davis
Lorraine Day
Stacy L. Dean
Arline P. Dell
Carol R. Dennis
Aurelia A. DeRubis
G. Edward Deseve
Cheree D. Desimone
Eugene J. Devine
Margaret W. DiBari
Elizabeth M. DiGennaro
Michael J. Discenza, Jr.
Arnold E. Donahue
Karen S. Dooley
William L. Dorotinsky
Michael C. Dost
Robert S. Dotson
Janice M. Drummond
James E. Duke
Sherron R. Duncan
Carter L. Dutch
Nancy J. Duykers
Marguerite D. Dyson

E

Jacqueline A. Easley
Marti E. Easton
Gary M. Ebert
Eugene M. Ebner
Mabel E. Echols
Christopher F. Edley, Jr.
Teresa F. Ellison
Kristina A. Emanuels
Richard P. Emery Jr.
Noah Engelberg
Michelle A. Enger
Adrienne C. Erbach
Jim R. Esquea
John L. Evans-Klock
Tina L. Evans-Mitchell
Suzann K. Evinger
Rowe Ewell
Quincy Ewing III
Allison H. Eydt

F

Timothy R. Fain
Chris Fairhall
Lisa B. Fairhall
Robert S. Fairweather
Jeffrey A. Farkas
William R. Feezle
Tanya M. Felder
Jack D. Fellows
Patricia A. Ferrell
Gayle A. Finch
Joseph Firschein
James F. Fish
Elyse H. Fitter
Darlene B. Fleming
Cecelia D. Fletcher
Dana L. Flower-Lake
Keith J. Fontenot
Anita D. Ford
Janet R. Forsgren
Roberta L. Foster
Wanda J. Foster
Andrew S. Freeman
Stephen M. Frerichs

G

Martha M. Gagne
Evett F. Gardner
Darcel D. Gayle
Darlene O. Gaymon
Michael D. Gerich
Donald E. Gessaman
Brian Gillis
Barbara A. Gils-Banks
T.J. Glauthier
Jonathan D. Gledhill
Kenneth G. Glozer
Michael L. Goad
Jo Ellen Godfrey
Debra Gold
Stephen M. Goldberg
Jeffrey D. Goldstein
Maria E. Gonzalez
Janet L. Graves
Arecia A. Grayton
Maryanne B. Green
Pamela B. Green
Richard E. Green
Judy L. Grew
Walter S. Groszyk Jr.
K. Lisa Grove
Norman E. Gunderson
Barbara Guttman

H

Lawrence J. Haas
Lauren Haber
Tobias J. Halliday
William A. Halter
Dianne M. Ham-McFarland
Michelle L. Hanson
Rebecca J. Hardy
Brenda F. Harper
David J. Haun
Audry V. Hawkins
Daniel D. Heath
Bryan E. Heid
Bruce C. Heide
Christopher Heiser
Renee P. Helm
Gregory G. Henry
Jefferson B. Hill

Timothy B. Hill
Troy S. Hillier
Janet L. Himler
James C. Ho
Marcel Hodak
Adam Hoffberg
Jean W. Holcombe
Christine P. Holmes
Linda L. Hoogeveen
Edith D. Hopkins
Sarah G. Horrigan
Laura J. Houseman
Kathy M. Hudgins
Paul W. Huelskamp
Robert H. Huie
Timothy G. Hunt
Lawrence W. Hush
Toni S. Hustead
Virginia A. Huth
Sherril L. Hyson

I

Laurel H. Illston
Steven J. Isakowitz

J

Norwood J. Jackson Jr.
Claire N. Jacobi
Laurence R. Jacobson
Lisa E. Jacobson
E. Irene James
Carline M. Jelsma
Carol D. Jenkins
Duane E. Jenkins
Carol S. Johnson
Darrell A. Johnson
Kim I. Johnson
Lorraine M. Johnson
Marilyn E. Jones
Ronald E. Jones
Christopher A. Jordan
James F. Jordan
James J. Jukes
Theodore A. Jump

K

Barbara F. Kahlow
Phyllis E. Kaiser-Dark
Stuart Kasdin
David E. Katague
Sally Katzen
Stanley Kaufman
Stephanie I. Kaufman
James B. Kazel
Alex S. Keenan
John W. Kelly
Kenneth S. Kelly
Steven Kelman
Farooq A. Khan
Charles E. Kieffer
Robert W. Kilpatrick
Tina M. Kirk-Frank
Carole Kitti
Karin L. Kizer
Ryan Kluft
Louisa Koch
Richard H. Kodl
Raymond P. Kogut
Alicia K. Kolaian
Charles S. Konigsberg
John A. Koskinen
Shannah Koss
Mark S. Kramer
Lori A. Krauss
Richard A. Kuzmack
Bradley W. Kyser

L

Joseph F. Lackey, Jr.
Leonard L. Lainhart
Neil F. Lamb
Brien J. Lasse
Edwin Lau
Wilson Lau
Mary Ann Leggett
Kelley A. Lehman
Patricia L. Lennon
Robert S. Lesher
Cameron M. Leuthy
Jacob J. Lew
Christopher M. Lewis
Thomas S. Lewis
Richard Lichtenberger
Linn M. Ligon
Tyrone C. Ligon
Henry E. Lilienthal
Diane G. Limo
Susanne D. Lind
Jenise Littlejohn
Lin C. Liu
Neil R. Lobron
Patrick G. Locke
Richard C. Loeb
Bruce D. Long
Jonna M. Long
Ron Longo
Janet Looney
Randall W. Lutter
Randolph M. Lyon
John L. Lyons

M

Jill M. Maccaferri
Donald J. MacMillan
James B. MacRae Jr.
Eric L. Macris
Larry D. Magid
Jennifer E. Main
Dalton L. Mann
Judith F. Mann
Josephine D. Marino
Karen A. Maris
Christine K. Markham
Bernard H. Martin
Timothy D. Martin
Patricia Mathews
Larry R. Matlack
Alexander J. McClelland
Bruce W. McConnell
Douglas D. McCormick
Yvonne A. McCoy
Michael J. McDermott
James H. McDivitt
Katrina A. McDonald
Richard S. McKay
William N. McLeod
William J. McQuaid
James B. Medica
Mark D. Menchik
William C. Menth
Katherine L. Meredith
Richard A. Mertens
Steven M. Mertens
Linda L. Mesaros
Harry G. Meyers
James D. Mietus
Alice McNutt Miller
Mark E. Miller
Matthew L. Miller
Nancy-Ann E. Min
Joseph Minarik
Janet W. Minkler
Matthew H. Mitchell
Ginger Moench
Gretina S. Monk
John B. Moore
Harry E. Moran
Linda F. Morgan
Elizabeth J. Mori
John F. Morrall, III
Delphine C. Motley
Jane T. Moy
Lydia Muniz
Rosalind S. Murphy
James C. Murr
Margaret A. Murray
Suzanne M. Murrin
Christopher J. Mustain
Leslie S. Mustain
Anne W. Mutti
David L. Muzio

N

Jonas E. Neihardt
Clifford S. Nelms
Nora H. Neureiter
Thomas B. Newgent
Kimberly A. Newman
Sheila D. Newman
Kevin F. Neyland
Melissa Nguyen
James A. Nix
S. Aromie Noe
Christine L. Nolin
Memphis A. Norman
Douglas A. Norwood

O

Dale P. Oak
Marcia D. Occomy
Kashira D. Oldes
Marvis G. Olfus
Laura A. Oliven
Ja-Na Oliver
Valerie M. Owens

P

William D. Palmer
Kristen E. Panerali
Anna K. Pannell
Darrell Park
Christopher W. Parker
Parashar B. Patel
Jacqueline M. Peay
Robert J. Pellicci
Emily D. Pelton
Kathleen Peroff
Michael J. Peters
Ronald K. Peterson
Genease E. Pettigrew
John R. Pfeiffer
Carolyn R. Phelps
Janet S. Piller
Joseph G. Pipan
Shirley C. Pipkin
Mila M. Plosky
Stuart W. Pollins
Keith J. Posen

Q

Iqbal Qazi

R

Bernice M. Randolph
Edward M. Rea
Francis S. Redburn
Arthur J. Reed Jr.
McGavock D. Reed
Franklin S. Reeder
Thomas M. Reilly
Rosalyn J. Rettman
Barbara A. Retzlaff
Jeeyang Rhee
Alan B. Rhinesmith
John M. Richardson
Sarah B. Richardson
Nancy S. Ridenour
Robert B. Rideout
Donna M. Rivelli
Alice M. Rivlin
Mary A. Robinson
Justine F. Rodriguez
Lara L. Roholt
Patrick L. Rooks
Annette E. Rooney
Christopher G. Rose
Lynn C. Ross
Elizabeth L. Rossman
Gary D. Rowe
Martha A. Rubenstein
Michael E. Ruffner
Kenneth F. Ryder, Jr.

S

Ashish Sahni
Cynthia R. Salavantis
Maria F. Salcedo
LaVonne D. Sampson
Mark S. Sandy
Bruce K. Sasser
Ruth D. Saunders
Isabel Sawhill
Thomas G. Schaaf
Lori R. Schack
Victoria L. Schaefer
Kevin J. Scheid
Glenn R. Schlarman
Andrew M. Schoenbach
Ingrid M. Schroeder
John T. Schuhart
Sarah C. Schulte
Kenneth L. Schwartz
Mark J. Schwartz
Nancy E. Schwartz
Ardy D. Scott
Walter L. Scott
Robyn L. Seaton
Jasmeet K. Seehra
Albert Seferian
Frank J. Seidl III
Barbara S. Selfridge
Andrew W. Sellgren
Neil K. Shapiro
Deborah L. Shaw

Margaret R. Shaw
Alice S. Sheck
Philip Sheuerman
Vanna J. Shields
Alice E. Shuffield
Mary Jo Siclari
Adrien L. Silas
Ronald L. Silberman
Angela C. Simmons
Pamula L. Simms
Margaret A. Simpkins
Jack A. Smalligan
Bryan R. Smith
Dennis E. Smith
Jeffrey K. Smith
Patricia A. Smith
Julie J. Sonier
Shaun D. Spencer
Edward C. Springer
Thomas P. Stack
Norman H. Starler
Randolph J. Steer
Douglas L. Steiger
Albert F. Stidman
Carla B. Stone
Dennis L. Stout
Barbara A. Stratton
Mark S. Streger
Eric J. Strucko
Milo B. Sunderhauf
E. S. Swain
Carolyn Swinney

T

Cynthia M. Taeuber-McIl-wain
Michael Talajkowski
Sahar Taman
Daniel M. Tangherlini
Vernetta Tanner
Nathan S. Tash
Wendy A. Taylor
Richard P. Theroux
Beverly B. Thierwechter
Sharon K. Thomas
Desiree Noble Thompson
Courtney B. Timberlake
Paul Tisdale
Elisabeth S. Topel
David E. Tornquist
Hai M. Tran
Moon T. Tran
Robert J. Tuccillo
Donald L. Tuck
Kathleen M. Turco
Richard J. Turman
Carla A. Turner
Katherine M. Tyer

V

Cynthia A. Vallina
Pamela B. VanWie
Valentina Veney
Areletha L. Venson
Stephen A. Verrecchia
Sandra L. Via
Phebe N. Vickers
Lori L. Victor
Frances W. Von Schilling
Kathleen M. Voorhees

W

Stanley R. Wallace
Katherine K. Wallman
Maureen H. Walsh
Sharon A. Warner
Theodore Wartell
Barbara E. Washington
Mark A. Wasserman
Iratha H. Waters
Patricia J. Watson
Gary Waxman
Rebecca A. Wayne
Mark A. Weatherly
Bessie M. Weaver
Tawana F. Webb
Stephen A. Weigler
Jeffrey A. Weinberg
Peter N. Weiss
Dianne M. Wells
Philip R. Wenger
Michael G. Wenk
Ophelia D. West
Tina L. Westby
Lisa F. Western
Arnette C. White
Barry White
Kim S. White
William G. White
Ora L. Whitman
Joseph S. Wholey
Linda K. Wiesman
Roxanne V. Willard
Debra L. Williams
Joyce M. Williams
Doris J. Wingard
Joseph M. Wire
Wayne A. Wittig
Christopher D. Wolz
Daren K. Wong
Herbert S. Wong
Thomas E. Woodley
Anthony B. Wu

Y

Margaret L. Yao
Cheryl G. Young
Louise D. Young
Julia E. Yuille

Z

David M. Zavada
Wendy B. Zenker
Gail S. Zimmerman
Leonard B. Zuza

Need Additional Copies ???

Copies of the Budget and related Office of Management and Budget documents may be purchased at any of the GPO bookstores listed below. (Paper copies only.)

GPO BOOKSTORES

ALABAMA
O'Neill Building
2021 Third Ave., North
Birmingham, Alabama 35203
(205) 731-1056
FAX (205) 731-3444

CALIFORNIA
ARCO Plaza, C-Level
505 South Flower Street
Los Angeles, California 90071
(213) 239-9844
FAX (213) 239-9848

Marathon Plaza, Room 141-S
3C3 Second Street
San Francisco, California 94107
(415) 512-2770
FAX (415) 512-2776

COLORADO
Room 117, Federal Building
1961 Stout Street
Denver, Colorado 80294
(303) 844-3964
FAX (303) 844-4000

Norwest Banks Building
201 West 8th Street
Pueblo, Colorado 81003
(719) 544-3142
FAX (719) 544-6719

DISTRICT OF COLUMBIA
U.S. Government Printing Office
710 North Capitol Street, NW.
Washington, DC 20401
(202) 512-0132
FAX (202) 512-1355

1510 H Street, NW.
Washington, DC 20005
(202) 653-5075
FAX (202) 376-5055

FLORIDA
100 West Bay Street
Suite 100
Jacksonville, Florida 32202
(904) 353-0569
FAX (904) 353-1280

GEORGIA
First Union Plaza
999 Peachtree Street, NE.
Suite 120
Atlanta, Georgia 30309
(404) 347-1900
FAX (404) 347-1897

ILLINOIS
One Congress Center, Suite 124
401 South State Street
Chicago, Illinois 60605
(312) 353-5133
FAX (312) 353-1590

MARYLAND
Retail Sales Outlet
8660 Cherry Lane
Laurel, Maryland 20707
(301) 953-7974
FAX (301) 498-8995

MASSACHUSETTS
Thomas P. O'Neill Fed. Bldg.
10 Causeway Street, Rm. 169
Boston, Massachusetts 02222
(617) 720-4180
FAX (617) 720-5753

MICHIGAN
Suite 160, Federal Building
477 Michigan Avenue
Detroit, Michigan 48226
(313) 226-7816
FAX (313) 226-4698

MISSOURI
120 Bannister Mall
5600 East Bannister Road
Kansas City, Missouri 64137
(816) 767-8225
FAX (816) 767-8233

NEW YORK
Room 110, Federal Building
26 Federal Plaza
New York, New York 10278
(212) 264-3825
FAX (212) 264-9318

OHIO
Room 1653, Federal Building
1240 East 9th Street
Cleveland, Ohio 44199
(216) 522-4922
FAX (216) 522-4714

Room 207, Federal Building
200 North High Street
Columbus, Ohio 43215
(614) 469-6956
FAX (614) 469-5374

OREGON
1305 SW. First Avenue
Portland, Oregon 97201
(503) 221-6217
FAX (503) 225-0563

PENNSYLVANIA
Robert Morris Building
100 North 17th Street
Philadelphia, Pennsylvania 19103
(215) 636-1900
FAX (215) 636-1903

Room 118, Federal Building
1000 Liberty Avenue
Pittsburgh, Pennsylvania 15222
(412) 644-2721
FAX (412) 644-4547

TEXAS
Room 1C50, Federal Building
1100 Commerce Street
Dallas, Texas 75242
(214) 767-0076
FAX (214) 767-3239

Texas Crude Building
801 Travis Street
Houston, Texas 77002
(713) 228-1187
FAX (713) 228-1186

WASHINGTON
Room 194, Federal Building
915 Second Avenue
Seattle, Washington 98174
(206) 553-4270
FAX (206) 553-6717

WISCONSIN
The Reuss Federal Plaza
310 West Wisconsin Avenue
Milwaukee, Wisconsin 53203
(414) 297-1304
FAX (414) 297-1300

There is a 25% discount on all orders for 100 or more copies of a single title mailed to a single address. No discount is allowed if such orders are mailed to multiple addresses.

Superintendent of Documents Publications Order Form

Order Processing Code: ***7275**

All prices include regular domestic postage and handling and are good through October 1995. After this date, please call the Order and Information Desk at (202) 783-3238 to verify prices. To fax your orders and inquiries—(202) 512-2250.

Qty.	Stock Number	Title	Price Each	Total Price
	041-001-00446-7	Budget of the United States Government, Fiscal Year 1996	$17.00	
	041-001-00447-5	Budget of the U.S. Government, Fiscal Year 1996—Appendix	42.00	
	041-001-00450-5	Analytical Perspectives, Fiscal Year 1996	24.00	
	041-001-00448-3	Historical Tables, Fiscal Year 1996	15.00	
	041-001-00451-3	A Citizen's Guide to the Federal Budget	2.75	
	041-001-00449-1	The Budget System and Concepts	1.00	
	041-001-00453-0	The Budget on CD-ROM	24.00	

(International customers—please add an additional 25%.) Total for Publications ______

Please Print or Type

(Company or personal name)

(Additional address/attention line)

(Street address)

(City, State, ZIP Code)

(   )
(Daytime phone—including area code)

Mail To: Superintendent of Documents
Government Printing Office,
Washington, DC 20402-9325

Please choose method of payment:

☐ Check payable to the Superintendent of Documents

☐ GPO Deposit Account ☐☐☐☐☐☐☐—☐

☐ VISA or MasterCard Account

☐☐☐☐☐☐☐☐☐☐☐☐☐☐☐☐☐☐☐☐

(Credit card expiration date)

Thank you for your order!

(Signature)

ISBN 0-16-045409-3
90000
9 780160 454097